ANDRE GIDE

ANDRE GIDE

ALBERT J. GUERARD

SECOND EDITION

HARVARD UNIVERSITY PRESS · CAMBRIDGE, MASSACHUSETTS

1969

FOR

JOHN HAWKES
TOM MOSER
JACK ROGERS
AUSTRYN WAINHOUSE

PREFACE

THIS BOOK WAS CONCEIVED AS ONE OF three studies which, taken together, might throw some light on the development of the modern novel, and on the modern novelist's perplexities. Thomas Hardy, Joseph Conrad, and André Gide were chosen as roughly representative of the progress of the novel between 1875 and 1925, and as interesting subjects for separate study.* In the Preface to *Thomas Hardy: The Novels and Stories,* I explained some of the resemblances and differences between the three novelists, and tried to justify the choice of this particular triad: my general intention was to record the impulse away from orthodox realism, classical psychology, and conventional structure; or, the impulse toward the somber and ironic distortions, the psychological explorations, and the dislocations in form of many novelists writing in the middle of the twentieth century. Our three writers clearly represented, it seemed to me, a movement from one state of art and mind to another.

My primary interest was nevertheless in Hardy as a writer not Hardy as a "historical presence." And so now my

---

* *Thomas Hardy: The Novels and Stories* and *Conrad the Novelist* were published by Harvard University Press in 1949 and 1958.

primary interest is in Gide's own work, rather than in his relationship to earlier novelists. But the critical problem is a very different one. We are no longer dealing with a "traditional teller of tales," and cannot dismiss so quickly the political and social background, or the author's own troubled personality. André Gide, like Joyce and Mann and Lawrence, exists as a "force," and one of his major subjects is the problem of conduct in our twentieth-century world. Unlike Hardy and Conrad, Gide has been a man of letters and explicit moralist, rather than a novelist only. His spiritual autobiographies are of interest to the reader of his novels, since one of his great novelistic problems was to transcend mere autobiography. But they are also works of art in a valid and separate genre, and self-explorations of considerable psychological importance. Gide's political, psychic, and aesthetic conflicts are closely related, and we shall find in them the same pattern of self-denial, of affirmation through renunciation. The critic of Gide, however much he may prefer to concentrate on the novels, finds such a limitation improper. The present book does not discuss Gide's "thought" systematically and at length; this has been done already by many others. It certainly does not propose to be a comprehensive study of all his work. But it is not, could not have been, a pure "essay in criticism" on the novelist.

We cannot approach Gide in the usual ways — dividing his career into "periods," or moving successively through the "mind," the "characterization," the "technique." Such a complicated and sinuous figure demands a series of separate assaults. The structure of the present book is therefore rather unusual. The first chapter describes Gide's career as representative in a very broad sense: representative of the modern intellectual's contradictory longing for individualist freedom and comforting submission to authority. The issues are political, moral, and religious. The second chapter comments on the inward conflicts which occupy so many of Gide's books. What, if looked at fairly closely, does the long series of spiritual autobiographies convey? Now, in place of the historical conflict between independence and commitment, we have a struggle between a longing to protect the self and a longing to destroy or dissolve it. The third and fourth chapters examine the novels as novels and emphasize Gide's effort to escape autobiography, realism, and conventional orderly structure — his effort to write, in fact, a kind of fiction for which he was little equipped. Our main concern is with the novels as works of art, the novels as they exist for one reader in 1951 and as they may exist for readers a century hence.

But what did Gide mean, as writer and as "representative man," for several generations? Why has he had such a great influence? My fifth and final chapter takes up what it would be customary to examine first: the personality of the living man, his relationship with other writers, the very strong and maieutic effect of his books. This chapter was undertaken at Gide's own suggestion * — and after long hesitation. I place little faith in the academic study of "influence," which often becomes vicious pseudo science. We cannot ignore Gide's place as a man who has modified our ideas and our image of the modern world. But it is foolish to pretend that his influence can be defined exactly. I examine one instance of alleged influence at some length (the notorious instance of Jacques Rivière), and reach a largely negative conclusion. This is the real value of such a full examination: to show how many intangibles, temperamental as well as literary, enter into the relationship of two closely associated writers. And if we cannot measure exactly Gide's influence on Rivière, how can we hope to fix the influence of one long-dead writer on another writer long dead?

My book thus offers a series of interlocking circles, and moves not once but several times from *Les Cahiers d'André Walter* to *Thésée*, and from Mallarmé's Paris to our own dark present. A few central episodes in this long career — the publication of *Si le grain ne meurt*, for instance — must return again and again. But only in this fashion can we begin to describe such an elusive figure without distortion.

* See Gide's letter of May 16, 1947, at the end of this book.

Two other matters may cause some surprise and discomfort. The first is the large number of pages devoted to *Le Voyage d'Urien* and to *L'Immoraliste*, two early works. Here I was frankly guided by what seemed to me lacking in other books on Gide. *Le Voyage d'Urien* — a symbolist work of considerable literary interest and nearly unique psychological interest — has been almost entirely overlooked. The present analysis is a first hazardous venture into very dark regions. *L'Immoraliste*, on the other hand, has been read widely but very often misread. It seems to me Gide's best novel and one of the masterpieces of modern fiction. *Le Voyage d'Urien* is not a greater work of art than *La Porte étroite* (which analysis can dispose of in a few pages), but *L'Immoraliste* most certainly is.

The other matter which may cause some uneasiness is a certain psychological emphasis: a minute attention to recurrent rationalizations and recurrent images in Gide's autobiographies, and to the structures of behavior dramatized in his novels. As novelist, essayist, and autobiographer, Gide was first of all a "lay psychologist." The conflict between the conscious life and the preconscious or unconscious was one of his great continuing subjects, and he analyzed or dramatized more fully than almost any other creative writer various impulses to self-destruction. To explore and perhaps expose buried aspects of personality was often the conscious ambition of his books, and not merely their unintended substance. This being so, what is the literary critic to do — who is *not* a professional psychologist or psychiatrist, and who is fully aware that even modest "psychiatric criticism" arouses in most readers a strong but ill-defined rage? Granted that Gide's subject matter and interests are (like those of Mann, Proust, Joyce, Kafka, and Faulkner) partly psychological — should not one leave these matters to the scrutiny of qualified professionals?

The answer is that the professionals are not interested. With very few exceptions, they place little importance on the novelist's deliberate studies of human behavior and human difficulties. Freud himself recognized the value of

Dostoevsky's insights — and how much truer Dostoevsky's picture of the mind was than that of his contemporary professionals! But most of Freud's descendants have been more exclusive and more severe. They attend least of all to what the novelist may say, consciously, about the more obvious patterns of the inner life: self-destructiveness, identification, repression and compensation, compulsive reënactment. They are interested rather in what the writer may unconsciously reveal of his own unconscious — and for this purpose a very slight artist often serves as well as a major one. They are also interested in the fact that a Sophocles or Shakespeare could, though unknowingly, arrive at certain fundamental structures of everyone's unconscious life. Their understandable practice in examining works of art is therefore to isolate and discuss these "fundamental structures" only. As a rule they pay little attention to what concerns the novelist himself first of all: the total complicated pattern of the invented human being. Even Gaston Bachelard, with his wide literary culture and his sensitive literary taste, is indifferent to conscious literary "psychologizing." The professionals' interest in wholly unconscious creation is important, of course, and no doubt only a trained psychiatrist or analyst could properly define the "content" of *Le Voyage d'Urien* and its multiple forms of "censorship."

There nevertheless remains a vast area of experience which the modern novelist writes about (and which, in novels, does not interest the professional) — precisely that area which daily affects us as happy or unhappy human beings. The novelist of the twentieth century has acquired, however imperfectly, a new conception of human nature and its needs, and this intimately affects his work. He has, whether we like it or not, a "psychology." His conceptions may resemble particular academic conceptions fairly closely. Or he may, like Faulkner, offer a peculiar amalgam drawn from many sources, and to which something personal has been added. But in all events he finds it impossible to think of his characters in terms of their conscious longings only. This being so, it is hypocritical and misleading to skirt all comment which smacks of "psychologizing," or to describe the literary efforts of André Gide as though they were the literary efforts of Henry Fielding. Beyond this one must state, as an article of faith, that the important psychological novelist — a Dostoevsky, a Conrad, even a Gide — can throw as much light as the average psychiatrist on these everyday human difficulties, and sometimes a great deal more.

This book raised one further problem: whether to preserve the French texts or to substitute English translations. The violation of translation seemed more than ever serious where it concerned one of the greatest of French stylists, and a writer whose very syntax and prose rhythms make a calculated assault on the reader's feelings. But Gide's general human significance, the fact that he was so much more than a stylist, counseled translation. I have as a rule followed the compromise recommended by my publisher: to use English translations in the body of my book, and the French text in the notes. I generally use the standard English translations, including Martha Winburn England's translation of *Le Voyage d'Urien*, published in *New Directions 14* (New York, 1953). But occasionally I substitute translations of my own, and these are identified in the notes by my initials.

This book was begun on fellowships granted by the Rockefeller Foundation and the Milton-Clark Fund of Harvard University. It was completed in Paris in February 1951, while I was on a Fulbright grant. I am grateful for the facilities offered by the Bibliothèque Nationale, the Stanford University Library, the University of California Library, and the Harvard College Library. My personal debts are even greater than usual. Joseph Warren Beach, Mark Schorer, John Hawkes, Chase J. Duffy, Thomas J. Wilson, Armand Pierhal, my father, and my mother read all or part of the book in manuscript, and made helpful suggestions. I particularly want to record the help given by the members of my Harvard seminar on the Modern Novel, which met in the spring of 1950; some of this help is acknowledged specifically in the notes. I am deeply grateful to André Gide, whose conversation and letters gave encouragement as well as advice. Finally: the Angèle who reappears in Gide's writings combats groundless fantasies with an inalienable yet sympathetic common sense. There has been, most important of all, my wife Maclin and own invaluable Angèle, who has read and commented on every version of this book.

POSTSCRIPT

The last lines of my preface were written on Thursday, February 16, and the manuscript sent off that afternoon. Gide died Monday night, February 19. Monday morning we decided to go down to Chartres with friends. On the way I read that Gide was very ill, presumably dying. Chartres was still beautiful, though hideous lights now top the towers to warn planes from the airfield nearby. But the day was very cold. We went home earlier than we had planned, I bought more newspapers, and the next morning read of Gide's death. I felt what many other strangers seem to have felt unaccountably — that someone very close to them had died. More abstractly, it was hard to believe that Gide had joined the company . . . of whom? Perhaps only of Amiel or of Benjamin Constant; perhaps even of Montaigne. In any event, my personal impression of Gide the man took on an interest which it lacked while he was still alive. Hundreds of people have known Gide well, where I knew him only slightly. Yet now I felt even my slight impression should be recorded.

I saw Gide only twice. The first time was in 1945, and I did not know then that I would write this book. I went to see him to transmit the *Kenyon Review's* offer of $25 for the American rights to his recent essay on Valéry. Twenty-five dollars! The figure seemed indeed absurd, when translated into francs at the artificial rate of exchange then current. I watched a secretary typing from manuscript, and tried to think of plausible arguments. Presently I was taken into Gide's study, a large shadowy room, and interviewed by Jean Amrouche (the editor of *L'Arche*). I had scarcely begun my eulogy of the *Kenyon Review* when Gide himself appeared; in his skullcap, very thin, his face a curious mixture of skepticism and friendly curiosity. No doubt he was amused to be offered $25 by an American soldier who was not even wearing his sergeant's stripes. We sat face to face across a small bare table; and, remembering his many attempts to stop smoking and his many failures, I offered him a cigarette. Some private devil prompted me to leave the pack on the table, though he had refused. Through the first minutes of our talk his eyes dropped repeatedly to the open pack, and at last (with a studied casualness?) the long fingers reached out.

Gide's speech was studied: slow and artfully seductive, the voice and rhythms of a man who loves words. I suspected that he knew the *Kenyon Review* as well as I, and that he would accept the offer. But he was not to be deprived of his fun. He pushed me on to more and more extravagant praises of the *Kenyon,* more and more elaborate reasonings on the poverty of American quarterlies and the distinction of their readers. And all the time I felt that Gide was gauging me rather than the *Kenyon Review.* I mention this because so many others have noticed the same thing — this incorrigible curiosity concerning any stranger who may happen along. "And if this review has such highly educated readers, couldn't they read my essay in French?" Couldn't one of our more commercial magazines publish it? Yes, I admitted that *Harper's* or the *Atlantic Monthly* might be interested. This went on and on, and at last Amrouche returned to say that A was waiting in room X, B in room Y, C in room Z. I had the impression of a busy doctor's office, with patients waiting in tiny cubicles. Gide stood up. "Then as I understand it, you are asking me to choose between art and money. I shall give you my answer on Monday." And on Monday he telephoned the decision which I am sure he had taken before I left. I remember the terror on my secretary's face as she held her hand over the mouthpiece of the phone. "C'est Monsieur Gide! Monsieur Gide lui-même!"

Since then Gide has written in answer to various queries, and two of his letters will be found at the end of this book. I did not see him again until December 1950, when I had finished a draft of my last chapter. I knew he had been tired and ill through the fall, and in any event I wanted to reach my own interpretations before consulting him. But I was not prepared to find him as tired as he was. His secretary phoned to ask me to come at four o'clock; it was a few days after the première of *Les Caves du Vatican*. I got caught in a traffic jam near the Chamber of Deputies, and was some minutes late. But Gide was still asleep; and once he fell asleep, these days, they never woke him. Would I mind waiting? I sat in a tiny bourgeois salon next to the reception room where I had waited in 1945. A postman arrived with a package. Then a maid scurried down a long hall to tell me that Gide was waking up. The phone rang: a Mrs. Gould. First the maid talked, then Elisabeth van Rysselberghe. "Yes, I know he would want to talk to you. But — can you believe it? — we can't find him. Yes, we've looked everywhere. Yes, we looked there. Do hold the phone: he has to be *somewhere* in the apartment!" I thought of the many forms of evasiveness Gide had mastered in his long life. Was he still, at eighty-one, the man who has just left?

But here he was — pausing, on his way to the phone, to apologize for keeping me waiting. I could not help hearing him talk into a telephone fifteen feet away. It was the voice of an exhausted and dying man, a kind of plaintive whisper. Mrs. Gould, I gather, was congratulating him on *Les Caves du Vatican*. And did she really enjoy the play? Didn't she find it too long? He was working on it day after day, to cut out a few more lines. Gide's voice found strength as the minutes passed; the phrases took on elegance, the voice its old charm and seductiveness. "Ah, c'est bien! Ah que vous êtes gentille!" Then he had hung up and was with me: in a shabby gray coat, a beret instead of the skullcap, and with a day's beard. He began by telling me how tired he was. And indeed the telephone conversation had exhausted him.

His memory seemed to be failing him. At first he remembered neither me, nor my book, nor the fact that he had proposed I come that day . . . all understandable enough. But also he seemed not to remember Jacques Rivière and his essay on "Le Roman d'aventure." I was obliged, at first,

to "fill him in" on everything. Then I had the impression
of a man recovering strength before my eyes. Were the ideas
in Rivière's essay really Gide's own, borrowed from various
conversations? The forty years gradually lessened as we dis-
cussed the essay, but Gide remained noncommittal. "Il est
bien difficile de préciser ces choses." We talked then about
Jean Schlumberger's *Saint-Saturnin*. Yes, Schlumberger may
have borrowed some of his technical innovations from *Les
Faux-Monnayeurs*, but I was right in assuming that Schlumberger had reached his own ethic independently. I had the
dismal impression that Gide would agree with anything I
said; that all these matters were too distant, too unimportant.
A few minutes later, on my way out, I saw Schlumberger
standing in the hall. Did he hear our discussion of his book?

With me, as with Mrs. Gould, Gide recovered energy as
the minutes passed. And suddenly he wanted to know about
my courses at Harvard, one of which examines his work in
some detail. Did I have many students? I recalled to him that
I seemed to value *L'Immoraliste* more highly than he did,
and that in my most elementary course three hundred students had read the novel with enthusiasm. I told him that
a kind of Gallup Poll on the final examination had put
Camus's *La Peste* at the summit of the modern novel, *L'Immoraliste* near the top — and *Madame Bovary* near the bottom. The failure of *Madame Bovary* gave him an ill-concealed
delight. "Can that be? Isn't that interesting? Interesting . . ."
I left him the manuscript of my final chapter and prepared
to leave. And now — many others have testified to this burst
of enthusiasm which speeds the parting guest — he was full
of personal solicitude. What did I think of Paris? How long
could I stay? Had I found a comfortable place to live? His
face lit up; his hands began to work up and down like those
of a cheerleader. "Allons, allons! Je suis content." His eyes
were shining with friendliness, his handshake was firm. And
I left him, for my overcoat and the dark hallway, where I
saw Jean Schlumberger waiting. Going down in the elevator
I felt, as I had felt in 1945, that an infinitely subtle mind
had played over and looked into me. But also I experienced

a new energy and enthusiasm, which had passed into me in some occult fashion. Gide was very old and very tired, yes. But he would always be able to collect his strength, prod his memory, pull himself together. Such a man, it seemed to me that afternoon, would certainly not die.

Albert J. Guerard

Paris
March 7, 1951

POSTSCRIPT (1969)

November 22, 1969, marks the hundredth anniversary of Gide's birth. Eighteen years have passed since his death, and since the first publication of this book. A number of scholarly and critical studies have appeared in the interim, as well as important collections of letters. There have been divers debates and questionings, and for a time the provocative or diabolic Gide came to seem, especially for some French readers, harmless and irrelevant. The struggle for sexual freedom and sincerity, at least, had long since been won. More recently Gide has taken on a larger, more timeless relevance: as a literary artist especially, as a master of language and living voice addressed less to his contemporaries (or to contemporary issues) than to young people of any epoch.

I have found no need to repudiate or alter the literary judgments I made in the first edition. It is now possible, on the other hand, to examine more fully the terms of Gide's psychosexual conflict, and to assess with more confidence the stresses and strains of his marriage. His own *Et nunc manet in te* (1951) casts a moving if sometimes deceptive light on the marriage. Jean Schlumberger's *Madeleine et André Gide* (1956) and Jean Delay's *La Jeunesse d'André Gide* (1956) provided thoughtful correctives to Gide's contrite self-incriminating narrative. Delay's book, translated in abridged form as *The Youth of André Gide* (1963), is a major work of humane and comprehensive scholarship.

My new appendix, "The Posthumous Revelations," examines some of these matters, and considers further the psychosexual background of *L'Immoraliste*, a novel still widely misinterpreted.

Albert J. Guerard

Stanford University
February 20, 1969

CONTENTS

GIDE'S UNENDING SEARCH FOR HARMONY *

BY THOMAS MANN

WHEN ANDRÉ GIDE HAD REACHED HIS SEVENTY-SECOND YEAR in 1941 there existed (according to the bibliography of Talvart and Place) some thirty books about him. Furthermore, there were 150 others, containing extensive essays on his work, and, finally, more than 500 articles and reviews scattered about in various magazines. This flood of literature on a contemporary writer, whether admiring, polemic, or both, was always of an emotional nature, and always betrayed a deep personal stake and concern. In the last decade, particularly around the time of his eightieth birthday, and now that he has passed away at the age of eighty-two (almost exactly the age of Goethe, one of his most beloved preceptors), this flood probably has expanded further.

Of course, it is France that has taken the most active part in a critical search and examination of Gide's complex and daring life, of his challenging work. America's contribution, despite the high level of literary criticism in this country, has been small: as far as I know (granted that I don't rely too much on my knowledge) there has been no major exploration of the intellectual phenomenon of Gide — as inviting to the art of criticism as it may be — since the incisive biography by Klaus Mann was published some eight years ago. Today the book, *André Gide,* by Albert J. Guerard (Harvard University Press, 1951), which I shall discuss here, will (surely for another eight years) make up for everything that American critics owe this extraordinary subject.

Albert J. Guerard, Associate Professor of English at Har-

* An essay-review first published in the *New York Times Book Review,* August 19, 1951. © 1951 by the New York Times Company. Reprinted by permission.

vard,[1] an American of European descent, a man of comprehensive literary erudition, intimately familiar with French intellectual currents, does understand and makes understandable America's aloofness toward a writer who has acquired the rank of a *contemporain capital* during a life conducted with magnificent and conscientious candor.

"We are no longer dealing," he says, "with a traditional teller of tales. . . . Unlike Hardy and Conrad, Gide has been a man of letters and explicit moralist, rather than a novelist only. . . . But the American novelist (and reader) of today deeply distrusts such versatility, and intimacy, such intellectual pretension. The novelist should rather be a craftsman, an impersonal and expert storyteller. . . . The very concept of the exemplary role or the exemplary conflict is foreign to our way of thinking."

There becomes apparent the dissimilarity between French, or general-European, and American cultural life; and just as it is Gide's over-all issue and design, so Mr. Guerard's book is but a single-minded attempt to lift Gide's most personal and intimate problems into universal ones, and, vice versa, "to interpret public dilemmas in the most personal terms." It was this, above all, that made Gide so representative. And yet Gide would not have been just this without one talent which counts nowhere so much as among the French: if he had not been an extraordinary virtuoso of prose, if he did not possess a unique style, capable of every nuance, and so persuasive that it triumphed over the most contrary materials.

It is always a happy aesthetic experience to find a book that equals in essence and performance the virtues of its subject. Mr. Guerard describes a life led under exacting predicaments; he portrays a man who won out over guilt and neurosis through the discipline of his art, for whom this art had become the saving instrument of self-control, and for whom language and style had turned into the blessed remedies for the anarchy within.

In a similar manner, the ordered, lucid intelligence of a

[1] Now Professor of English at Stanford University.

sagacious critic is needed to conquer the contradictions and
paradoxes of the *oeuvre* born from this anarchy — and Mr.
Guerard's book possesses and practices this skill. Its author
is precisely the stylist which the task requires. A thoroughly
Americanized Frenchman, he uses his rich vocabulary to
write an English of utmost flexibility that matches achievement with achievement and is able to follow the tortured
twists of its theme, since it is both progeny and instrument of
the determination to simplify the complex and bring order
into the chaos.

The volume in which this is done contains first a preface,
spiced with personal anecdotes, and then five chapters of
about the same length. The first is a psychological study of
"The Crisis of Individualism" in our time; the second treats
of Gide's "Spiritual Autobiographies" — such books as *The
Notebooks of André Walter* and *If It Die* (Random House,
1935); the third is dedicated to the earlier novels, particularly
The Immoralist (Alfred A. Knopf, 1930); and the fourth to
the narratives of the later years, especially *The Counterfeiters* (also Knopf, 1927).

The concluding fifth chapter bears the ironical title, *The
Corruptor of Youth* — an unmistakable allusion to Socrates'
trial, and a very fitting one. For at each step, Gide's "corrupting" effect — corrupting because it is morally disquieting and
undermines tradition — is reminiscent of Socrates and the
radical-Protestant confessionalism of J. J. Rousseau. It stands,
so to speak, in this mythical tradition.

The five sections of the book could have been published as
independent essays; however, they overlap. *If It Die*, for
instance, is drawn upon at different places; the same psychological motive appears again and again, in new contexts and
newly illuminated, and thus the chapters join, after all, into
an interconnected unit — just as does the lifework which they
interpret and which, like few others, demonstrates that what
counts is not the single book, even though it makes a claim
to finality, but the opus in its entirety.

"A single book," Mr. Guerard says quite accurately, "may
save or corrupt us by a single message or particular energies.

Only a series of books is likely to provide the contours of an attitude and a full image of our age."

Mr. Guerard's wide-ranging appraisal of Gide's interesting — some may say all-too-interesting — personality is by no means a panegyric; he is American enough to abhor unconditional glorification. Mr. Guerard does criticize. And his reservations concern something fundamental: the purely creative powers of his hero which he calls "intermittent and slight." Repeatedly, he admits "the unevenness of Gide's achievement as a novelist," caused chiefly by a special brand of subjectivity, "an introspectiveness of talent and imagination," and a resulting inability to identify himself with minds radically different from his own.

There is even a certain lack of talent for keeping alive the experiences of his own youth, for re-creating them in his ripe age with convincing freshness. And certainly, other modern writers have been able to conquer larger epic fields, to fashion their creations into the image of a wider cosmos and populate them with a greater number of living characters.

And yet Mr. Guerard quite correctly calls the author of *The Immoralist, The Counterfeiters,* and *The Vatican Swindle* (Knopf, 1925) one "of the most important novelists of our century, who has modified our ideas and our image of the modern world," and he supports this statement chiefly with *The Immoralist,* to him Gide's best novel and one of the masterpieces of modern fiction. He puts this early work not only above the impudent, entertaining *The Vatican Swindle,* but above *The Counterfeiters.*

It is not easy for me to concur with Mr. Guerard's judgment, which, incidentally, presents a somewhat humorous contradiction to the fact that it is *The Counterfeiters* to which Mr. Guerard dedicates, in his fourth chapter, the most extensive interpretation — the truly critical virtuoso piece of the book. Isn't *The Immoralist* of 1902 a first novel of rather faded originality, whose capacity to shock has largely been lost through the decades, and whose title, inspired by Nietzsche, smothers the content by sheer philosophical dead weight?

And, after all, isn't it *The Counterfeiters* which plays a more important role in the history of the European novel than *The Immoralist?* And the name of André Gide, the novelist, won't it be rather connected with the great, experimental *Counterfeiters* of a man of almost sixty? Today (and it has been like this for quite some time) we need more "sense of history," more distance from our actual knowledge of psychology — not to say sexual pathology — in order to appreciate the earlier work.

True, long before Freud's research data had reached the public's consciousness, the story of *The Immoralist* anticipated a complete insight into the conflict between conscious and pre- or sub-conscious life. This insight stems from Gide's homosexual disposition — which remained latent and misunderstood for a surprisingly long time — a disposition which has been the root and fount of his moral dynamism, of his revolutionary disavowal of everything respectable-traditional, and of all conformist security. It has made him into a great mover and shaker who, in the long run, will have served human progress, and who could say of himself: "To disturb, that is my role."

In an admirable manner, Mr. Guerard puts into bold relief the basic procreative dilemma of this mind. He makes us experience this dilemma between an inherited puritanism, never denied and never to be denied, and the self-preservation of a natural drive that deviates from the so-called "natural." Incapable of both a nonchalant hedonism (which he pursued occasionally and made predominant in *The Fruits of the Earth*) and of an unfettered puritanism, this mind oscillates — or plays — between the realm of order, which he needs desperately, and that of anarchy, to which he is equally heir. Until at the end he makes this very state of oscillation the basis of a new ethics.

Gide is not the man of the "golden middle" — this is precisely what he despises most. His task is the cultivation of the extremes; to hold them in precarious harmony is the mission of his life, and a rather tricky one. If out of all this a moral could be pointed — if Gide himself had wanted us to point one — it could only be this: that every principle is nothing but the corrective of its opposite.

It is worth watching how the ascetic element dominates in such a life as Gide's, which, willingly or unwillingly, has become a precept; for such a life demands an unceasing self-restraint, a discipline of its basic nature or of that which it assumes to conform with its nature. It demands the sacrifice of the ego, an abandon of "self-esteem," in the sense of finding peace in one's unique way of existence, in the sense of a completed, straightforward personality.

"He who loves life loses it, but he who hates it will win it forever." And: *"Si le grain ne meurt . . ."* These are Gide's favorite recurring mottoes from the Bible. Without knowing Nietzsche, the immoralist out of morality, Gide arrived at the tenet that "virtue demands its own sacrifice." Before having been aware of the more imposing parallel phenomenon of the German philosopher, he insisted he had "to spoil everything he cared for," and just as with Nietzsche, the puzzled spectators have asked themselves how someone could live who kept sawing off the branch on which he was sitting.

But he has lived, and as an artist he has made creative this very contradiction. It cannot be denied that he sublimated a good deal of prankishness, a tendency to hoax and mystification, into this special type of morality. There exists a demonic unfaithfulness, a fickle and protean tergiversation, a slippery elusion and vexing refusal to be defined and tied down; and, finally, a delight in teasing the good people by bewitching them with ideas for whose possible wickedness the writer finds equally convincing words.

This hobgoblinism implies really a high sincerity, an unconditional candor; and its intellectual restlessness is quite different from the relativism of such skeptics as Renan and Anatole France; it is truly an unending search for truth, and a readiness to suffer the solitude of freedom which could be called heroic.

There beckoned for the dear soul the two ports and comforting shelters that have served as an escape to many a contemporary: Communism and the Catholic Church. Gide, whose nature needs commitment as much as freedom from it, experimented with Communism out of sheer rebellious spirit, and for a short while; but very soon he discovered that it was "only relatively justifiable." Often he held out hope to his worried friend, Paul Claudel, that he might become a convert to Catholicism; yet, although a thorough Christian and a traditionalist as well as a revolutionary, he nourished a pronounced aversion to pragmatic Catholicism as represented by the nationalist Barrès.

He wrote *The Prodigal Son* — which helped him, as Guerard says, to avoid real conversion. He was religious, but he found Catholicism "inadmissible" and Protestantism "insufferable." He knew how difficult it is to bear freedom, but his fear of it was outweighed by fear of mental luxuries, of all conformism, of the slackening of vital tensions and the slothful submission to authority. Whenever he was tempted to feel satisfaction, he quickly withdrew into the wilderness of his proud and cunning individualism; as a man and alone he looked the Sphinx in the eye and put up his riddle against hers.

This is infinitely sympathetic, and even though it adds to his personality a few whimsical, erratic traits — traits familiar to everyone who knew him — it still awakens brotherly feelings. His work struck out in favor of realism, and against it; it was filled with experimentation, and at the same time stimulated a new classicism — although a classicism purposely standing aloof from that of the conservatives, Maurras and Brunetière, in politics as well as morals.

Mr. Guerard says of *The Counterfeiters* that it is much less radical an experiment than *Ulysses*, yet at the same time less realistic. In a fitting phrase, he calls Gide "a cautious radical and a daring conservative" — and precisely this mixture made me confess to brotherly feelings.

Gide's famous "curiosity" was as strong in the realm of literature as of morality, and it conferred on France considerable benefits. It was this curiosity that helped most to break through the Chinese Wall which, until recently, has surrounded the exclusive and precious culture of France.

Gide insisted that classical French tradition needed, more than anything else, a rejuvenation and renascence through strong and demonic energies, imported from without, and as a vigorous propagandist of such ideas he let the fresh air stream in from everywhere.

Without Gide, the French might still be looking at Dostoevsky as an odd, unfathomable genius. And if Henry James appeared too rational, too distinguished, too "French" to benefit France, Conrad's reputation was considerably increased by Gide's appreciation. The United States owes him a debt for his efforts to bring Whitman and Melville to the French public, and if this public today is familiar with the names of Faulkner, Hemingway, Steinbeck, Caldwell, a good part of the credit must go to Gide's "curiosity."

On the reverse side, Gide's name, reputation, and influence have never been spread far in the United States. Mr. Guerard ventures that this should be changed — that's probably why he has written his book. He believes that a "demoralizer" of this format, a destructive but controlled intellect, questioning all preconceptions, yet with a natural feeling for tradition and order, would be quite useful in this country "with its lingering puritanism and its tendency to slogan thinking." Yes, he even declares that "it would hardly be possible to overestimate the benefits an American Gide would confer."

One cannot help being touched by the author's concluding phrases, in which he speaks of the "expedient decision and convenient fiction, the virtuous rationalization of impulses to power or survival, the collective hypnotic illusion," which the pressure of events has forced upon this country, its education, its government within a few years.

He says:

"We have become pragmatists on a monstrous scale, and are much closer than most people think to the world of Orwell's *1984* where what ought to be is 'honestly' mistaken for what is. The pragmatist's truth (which Gide hated more than anything else) has gradually come to seem more true than fact. The mechanisms of propaganda grow constantly more powerful, and with them our capacities for self-flattery and self-delusion. It is hard to see how, in the years that face us, young people will learn to think truthfully, rather than to think usefully or patriotically. In such a world, we can be sure, there will be few demoralizers to combat the radio, the newspaper, the communiqué, the leaflet. These few may seem merely decadent, and Gide himself the product of a dead culture and leisure class. Yet perhaps only these few demoralizers shall save us."

ANDRE GIDE

1

THE CRISIS
OF INDIVIDUALISM

TO GIVE MUCH ATTENTION TO A WRITER'S
life is, as a rule, an easy way to escape his significance
as an artist. It has been said, in defense of biography
and minute scholarship, that they prepare the way for criticism. Yet the monographs on a Dickens or a Dostoevsky accumulate appallingly, while fewer and fewer critics are willing
to attempt comprehensive studies of their work. Beyond this
biographers have actively misled us: not merely by offering
so much amusing atmosphere and gossip, but by documenting
so heavily the writer's "sources" and his rational "intentions."
The rare first-rate critical biography reminds us, instead,
that the real sources of a work of art are irrecoverable, that
a great novel or poem often triumphs over its author's intentions, and that the personality of the artist may be very different from the public personality of the citizen. Thus a record
of Thomas Hardy's uneventful life and stolid public manner
tells us little of his love for the whimsical, the macabre, the
strange. And a romantic interest in Joseph Conrad's career
as a master mariner makes it all the more difficult to perceive
his profoundly intellectual genius.

Faced by André Gide, however, we must for once concede
a real relevance to biography: to the actual recorded curve
and particular events of the writer's life. This is true not

merely because an intense subjectivity imperiled Gide the
novelist, or because Gide the man triumphed over guilt and
neurosis only through the discipline of art. Actual events,
actual divagations and sufferings, both energized his books
and made their writing difficult. In still larger terms, Gide's
life — refashioned symbolically in his books — has reflected
minutely the drama of modern individualism and therefore
has a general interest. Neither Conrad's life nor his austere
ethic of rejection has much immediate significance for the
modern world. We must look instead to his previsions, in
Nostromo and *Heart of Darkness* and *Secret Agent,* of our
present capacities for violence and collective self-delusion.
With Gide, on the other hand, the issues are particular and
immediate. Since 1897 France has been, thanks to the Dreyfus
case and to two wars, and thanks also to the French passion
for debate, the "conscience" of Western civilization; the
country, that is, where moral consequences have been recognized and debated most ruthlessly. And the most representative French novelist and moralist of the twentieth century
has certainly been André Gide. The timid young puritan
who attended the salon of Stéphane Mallarmé, there to discuss how literature could best avoid the contamination of
life, was by 1934 a public figure of enough importance to
plead with Goebbels for Dimitrov. His political essays, letters,
and speeches between 1930 and 1938 were sufficient — together with a play on labor relations — to supply a volume
called *Littérature engagée.* To be sure, Gide has long since
returned to the conviction that literature must remain dis-
engaged. Yet in 1950, at eighty-one, he could take a rightful
place in the film *La Vie commence demain* — with Picasso,
Le Corbusier, Jean Rostand, and a very few others — as one
of the makers of the modern mind. He had been the intellectual descendant of Dostoevsky and Nietzsche; he was to
be, in a sense, the intellectual father of Jean-Paul Sartre
and especially of Albert Camus. It is given to few persons to
live such markedly symbolic lives.

The hidden (not outward) stresses of Conrad's life helped
him to dramatize the condition of "modern man": skeptical,

homeless, and neurotic; tormented by guilt and tempted to self-destruction. This is even more true with Gide, whose personal conflicts required a rationalization of anxiety; it is characteristic of the modern temperament that the most particular should become the most general. The essential conflict seems to have been, at a first glance, between a strong ascetic impulse and the imperious demands of homosexual desire; or, perhaps, between a succession of saintly and inflexible women and a succession of charming Arab boys. Some rebels can exist outside the Law, but Gide could not. He was therefore obliged to demonstrate a Law which would justify his anomaly and admit his most contradictory impulses. He was equally incapable of casual hedonism and of untroubled puritanism and constantly oscillated between order and anarchy — until at last he made the very state of oscillation the foundation for a new ethic.

Gide was born in Paris on November 22, 1869. "Born in Paris, of an Uzès father and a Norman mother — where, Mr. Barrès, will you have me become 'rooted'?" [1] His father, who died when André was eleven, was a professor in the faculty of law at the University of Paris; he was descended from an unbroken Protestant line and was appropriately named by his colleagues *Vir Probus*. André Gide's mother came from the Rondeaux family of Rouen, which had included a few Catholics, but she herself was brought up as a Protestant. French protestantism has always shown the passionate austerity of a threatened minority group, yet has had a long tradition of intellectual distinction. As a child Gide saw the faithful of Uzès keep their hats on during worship, in memory of the days when they had been forced to meet out-of-doors and secretly, under the torrid skies of Languedoc. Gide was always determined to prove himself a creature of contradiction and insists perhaps too strongly on the difference between the two families and the two regions. Georges Lemaitre contrasts the "pure intellectuality" of the Uzès region, "where even asceticism is not out of place," with the cheerful hedonism and "fundamental sensuousness" of Normandy; [2] but many visitors at least would be tempted to reverse the terms.

Gide describes his mother as an uncompromising puritan; Normandy would often seem to him a land of fog and gloom.

Gide's sickly childhood was largely surrounded by pious and austere women; he saw his uncle, the economist Charles Gide, only rarely. There was Anna Shackleton, the retiring Scottish spinster who had been Madame Gide's governess, and whose humble resignation was to be remembered in *La Porte étroite*; there were the Misses Fleur and de Gœcklin, teachers; there was Aunt Claire, who devoted her life to keeping up bourgeois appearance. And there was above all Madame Gide herself, determined that her only son should have every advantage and determined also that he should be protected from every contaminating influence. She saw to it that he had piano lessons and took him to concerts, but forbade Chopin as "unwholesome." She spared no expense for private tutors or for trips intended to improve her son's health. But even after his literary career had begun she made him account strictly for a three-hundred-franc monthly allowance. Resistance to the mother's moral tyranny — "this continual pressure which she exerted on others" — is the concealed undercurrent which runs through Gide's *Si le grain ne meurt* and comes violently to the surface of its final pages.

One other woman played an extremely important part in Gide's childhood and later life, his cousin Madeleine Rondeaux, the Emmanuèle of *Si le grain ne meurt*.* When he was eight years old, Gide had been expelled from the Ecole Alsacienne for masturbating in the classroom; the family doctor had tried to cure him by threatening a surgical operation. The boy of thirteen, still haunted by a sense of guilt, directed all his longing for purity toward Madeleine, the most idealistic and most reserved of his vacation companions. Her mother's infidelity had saddened her, and given her an extreme horror of anything that suggested "sin." Gide did not understand this fully until some time later, but one day he found Madeleine kneeling at the side of her bed and in tears; and then and there discovered the "mystic orient" of

---

* See Appendix (1969), "The Posthumous Revelations," for new light on the marriage. See also Gide's *Et nunc manet in te.*

his life. "No, I should understand nothing of all that until later. But I knew a great, an intolerable distress dwelt in this little being I already cherished — such an affliction as would demand all my love and all my life to cure." [3] Together the two little puritans planned a life of piety and austere heroism. In his most somber and tormented hours Gide never gave up the idea that he would eventually marry Madeleine and in 1890 he naïvely hoped his first published book would overcome her scruples — which were those of Alissa Bucolin in *La Porte étroite*. Gide's own feelings seemed to have remained as ethereal as those of the thirteen-year-old boy. He married Madeleine at last, in 1895, but only after having discovered and liberated his homosexual inclinations.

The sexual conflict, both before and after this curious marriage, was of course a crucial chapter in Gide's life; it was the concealed subject of most of his early books and the admitted subject of *Si le grain ne meurt*. Was Gide driven to homosexuality by a quasi-religious veneration for Madeleine, the only woman he had ever thought of marrying; and by the fact that his childhood had been surrounded by saintly and austere women? Or did the still unsuspected homosexual inclinations determine his chaste feelings toward Madeleine? These are among the few questions which Gide has made no real effort to answer. The remainder of the self-portrait is so full and so familiar that it requires only the briefest summary here, though later we shall consider in detail how frustration expressed itself through the symbolic action of art. We need only recall that at the age of twenty Gide was tormented by erotic reveries yet refused himself normal sexual experience — whether out of homosexual distaste or puritan distrust of the flesh. In this dilemma he reverted again to masturbation, and was again tormented by guilt. The struggle to overcome masturbation is, Gide tells us, the real "subject" of his first book, *Les Cahiers d'André Walter*.[4] But even while writing this book he wondered whether sin had not invaded him in another guise. Was not the egotistical pride which he took in his occasional victories over the flesh more corrupt than the flesh itself? The weari-

ness of the debate drove André Walter mad. It made Gide
want to "dissolve" the conscience which did the debating.

Pierre Loüys introduced Gide to some of his literary
friends; Gide went to Mallarmé's Tuesday evenings and to
Hérédia's Saturday afternoons, carrying a Bible in his pocket.
At this time he seems to have had no suspicion of his latent
homosexuality; he had long felt a horror of the abnormal.
He was aware only that somewhere beneath the stiff and un-
comfortable self which faced the world, and which thus
courted both God and the symbolist poets, lay another, a
mysterious and *real* self, which longed to make its appearance.
He began to wonder, then, whether God wanted him to suffer
so: divided within himself, torn between undefined but certainly contradictory needs. And having taken this first step,
he imagined a possible state of being which would harmonize
the discord. When he left for Algeria in October of 1893,
with Paul-Albert Laurens, it was with the deliberate intention
of discovering the imagined harmony. At Sousse a native boy,
who discerned Gide's inclinations more clearly than he did
himself, provided a first and clandestine experience. At Biskra,
determined to "normalize" his desires, Gide regularly shared
an Oulad Naïl prostitute, Mériem, with Laurens. Even this
symbolic victory over the puritan enemy, though not wholly
satisfactory, calmed his taut nerves. Meanwhile, however,
Gide had begun to spit blood, and Laurens wrote home in
alarm. The anxious and implacable mother came to Biskra
at once, and discovered the "ménage-à-trois." Gide even went
out of his way to explain that Mériem came for him as well
as for Laurens; this was the first of his important confessions.

From Biskra, Gide went to Champel, for the cure, and
then returned to France — with some of the anguish "Lazarus
must have felt when he escaped from the tomb." The things
that had hitherto interested him no longer seemed of any
importance; he now felt himself a stranger in the pretentious
atmosphere of the literary salons. He went to La Brévine in
Switzerland for further months of cure, and was repelled
by the sullen hostility of the peasants. In January 1895 he
went to Algeria again — and at Blida discovered the names

of Oscar Wilde and Lord Alfred Douglas on the hotel black-
board which served as a guests' register. Gide immediately
erased his own name and left for the station. He had met
Wilde in Paris, but had not heard of his homosexuality until
later. Before he reached the station, however, Gide regretted
what seemed to him an act of pharisaical cowardice. He returned to the hotel, and that night joined Wilde and Douglas
in a tour of the Blida cafés. But it was only some days later,
in Algiers, that Wilde forced him to acknowledge his desires.
Why does Gide so emphasize the part played by Wilde, since
the night spent with the little native musician in Algiers was
not his first homosexual experience? Precisely because Wilde's
direct question demanded a direct answer; a frank admission
to someone else, and therefore to himself, that he *was* a homosexual. The one word "Oui" — spoken in the dark street
and "with what a strangled voice" — was a recognition of the
suspected but suppressed self.

Thereafter Gide's task was one of self-justification and ad-
justment rather than of self-discovery. He had to preach to
others the gospel of liberation from repression and childhood
influence. But beyond this he had to construct an ethical
system which would not exclude him, which would admit
the existence of his anomaly. The first notable attempt was
his manual of affirmation, escape, and hedonistic joy, *Les
Nourritures terrestres* (1897). Its essential message was this:
various forces — a person's moral and intellectual heritage;
his family and books and whole childhood; his obligations,
principles, and habits — conspire to impose on each man a
mechanical and factitious self. They simply prevent him from
living. The only way to bring the true self to the surface,
and thus give it life, is to discard ruthlessly everything acquired and very nearly everything inherited. The first step
toward liberating the real self is to destroy or dissolve the
self which conceals or suppresses it.

In summarizing thus briefly, it is hard to avoid the impression that Gide merely did what he wanted to do in a rather
roundabout way. But no such simple explanation can cope
with the complex movement of these years. At the time he

wrote *Les Nourritures terrestres,* Gide had already sacrificed
his hard-won liberty. He had married Madeleine Rondeaux.
Why? Gide explains on the last page of *Si le grain ne meurt*
that he hoped to lead her to his own faith in a freer life. His
love for her remained, after his mother's death, the first thing
he could fall back on and, no doubt, the strongest possible
counterweight to an alarmingly full liberty. We can never
hope to understand Gide unless we recognize that his "dread
of comfort" (of spiritual inertia, of easy conformity, of lazy
submission to authority) was no stronger than his "dread
of liberty"; [5] and that he could entertain the two fears simultaneously. But Gide acknowledges that his marriage cannot
be easily explained:

> Our most sincere acts are also the least calculated, and the ex-
> planations we later seek for them are futile. Fate drove me on;
> also perhaps a secret need to challenge my own nature; for in
> Emmanuèle was it not virtue itself I loved? This was heaven,
> which my insatiable hell was marrying, but I would not acknowl-
> edge this hell at the time. The tears of my mourning had
> quenched . its fires. I was as dazzled by heavenly light, and
> what I no onger consented to see had simply ceased to exist. I
> thought I could give to her my whole self, and did so without
> reserve. Some time after that we became engaged.[6]

The biographer who some day tries, perhaps irrelevantly,
to recreate Gide's actual life will no doubt have to give this
marriage an important place in his story. The critic concerned
with something very different (Gide's generalized image of
himself) would falsify his data by doing so. Only a few entries
in the *Journal* suggest what the marriage may have, in particular, signified. Gide always returned to Madeleine and to
Cuverville, their Norman estate, after his longest journeys.
He appears to have loved his wife until her death in 1938
with some of the thirteen-year-old boy's pity, awe, and reverence — and with no little exasperation. For no woman could
have been less suited to join him in the journeys themselves,
the daring individualistic adventures. The moving portrait
in the *Journal* for 1931 unmistakably recalls the self-denying
Alissa of *La Porte étroite*: "Her natural humility would not

admit that she could be superior in anything, and thus she condemned herself to the most ordinary occupations, in which nevertheless her superiority was obvious. From witnessing, powerless, this progressive renunciation, which she even refused to recognize, I suffered unspeakably." [7] Gide's restless, questioning mind tried without success to overcome his wife's modest but inflexible puritanism. He says that all his books prior to *Les Faux-Monnayeurs* were written under her influence and "in the vain hope of convincing her." She represented the force of piety which underlies *André Walter*, *L'Immoraliste*, *La Porte étroite*, and *La Symphonie pastorale*, and which provoked the sharply reacting hedonism of *Les Caves du Vatican*.[8] She was always there, to call the Prodigal Son back to his home and his Christian inheritance. It was perhaps chiefly for Madeleine that Gide argued he had rejected puritan virtue out of love for a more genuine virtue.

We can estimate the effect of Gide's marriage in a very general way. Most obviously it forced him to work out a theory of love which argued a complete divorce of the mind and the body, of homosexual pleasure and heterosexual love. (In 1924, after reading Freud, Gide speculated on the possible dangers of such a separation,[9] but he had dramatized them long since in *L'Immoraliste*.) He struggled at various times against his homosexual inclinations, and more than once reverted to onanism as a result of too harsh repression. He was frequently moved by pity for Madeleine (an emotion which in theory he disapproved), and most of his novels present sympathetically the plight of neglected wives. He had furthermore a very real distaste for obvious self-indulgence. But against these restrictive forces stood the inclinations themselves, which were no doubt unusually strong, as well as the recurring conviction that restraint helps the devil accomplish his work. Eventually he decided that it was useless to resist the temptations of the flesh, which he found far less distracting than those of the mind and heart. But for many years the conflict induced long sieges of alternating lassitude and nervous tension. The *Journal* records many of these bouts with "ennui" (which in French suggests both disquiet and apathy) — though here the biographer must recall that Gide seldom kept a full diary during his happy or productive periods. A common remedy for ennui was to take a trip, and more often than not the destination was North Africa; Biskra was as symbolic of freedom as Cuverville of constraint. The *Journal* leaves the impression that Gide's were less journeys in space than in time. He hoped by them, and generally in vain, to recover the hour of his first "liberation"; the sense of plenitude and fulfillment, of energy married to repose. The *Journal* is a record of uneasiness, insomnia, and headaches; of books read or piano compositions played, often for "hygienic reasons." But it is also, to an extraordinary degree, a record of arrivals and departures. The detailed history of Gide's sexual difficulties need not concern us, and it is very probably irrecoverable. But these difficulties certainly contributed to the various self-portraits he chose to give us; and which constitute a remarkable study of the restless and divided mind.*

Gide's reiterated desire to "dissolve the self" was thus partly a desire to destroy or overcome inhibition. But it was also a desire to abolish the sense of guilt, to liquidate it through confession. The child's abrupt expulsion from the Ecole Alsacienne and the stupidity of the family doctor may be at the root of these guilt feelings. The struggle against

---

* I do not mean to imply that the self-portraits are "insincere"; but autobiography, when it reaches the level of art, is very nearly as selective as fiction. A writer's general feeling of unrest at a particular moment may be due to many concurrent irritations: poor digestion, sexual frustration, bad weather, the fact that a book is "germinating" somewhere beneath the level of full consciousness, a sharp disappointment, etc. The author-diarist, since he is an artist, will necessarily bring some order out of this chaos, and will perhaps convince himself that sexual frustration is the only irritation to have any significance. This very act of choice at least minutely affects his total personality; creates a "new" personality. And it is this second personality which, more often than not, is "reflected" in his later works of art. The author's life as he actually lived it is very different from the author's life as he conceives, perceives it to have been. But only this second and already fictitious life has a real usefulness to the critic. Our hypothetical biographer will, no doubt, analyze Gide's long association with Elisabeth van Rysselberghe, the mother of Catherine Gide. Yet the more exact our information becomes, the more difficult it may be to recover the "reflective" Gide described in the autobiographies and "translated" in the novels.

onanism left its mark on *André Walter* and *Le Voyage d'Urien*, as we know from *Si le grain ne meurt*. But it was the homosexual liberation of 1893–1895 which Gide felt particularly bound to confess. He was long restrained from a complete and public admission by the fear of hurting his wife, though he had the true puritan's horror of presenting a false face to the world. The oblique confession of his early books failed to dispel Gide's reputation for saintly asceticism. *Corydon*, a theoretical defense of homosexuality, was first published anonymously in 1911; its judicious distribution illumined some of Gide's literary friends but not all. And soon he was convinced that he would occupy an important position in French literature and felt obliged to confess to the wide world. The writing of *Si le grain ne meurt* served a very real therapeutic function; it was an act of self-discovery as well as a revelation. But it was also intended to fix the truth for posterity. The public and full edition of *Si le grain ne meurt* did not appear until 1926, but Gide began writing the second and crucial part in 1919. Thereafter the extraordinary note of personal tension, the urgency of concealed forces, largely disappears from Gide's work. Complete confession resulted in a happier equanimity, but this very equanimity made his last novels uninteresting problem studies.

Thus, as with Conrad, the stress of very personal conflicts helped Gide to dramatize the isolation, the sense of guilt, the schizoid anxiety of the modern intellectual — and his alternating impulses toward order and anarchy. There was the significant difference that Gide lived in the intellectual center of the world and witnessed the birth of new ideas. He became involved, often against his will, in the most impassioned moral debates of modern times; he could not, like Conrad, reduce the question of social obligation to the clear-cut issue of traditional and undisciplined seamanship. And his effort as an artist was not a lonely and blundering one to the extent that Conrad's was. Conrad took up authorship late, persisted only because his first book chanced to fall into the hands of Edward Garnett, and thereafter tried by unremitting and agonized work to keep a balanced budget. Gide, on the other hand, was still a young *lycéen* when he determined on a literary career, and an independent income freed him from the necessity of commercial success. Once *André Walter* had disappointed his naïve expectations of immediate and universal celebrity, he resolved to bide his time. In 1893 he wrote that in spite of his great desire to get started he would not yet permit himself to begin writing again: "All day long I read, I go for walks, I seek pleasure; at night I go out again; I am thirsty and I quench my thirst . . ." [10] A year later, and with a patience exceeded only by Valéry's, Gide voluntarily postponed his important work to his fourth decade: "I have six more years of prefaces." And where Conrad depended until very late on the encouragement of a few friends who often misunderstood his work, even a brief list of Gide's friends reads like a dictionary of French and European literature from Stéphane Mallarmé to Albert Camus.

Gide nevertheless refused to capitalize on friendship to advance his literary career. He never became a docile member of any literary school, and engaged in his first and one of his last political maneuvers on his own behalf when he urged Loüys to distribute *André Walter* in the proper symbolist salons.* Even in these early years Gide was only a half-hearted symbolist, and the earthy *Nourritures terrestres* alienated his first admirers. He maintained cordial relations with Mallarmé until the master's death, but definitely broke with the irresponsible Loüys. In 1897 Léon Blum, then literary critic for the *Revue blanche*, welcomed Gide to the ranks of the *naturistes* whose vague affirmations were becoming fashionable, as did Saint-Georges de Bouhélier himself (the adolescent director of the school). But Gide responded with a very lukewarm comment on Bouhélier and Eugène Montfort. [11] He reacted in a similar fashion to the admirers of his later books. He welcomed pupils, whose complacency he wished to disturb, but he insisted that he always discouraged

---

* Gide's *Journal* perhaps exaggerates this reticence. He did not campaign as actively as others, but he did send copies of his books to influential people. And he was very disappointed when Francis Jammes decided not to write a promised article on his work.

disciples. Where authors normally seek to consolidate, from
book to book, both their publics and their own literary discoveries, Gide refused to profit by acquired momentum:
"Before each new book I am as uneasy as if I had never written
anything, and I reconsider the whole problem of art as for
the first time." [12] Gide recognized the dangers of such un-
orthodox strategy, but he was confident that his work would
prevail at last. He long thought, however, that this would
occur only after his death.

Until 1910, and to some extent until after the First World
War, Gide's reputation was that of a "coterie writer," though
with each new book the coterie underwent slight changes in
membership. A few die-hard symbolists forgave his novels
for the sake of his cloudy travelogues; a few decadents mis-
took his curiosity for a Satanic love of evil.[13] But even some
of his most friendly readers considered him perverse, delicate,
almost willfully minor. They cherished his books, as only
French readers can, for their exquisite prose style. In January
1907 Gide wrote that he had *created* the silence which surrounded his work by discouraging reviews in friendly magazines. Octave Mirbeau's belated mention of *L'Immoraliste*
and the unexpected success of *La Porte étroite* were perhaps
the first notable steps toward a less private reputation.[14] Yet
by 1925 Gide was already a living classic. *Vingt-cinq Ans de
littérature française*, edited by the unforgiving Eugène Montfort, could still dismiss him as a minor diabolic and the idol
of a clique, but René Lalou spoke for the unprejudiced in
describing him, in his *Histoire de la littérature française
contemporaine*, as the foremost prose writer of his generation.
Since 1925 he has been considered the most important intellectual influence of the period; and, with Proust and
Valéry, one of the greatest French writers of the century.

To understand how this emergence from obscurity could
have occurred, and so gradually that it took Gide's antagonists
by surprise, it is necessary to recall the peculiar importance
of the French literary magazine. Gide said, no doubt to torment them further, that Henri Massis and Henri Béraud had
made him famous by their attacks: the one criticizing his

destruction of the classical-Christian psychology and ethic, the other his puritan concern with inner torment.[15] The real explanation seems to lie in the historic and preëminent position of *La Nouvelle Revue française*, virtually founded by Gide, and which (with its attendant publishing house, Gallimard) attracted nearly all the great writers of the time.* In 1908 Gide started the new magazine, in association with a few friends who admired him.

The first issue, entrusted to Eugène Montfort because of his experience as an editor-publisher, was a disappointing false start; two articles were not in accord with the austerity of Gide's intention. A second beginning was made in February 1909, with Jean Schlumberger, Jacques Copeau, and André Ruyters as the nominal editors, but with Ghéon and Michel Arnauld as fellow-supervisors, and with Gide as the real moving spirit. The subsequent and complex development of the magazine, which became perhaps the most important literary periodical in the world, must furnish the central chapter of any history of modern French literature. The *Nouvelle Revue française* reflected the great moral and literary crises between the two wars and significantly was succeeded, after the Second World War, by the existentialist *Temps modernes*. From the first the *Nouvelle Revue française* followed a policy of ruthless opposition to literary commercialism and sophistication and welcomed genuine talent from any ideological quarter, even that of Claudel. It thus offered the combination, which became so common between the two wars and which still disturbs the old-fashioned conservative, of an experimental classicism and a relativistic moralism. Many of its later hesitations were those of Jacques Rivière, an editor who reflected even more than Gide the contradictions of the modern temperament. How could the same magazine preach order in art yet greet radical innovators with

* After 1896 Gide became one of the chief contributors to *L'Ermitage*, a small but important symbolist magazine, and eventually one of its editors. Here, for a public which remained very limited, Gide wrote his *Lettres à Angèle* and other critical essays. But the review was handicapped by its symbolist origin and divided aims, and in 1908 expired. *L'Ermitage* remains historically important as the parent of the *Nouvelle Revue française*.

interest? Precisely because it combined a belief in art as an instrument of control with the spirit of free inquiry; it remained faithful to the essential contradictions of Gide himself. While becoming more and more ethical and finally more and more political in interest, it honored the one lasting symbolist doctrine: respect for the work of art.

The magazine was successful beyond the dreams of its founders, and in 1911 gave birth to a publishing house directed by Gaston Gallimard. Its perspicacity in attracting important new authors soon created an enviable situation which has persisted to this day: ambitious beginners send their manuscripts to Gallimard first.[16] Both the magazine and the publishing house, here again prompted by Gide, made a point of translating foreign authors, especially those who brought something lacking in French literature itself. The issue devoted to Conrad was the most impressive tribute his work has yet received. Gide himself translated *Typhoon* and, at the cost of many exasperating hours, supervised and corrected the translation of other Conrad books. He was largely responsible for the French interest in authors as different as Whitman and Melville, and at least partly responsible for the recent interest in living American novelists, as well as for the continuing attention to Goethe, Dostoevsky, and Nietzsche. Whenever a Malraux or a Sartre makes some pronouncement on foreign literature, he seems to be rephrasing an earlier pronouncement of Gide. Here at least he has been the seminal mind of his generation.*

* Gide's theoretical criticism shows, at every moment of his career, an awareness of the particular needs of French literature at the time. It is relative to surrounding conditions, and may therefore seem startlingly self-contradictory. Thus in 1905 Gide argued (against a conservative "interviewer") that the writer should be in tune with his time: "Malheur à ceux qui n'ont pas faim précisément pour le plat que le temps nous présente" ("Chroniques de l'Ermitage," *Œuvres complètes*, IV, 389). More frequently, of course, he maintained that the writer should separate himself from his age and oppose it (see for instance "Feuillets: Taine," *OC*, XIII, 431–432). And so too, at a very short interval, Gide argued that art thrives in an age of confusion ("Lettres à Angèle," *OC*, III, 196) and that it thrives in an age of harmony, authority, and belief ("L'Importance du public," *OC*, IV, 188–189, 193). He was curiously attached to an epigram which contradicted his own relativism: "Le scepticisme est peut-être parfois le commencement de la sagesse;

For the future historian, much of Gide's importance may come to rest on these literary grounds. But to the writer and critic of today, who is still very much involved in the problem of individualism, Gide appears to reflect more strikingly than anyone else the twentieth-century intellectual's oscillations between isolation and identification. Where one writer after another despairingly fell into the arms of communism or the Church, Gide refused to commit himself, or withdrew from each commitment. He was to find, poignantly, that if one refuses to transfer his burden to some protecting institution, he must carry the burden himself. And the burden is the ego, a prey to loneliness, pride, and ennui. But he was tempted at least briefly by each impulse toward identification which the intellectuals of his generation experienced.

We cannot hope to summarize adequately, in a few paragraphs, the problems faced by intellectuals since Gide made his timid entry into the symbolist salons. Throughout the nineteenth century, the struggle between the modern world and the upholders of tradition — the Red and the Black, to distort perhaps Stendhal's convenient terms — had never ceased. But in the nineties, a weary and precarious peace had been reached: the most prominent writers had agreed that burning issues were not within their domain. The great disturber of this literary detachment was the Dreyfus case. In 1894 Captain Dreyfus had been condemned on forged evidence; and, *for the sake of the principle of authority*, the army was determined to uphold the conviction at any cost.

The issue of anti-Semitism was at first a minor one. Thus

---

mais c'est souvent la fin de l'art" ("'L'Amateur' de M. Rémy de Gourmont," *OC*, VI, 291–292). Gide recognized the prevailing Byzantine preciosity of modern literature, and to a degree deplored it. But he felt that Roger Martin du Gard alone among the *non-précieux* counted (Letter to Madame X, April 17, 1928, *OC*, XV, 537). Gide's attitude toward tradition and experiment varied according to whether literature seemed, at the moment, too conservative or too radical; and he was always aware that the most startling innovation may soon be reduced to a formula (see for instance "Les Limites de l'art," *OC*, III, 403). His essay on Heredia expresses succinctly his feeling that art needs both the traditionalist and the innovator ("José-María de Hérédia," *OC*, IV, 443–446). Gide's criticism was thus as relativistic as his ethics; it is criticism by reaction against excess in any direction.

Gide was able to join the supporters of Dreyfus, although he had privately expressed some misgivings about the influence of the Jews. The choice (and it was the choice posited later in so many of Gide's books) was between the quest of *truth* as a moral obligation and a *duty* to the group transcending mere truth. The liberals trusted free individuals to work out peacefully a society devoted to the enjoyment and betterment of this life. The authoritarians distrusted the individual; they felt that only institutions placed above dispute — church, state, army, family — could save man from self-destructive anarchy.

In 1898, the Dreyfusists included Zola, Anatole France, Péguy, Proust, Maeterlinck, Verhaeren, André Gide, and his uncle Charles Gide. Among the anti-Dreyfusists were Charles Maurras, Maurice Barrès, Jules Lemaître, François Coppée, Pierre Loüys, the anti-Semite Edouard Drumont, and ("non sans réflexions") Paul Valéry.[17] The Dreyfusists included many Catholics as well as Protestants, and capitalists as well as socialists; the struggle of liberalism and reaction transcended party lines.

Why did Gide join the Dreyfusist movement? Out of a love of justice and truth, no doubt; but also because the Dreyfusist attitude implied the rejection of conservative ethics. So too he would later move toward communism, not only because he found his own privileged position intolerable, but because he was attracted by Russia's threat to Christianity and the family as institutions. The "Affair," however, left but few traces in his writings. Apart from his letters, the only direct allusion to it — and it remains ambiguous — is in the play *Philoctète* (1899). There Philoctetes, abandoned on his desert island, is at once a figure of splendid isolation and of monstrous conceit. Ulysses appears as the representative of those prompted solely by the interests of the state, while Neoptolemus is moved by Christian sympathy and love of justice. It is difficult to decide who wins the argument: like Jean Anouilh's *Antigone*, the play could be taken as liberal or reactionary, according to the way in which it is acted, and according to the temper of the audience. Gide's Dreyfusist individualism reveals itself rather in his attacks on Barrès. Barrès was preaching "the acceptance of a determinism"; he defended the family rooted in its native soil; and his nationalistic doctrine was an extreme form of cultural autarchy.*

The Dreyfusists won; although the anti-Dreyfusists had their inglorious revenge, forty years later, when Charles Maurras became the philosopher of Pétain's "national revolution." But the Dreyfusist victory was personal and political: justice and truth were soon forgotten in the sordid scramble for spoils. The intellectuals felt a disillusionment as sharp as that of the resistance writers who, in 1945, saw the gradual resurgence of the mouldy political parties. A sacred cause binds faith, releases energies, imposes unity: with victory comes discord. There is something symbolic in the fact that Péguy — when the socialists refused financial support for his projected review because he would not follow the party line — went on to found his solitary Cahiers de la quinzaine. There seemed no place for the intellectual in the realities of political life. If some Dreyfusists proposed workers' universities and popular lectures on culture, others felt with Gide that this would irretrievably debase literature and art.[18]

The Dreyfusists, although individualists first of all, had

---

* How far Gide could be, on occasion, from the true Dreyfusist spirit is revealed only too plainly in a letter written in January 1898. He was moved most of all by the dishonesty of his opponents' methods: "Je veux bien que, dans l'intérêt de la chose publique, il est des coquineries qu'on doive taire après qu'elles sont faites . . . et la question Dreyfus se pose pour moi assez bien comme la formulait Degas — à peu près: 'Dreyfus innocent? Dreyfus coupable? La France m'importe plus qu'un individu' . . . Mais alors il fallait agir d'autorité et ne pas laisser commencer les clabauderies. Maintenant qu'ils ont commencé tu ne les arrêteras pas . . . Trop tard maintenant, cher ami, pour étouffer l'affaire: vous enfermez le feu sous votre manteau — et le doute dans nos esprits, la suspicion des chefs — et tandis que par une allure plus franche, (et plus brutale si tu veux), vous n'auriez mis contre vous que des syndiqués, des anti- ou pseudo-patriotes, vous allez vous aliéner quantité de gens simplement honnêtes et de grande valeur, en dehors de la question politique, comme M.D., comme moi, comme XXX révoltés par vos façons, non par votre cause, et qui vont, à vos yeux, grossir le nombre des syndiqués; bien malgré eux je t'assure, et désolés, complètement désolés de ne pouvoir faire cause commune avec vous.

"Car je n'aime pas les Juifs . . . je t'assure; et au contraire ne les ai jamais crus plus dangereux" (Letter to E. R., January 24, 1898, OC, II, 486, 488).

yet known the joy of identification, of working for a common cause. Now they felt intensely alone. They needed to submerge themselves once more in something larger than themselves. Many, and Gide's friends especially, followed Claudel and Péguy into the Church. The conversion of Huysmans, Brunetière, and Bourget in the 1890's showed the way. Jacques Maritain, converted in 1906, was to convert Jean Cocteau. Christ appeared twice to Max Jacob; in 1909 in the Rue de Ravignan and in 1914 at the movies. So far as Gide was concerned, the most regrettable conversion was that of his friend Henri Ghéon. This was a sharp defeat in the struggle for souls he waged with Paul Claudel.

Gide himself was never tempted by the purely pragmatic and nominal Catholicism of Charles Maurras, Bourget, and Lemaître,[19] but he found the genuine apostolic zeal of a Claudel harder to resist. The very separation of Church and state which had been one of the consequences of the Dreyfus case revitalized liberal Christianity; Gide's friends repeatedly emphasized how easy it would be to join them. Why did they work so hard, and at the possible cost of friendship, to save this particular soul? They pitied Gide's anxiety, which they felt only the offices of the Church could assuage. But beyond this they respected his obvious Christian sympathy. They held out, at the darkest hour of his guilt, anxiety, and solitude, the promise of absolution, rest, and companionship. Finally, they thought his apparently antinomian Christianity, with its diabolic verbal legerdemain, more dangerous than obvious materialism. To judge by his writings — though not the most detailed diary can record all the waverings of a mind — Gide was twice strongly tempted, in 1906 and in 1916. In 1906 — though much more than this lies behind Gide's religious impulse of that year — the victorious Dreyfusist cause was stained by scandal and profiteering. In 1916, when the morale of France was at its lowest, many again sought refuge in the Church. Gide, looking back on this later crisis, wrote that his individualism was preserved by the example of Henri Massis. The hypocrisy and surly temper of Massis's Catholicism persuaded him that such a religion could never be his.[20]

The religious attitude of Gide is hard to define. He had preached, as early as 1897, the sacrifice of self, the annihilation of egotism and pride. But he had also advocated the abandonment of virtue, for virtue is a source of pride. He had sacrificed not merely the Church, but St. Paul, to a very personal interpretation of Christ's words; he even argued — again as early as 1897 — that Christ was opposed to the institutions of marriage, the family, and the home. The most interesting aspect of his religious thought is its postulation of the Devil's existence; of an occult, energizing and corrupting force, within the individual, which alone can account for certain human perversities. The reading of Dostoevsky added humility to his doctrine of affirmation through renunciation, and led him to argue — never very coherently — that eternal life begins here and now. Once his own perplexities were solved, Gide settled into a banal religion of emergent evolution which put God at the end rather than at the beginning of the evolutionary process. His latest religious essays reject any belief in personal immortality.

Gide, less radical in politics than many of his fellow Dreyfusists, was more thoroughly emancipated than they from traditional ethics. The very fact of his indifference to politics may have protected him from Péguy's severe disillusionment. But this indifference increased his sense of isolation. He had no regular job to save him from weary hours of introspection; and he still refused, on principle, to put his art at the service of a cause. It was more or less by chance that he was finally moved to do so. Law courts had always had a fascination for him. In 1912, he served as a juror on the Rouen Cour d'Assises. To all appearances, he had no intention of being a reformer when he welcomed the assignment. But the twelve days that he spent in court, this time as actor rather than spectator, persuaded him that justice was constantly impeded by an outworn psychology, by the necessity of establishing an obvious *external* cause for every crime. Thus the court was totally unequipped to judge an incendiary who disclaimed any motive for setting fires. Gide was afraid that his own interpretation (that the crimes may have given sexual satisfaction) would seem absurd to the other jurors. On this occasion, he kept silent; but when an obvious miscarriage of justice occurred a few days later, he went out of his way to arrange for an appeal and made a private investigation at Le Hâvre.[21]

The direct result of his experience was a proposal to reform certain court procedures.[22] But Gide's real conclusion was that it often is impossible to pass judgment at all. In 1930, he founded a series of books, "Ne Jugez Pas," which describes crimes so complex and so contradictory that the first and obvious reactions to them are ultimately proved untenable. In that year he contributed to the series two inquiries of his own, *L'Affaire Redureau* and *La Séquestrée de Poitiers*. While Gide's fascination with the abnormal and apparently unmotivated act may seem as strong as his thirst for justice, especially in the second of these volumes, his collection no doubt contributed to a more scientific attitude toward criminology. It is perhaps the direct antecedent of the valuable "témoignages" published by *Temps modernes*.

Gide's humanitarian impulses before the First World War were thus restricted to individual acts of charity, or to the problem of justice as it affected particular and unusual cases. The impulse to identification which made Gide seem close to conversion in 1916 did take him briefly into the Action Française. Once again the moral compulsion may seem incomprehensible to American readers who do not recall the collective anguish of that year. Four years before the war Gide had pondered the arguments of the royalists, who could perhaps restore government by an élite; he certainly agreed with them that wholesale "leveling" led to tyranny.[23] In April and May of 1914, on a trip to Turkey, he talked over with Ghéon the "slow decomposition" of France, and wondered whether only a war could save her from this "abominable decline." When Gide at last gave his nominal adherence to the Action Française he was by no means a royalist, but he felt that Maurras's group represented the only unifying force in the nation and the only bulwark against socialism.[24]

In April of 1921 he explained that the war crisis had forced
him to check his natural inclination to the Left, and argued
that the time had come to demobilize intellects.[25] He resigned, of course, from the Action Française.

With the writing of *Si le grain ne meurt* Gide's most intimate anxieties ceased. His renewed faith in a purely individualist ethic is best expressed in *Les Faux-Monnayeurs*,
which is notably free of economic and political concerns. It
may seem a long road from the Paris of this novel to Moscow,
but Gide stumbled onto it almost at once. He finished *Les
Faux-Monnayeurs* on June 8, 1925, and on July 14 left for
the Congo: armed with an official mission from the Minister
of Colonies, but with a vacationist's curiosity rather than a
reformer's zeal. He remained in Africa until May 1926 and
on his return launched a government inquiry into the exploitation of natives which had wide repercussions. The detailed diaries of his journey, *Voyage au Congo* (1927) and
Le Retour du Tchad (1928), have of course no particular
literary significance, though the fragment "Dindiki" is one
of Gide's most charming essays.[26] They do have considerable
value for the biographer, since they largely correct the gloomy
impression left by the *Journal*. They suggest, quite unin-
tentionally, the very companionable person of whom Gide's
friends speak: his childlike curiosity and eagerness for adventure, his freedom from any kind of snobbishness, the ex-
ceptionally free play of his mind. It cannot be affirmed too
often that the personality which even a Boswell can record is
often very different from an author's generalized picture of
himself, and that the "material reality" of the former may
have no strong connection with the "psychic reality" which
expresses or contradicts itself in art.

The journey began pleasantly enough, and Gide could
take time to admire Conrad for omitting the worst of the
storm in *Typhoon*, or to discover that he himself had long
been a Bergsonian without knowing it. At most he felt the
colonials would do well to show a little more kindness and
courtesy to the natives; he himself got on splendidly with
his porters and guides. But late in October he met a native

with sufficient courage or despair to tell the truth, and from him learned of a retaliatory massacre by an agent of the great concessionary company. Thereafter he could know no peace until he had discovered the full horror of exploitation and disguised slavery, of a system so cruel and so sweeping that it threatened to depopulate the region. Gide had witnessed some abuses in North Africa in the 1890's, but felt that they were no concern of a writer. Now for the first time he wanted to write for his own age:

> Henceforth a great lament inhabits me; I know things to which I cannot remain indifferent. What demon drove me to Africa? Why did I have to go there? I was at peace. And now I know. I have to speak out.
> But how make myself heard? Hitherto I have always spoken without troubling as to whether anyone listened; have always written for those who would come later, and with the one ambition to survive. I envy the journalist whose voice, consenting to be forgotten immediately afterward, yet carries right away. Have I moved until now between the panels . . . of lies? I want to go behind the wings, behind stage appearance, and know at last what is hidden, however horrible it be. It is this "horrible" that I suspect, that I intend to see.[27]

When Gide returned to France nine months later he was not opposed to either colonial or capitalistic enterprise. He believed the colonial administrators were doing the best they could on a slender budget; he even thought that some concessionary companies were beneficial to the natives.[28] His sole purpose was to call attention to the flagrant abuses of the large companies in French Equatorial Africa, especially those of the CFSO, the Compagnie Forestière Sangha-Oubanghi. And at first he seemed to be successful. His accusations were taken up by Léon Blum in *Le Populaire*; he was called in by the Minister of Colonies; a government investigation was initiated and a committee sent to the Congo. On November 23, 1927, the minister announced to the Chamber of Deputies that the concessions of the great companies *which were to expire in 1929* would not be renewed, or not under the same conditions. But six days later the CFSO announced an increase in capitalization. Since its concession expired in 1935 rather than 1929, it was unaffected by the minister's ruling.

This was Gide's first direct experience with the worst abuses of monopoly capitalism, and his first realization of the occult power which it exerts on government and on all but the radical press. He now understood that individual effort could do little to correct grievances and that the big companies would defend their errors with the same jealousy that the army had defended its errors in 1897. It would nevertheless be wrong to assert that Gide's chance discoveries in the Congo led directly to his communist adherence; the *Journal* for 1929–1935 reveals how indirect and hesitant his progress was. And it was of course the progress of an individualist of 1897, rather than the unquestioning revolutionary impulse of a man thirty years younger. Gide himself admitted only one great change in direction. Where he had long felt that progress depended on man's individual effort to surpass himself, he believed in 1935 that this could occur only if social conditions were so changed as to encourage this individual effort. In his long pilgrimage he had seen before him only space and the projection of his own *ferveur*; now he saw the possibility of his dream being realized. And the dream was still that of the freer individual, emancipated from illusion, authority, fear.

Perhaps the strongest emotional force at work was class-guilt; the intolerable feeling that he was one of the favored. Only privilege had made possible his voyages, his quiet and civilized pleasures, and the prolonged self-examination which nourished his books. "Wherever I look I see around me only distress. He who remains contemplative today evinces an inhuman philosophy or a monstrous blindness." This sense of unmerited privilege and of surrounding distress, together with the old faith in progress, pushed Gide toward communism; hatred of intellectual conformity held him back. His earnest rationalizations were those of an entire generation of liberals; and his dream, which may yet be realized, was of a free individual and a pluralistic culture within a rationally organized state. Thus he argued that Russian communism was unfriendly only to the old bourgeois individualism of jealous self-interest; and that equality of opportunity would help rather than hinder the exceptional individual to rise. He was not interested in the common man but in the uncommon man who, thanks to a fair chance, would assert his individual worth. He was quite willing to accept cruel expedients as temporarily necessary, and he had no trouble visualizing a communism which would reconcile itself with the essential teachings of Christ. The very destruction of family and orthodox church would prepare the way for a truer Christianity.

Here again, in declaring his sympathy with communism, Gide may have satisfied a need for identification which he had long resisted. Nothing is more significant than the disgust which he felt early in 1928 for exclusive preoccupation with self. Since 1893 at least he had doubted the egotism which applauds its own virtue. Yet he had also pursued deliberately a solitary path. Whatever satisfaction submission to authority gave, it cost an enormous effort. In 1932 and 1933 he refused to join the Association des Ecrivains et Artistes Révolutionnaires, saying that he would be unable to write, and so would lose all usefulness, once he had been "enrolled." In June of 1933 he observed that if one takes a position, he is at once "taken" by that position. A year later he was interested to learn that his *Prétextes* had a pure Marxist spirit. "Well, so much the better! So be it. But if I am a Marxist, I beg you to let me be one without realizing it." But in January of 1935 (at a meeting of the Union pour la Vérité) he acknowledged that the fear of not being "in the norm," rather than a fear of the communist index, had forced him to stop writing completely. Marxist orthodoxy was perhaps as intrinsically dangerous as any orthodoxy, but at this particular hour it was expedient. He could not write orthodox books; his truest service to the cause would therefore be to stop writing. He even acknowledged that he had been unable to do any serious writing during the last four years.[29]

The verbatim report of this round-table discussion of his work, published as *André Gide et notre temps*, is one of the best possible introductions to a study of Gide; Fernandez, Halévy, Marcel, Maritain, Massis, Mauriac, and others ask most of the fundamental questions, and Gide answers them simply and with humility. But the discussion centers too often on his earlier attitude to throw much light on his contemporary anxieties. Gide said enough, however, to convince Gabriel Marcel that communism could be for him only a "resting place," that his pilgrimage was not yet ended. The account of his trip to Russia and of his sharp disillusionment — recorded in *Retour de l'U.R.S.S.* (1936) and *Retouches à mon Retour de l'U.R.S.S.* (1937) — is too well known to require comment.* He returned to France still faithful to the ideal of a free man in a planned economy, but persuaded that the Soviet experiment had failed. Intellectual conformity and inertia were there even more striking than in bourgeois countries, and the true revolutionary spirit was lost.

Neither Gide's adherence to communism nor his swift withdrawal has other than a personal and symbolic interest; his arguments reveal all the naïveté of an honest but highly "unpolitical" mind. "The social problem . . . If I had stumbled on this great trap at the beginning of my career, I should never have written anything worth while." [30] Thus Gide wrote in his diary for May 30, 1940, and even the most socially conscious critic must agree. The biographer would be rash indeed who argued that Gide's attitude is conducive to foresighted political action and choice at a time of crisis. Gide himself acknowledged, early in 1941, that his lifelong relativism, his constant effort to understand the other side of every question, must finally exact its price. The record of Gide's hesitations both before and after the fall of France, which he has had the courage to publish, is that of a mind

* *Littérature engagée* (Paris, 1950) — a selection of speeches, essays, letters, etc., edited by Yvonne Davet — helps us to follow the movement of Gide's political thought and feeling between 1930 and 1938. This volume also contains his wretched melodrama of labor relations, *Robert ou l'intérêt général*.

which resents mobilization and which is yet willing, in the hour of disaster, to believe in the obvious authoritarian remedy. It can scarcely be called the diary of a "resistance" writer. The articles and "imaginary interviews" that Gide contributed to *Le Figaro* in 1941 and 1942 — especially the ingenious interview on French usage — show a daring willingness to taunt the German occupiers. But the problem (especially where it concerns a writer over seventy) is less one of courage than of foresight. And from the point of view of the French resistance the foresighted course was not to publish in the officially sanctioned press at all.

On June 24, 1940, Gide was stupefied by Pétain's ridiculous assertion that France remained "intact." But on July 10 he was willing to accept a French dictatorship that would save France from decomposition, and on September 5 he argued that to make up with yesterday's enemy is not cowardice but wisdom. "He who resists destiny is taken in a trap. What is to be gained from bruising oneself against the bars of his cage? For the intellect, the risk of letting itself be dominated by hatred is too great." On October 14 he showed that he was aware of all the cynical opportunism which the word "collaboration" might cover. And yet . . .

He would be wise today, I think, who would not show too clearly that he knows himself to be duped — and who would cease to be duped in the very gesture of acting as though he were. This is a dangerous game, to be sure — but less dangerous that a desperate resistance or than, worse still, a revolt. The least you can say of a revolt is that it would be premature, and would involve in terrible reprisals even those who had not participated.[31]

This was of course the familiar argument which the Resistance found more demoralizing than the most blatant "collaboration." It was the argument for which Montherlant has been so severely condemned. The great difference was that Montherlant published his counsel of despair during the Occupation and that he showed, in a few isolated pages, a certain relish in the humiliation of his bourgeois and Christian countrymen.

Gide's hesitations were those of innumerable honest but confused Frenchmen. Like them he could not, in 1940, conceive of an effective Resistance movement. And like many of them he was saved from his own errors by seeing those errors glaringly magnified in the behavior of opportunists. Jacques Chardonne's *Chronique privée de l'an 1940* — an apologia of collaboration all the more shocking because of the author's earlier liberalism — served to disabuse him. Gide recognized in Chardonne an alarmingly kindred spirit, and a relativist who had carried relativism to treason. Was this the logical consequence of his own impulse to see a "no" accompanying every "yes"? The very nebulousness of Chardonne's argument reminded him that the French excel in the art of definition. "When he affirms himself by non-affirmation, by reticence and abstruseness, by 'the contrary might also be demonstrated,' he plays the part of the drunken helot, warning me against the wine for which I too might have had a weakness. Seeing him reel and stagger, at once I stand erect." [32] Gide immediately resigned from the *Nouvelle Revue française*, edited now by the collaborationist Drieu La Rochelle, and wrote for *Le Figaro* his famous review of Chardonne's book. If he still felt, in September of the same year, that the nation needed order and discipline — those catchwords of Pétain — he was not again tempted to collaboration. By January 1, 1942, he referred to the "national revolution" as a *singerie*, though he still could not see what form the future would take.

Through all these changes, these complex suasions of temperament and circumstance, there appears a certain constancy: what is called the Gidean "attitude." It can perhaps best be summarized by saying that Gide wanted to be, like Flaubert, a "demoralizer" [33] — a destroyer, that is, of pragmatist pretense, of abstract or inherited authority, and of flattering self-delusion. He wanted to throw open all questions which men are tempted to consider closed; to challenge all received opinions, all restrictive institutions, all *a priori* notions concerning the nature of man. He had the puritan's horror of spiritual inertia, the scientist's skepticism of conclusions, and the optimist's faith that man achieves a higher destiny if he works it out unaided. Perhaps his most characteristic gesture is to refuse to profit from the *élan acquis*; from the acquired momentum of what others have discovered and codified, or of what one has himself discovered in the past. The ardently critical spirit thus advances into an always fresh, perilous, and unpredictable future, though constantly menaced by nostalgia for a comfortable and inherited past. The shadow of Renan as well as of Nietzsche and Blake may appear to hang over this attitude and effort, though Gide sharply criticized the dilettantism of Renan and the pseudo-scientific relativism of Rémy de Gourmont.[34] Temperamentally, Gide was inclined both to mysticism and to rationalism; to destroy both therefore required an unusually severe effort. He was harried as often by the nemesis of belief as by the nemesis of faith.

To "demoralize" meant to disturb faith in every institution which depends on compromise or submission and which is rooted in ancient habit: the church, family, and home most obviously, but also all political and intellectual "parties," the Cartesian and kindred traditions, and the elaborate ethics of custom. Gide believed in progress, but where others sought progress through provisional order, he preached provisional anarchy. Like Nietzsche he offered a startling parody of the golden mean. Rather than seek the midpoint between two extremes (which vary with each individual), man should cultivate both extremes, and hold them in precarious harmony. Suppression and fear may, paradoxically, induce comfort: the comfort of mediocrity and ignorance. But only the most ruthless and most adventurous *self-exploitation* can create new energy. "Descend to the bottom of the pit if you wish to see the stars." Gide called this a "Proverb of Hell," which by no means implied disapproval. Why did he insist on the educative value of what men normally call "evil"?[35] Primarily because the "evil act" is often independent and insubordinate, and sometimes so spontaneous as to appear gratuitous. However dangerous in itself, it promises a possible progress to a different state of being. The lawless individual, if he does not rest in lawlessness, has a chance to transcend himself.

For Gide did not preach mere nihilism and anarchy; he criticized rather than transvalued values. What he wanted of course was to put the ethical problem, which concerned him more than any other, squarely to the individual. And he was persuaded that the emancipated individual could endure and survive his freedom. The price of success is eternal vigilance, which can be a weariness to both flesh and spirit. Gide's is essentially an ethics of reaction, the most sophisticated of puritanisms. His famous adage — that *man should follow his slope* (his natural inclinations), *upward* — implies not merely that a goal of diversified harmony should be kept in mind, but that the hardest way is the best. The Apollonian by birth should explore and develop all his Dionysian impulses; the born Dionysian should seek coolness and wisdom. The extremes of traditionalism and experiment in art, and of order and anarchy in conduct, have no value in themselves, but are alike useful as educators and correctives. The true individualist cultivates a rich eclecticism of the inner life and respects the spirit's dialogue with itself. To suppress one voice at the expense of another is to cease to be fully alive. The great enemy of *individualism* (a personal complex of often heterogeneous tendencies) is *individuality* (the exclusive and tyrannical predominance of one tendency). But even the most rewarding state of being must be destroyed, *must die*, so that a new one can be born; even one good custom can corrupt the man. "Except a corn of wheat fall into the ground and die, it abideth alone: but if it die it bringeth forth much fruit. He that loveth his life shall lose it; and he that hateth his life in this world shall keep it unto life eternal." These were the scriptural passages to which Gide constantly returned, and which he could use to serve any argument. But he repeatedly insisted that "eternal life" was not a future life. Eternal life must begin here and now and in this world — the only world we have. The condition of man is one of restless change and courageous seeking; of institutions and values and selves incessantly dying, and incessantly being born.

Such, in the briefest terms, is Gide's ethics of movement and politics of evasion. Unlike the dilettante or casual skeptic, Gide understood as well as any of his contemporaries the comforts of identification and commitment, the enormous relief which comes from referring all questions to a higher authority. But stronger still was his distrust of comfort, inertia, and compromise. On the political level (since institutions must die so that others may be born) he refused to settle down and thus dramatized, half unwittingly, the political and moral dilemma of the twentieth-century individualist. But so too, on a wholly inward level, he refused to settle down. A very similar struggle, between detachment and commitment, between cold isolation and Dionysian submersion, could occur within the self, within the unpolitical "ego." Perhaps the outward and inward struggles are very closely allied. Thus the psychologist Otto Rank, seeing in everyone these impulses to protect the ego and to destroy it, traces them upward to men's highest moral achievements and downward to the trauma of birth. Do all men symbolically reënact, throughout their lives, the painful separating experience of birth (to "prove" that it was not too painful); yet always incorrigibly long for the unconscious warmth of the womb? Do these deepest human impulses account for all our outward acts? Perhaps. But for coherence we must treat the political and the psychological conflicts separately. Gide's long debate with the political forces of his age was doubled by a long inward dialogue. Here too — in the lonely region of the self, of the abstracted untemporal ego — selves must incessantly be destroyed, must die, so that others may be born. And here, when we review the autobiographies and quasi-autobiographies, we must remember once again that we are not concerned with the Gide known to his friends — a cheerful, companionable person, who in certain years did certain things — but rather with the adventurer into depths no friend could see.

2 THE SPIRITUAL AUTOBIOGRAPHIES

THE PARTS IN GIDE'S FAMOUS "INTERIOR dialogue" can be assigned only too easily to obviously opposed voices: Biskra and Cuverville, Paganism and Christianity, the longing for sexual freedom and the longing for salvation, liberty and restraint. On the Congo journey Gide could go no farther north than Lake Tchad, and there dreamed nostalgically of an oasis across the desert. But the end of this as of every journey was Cuverville. Biskra and Cuverville were the extreme poles of Gide's wanderings, but these were poles within his mind, and had been from early youth. More exactly, the dialogue was between the impulse to unify or concentrate the self, and the impulse to destroy or dissolve it. Here above all Gide, most modern of the moderns, was the heir of the nineteenth century. He deliberately aggravated in himself the unrest from which our age has suffered, and was a loyal interpreter of the nineteenth-century writers who tried to work out a metaphysic of the divided ego: Baudelaire, Dostoevsky, Nietzsche. He always sought to avoid pride and ennui, at once "the two most authentic products of Hell" and "the two great springs of romanticism"; it is wholly appropriate that his earliest

fragment should echo St. Anthony's longing to become
"matter." *
Gide's plight is the plight of the romantic (or modern)
ego. To escape vanity and ennui ("the isolating screen of the
soul") he cultivated disintegration — with such success, indeed, that he finally had to consult a doctor. How can one
satisfy impulses which are simultaneously outward and inward? How can one destroy the isolated ego without falling
into sheerest anarchy? To understand the paradox is not
absolutely essential to a first appreciation of Gide's novels —
though it may be argued that Gide solved the paradox only
on the level of art, of a classically controlling form. Gide's
analysis of the ego is contained rather in the *Journal* and
other autobiographical writings. They dramatize the paradox and offer a prolonged expression and analysis of that
willed disintegration of the personality which only psychol-

* These contradictory impulses to protect and to dissolve the ego appear
in many writers of the so-called Romantic period. See my article, "Prometheus and the Aeolian Lyre," *Yale Review*, Spring 1944, pp. 482–497. Two
quotations from Flaubert will help us to define these impulses at the outset.
"J'ai pris plaisir à combattre mes sens et à me torturer le cœur," he wrote to
Mlle de Chantepie in 1857, describing his youthful effort to fashion an independent ego; an ego which had, so to speak, freed itself from circumscribing
matter: "J'ai repoussé les ivresses humaines qui s'offraient. Acharné contre
moi-même, je déracinais l'homme à deux mains, deux mains pleines de force
et d'orgueil. De cet arbre au feuillage verdoyant je voulais faire une colonne
toute nue pour y poser tout en haut, comme sur un autel, je ne sais quelle
flamme céleste . . . Voilà pourquoi je me trouve à trente six ans si vide et
parfois si fatigué" (*Correspondance* [Paris, 1928], II, 88, Nov. 4, 1857).
Flaubert's counsel to Mlle de Chantepie is to think less about herself; to
escape the imprisoning present and the sterilizing ego through art. The very
last speech of St. Anthony conveys the longing for complete dissolution of
the personality: "J'ai envie de voler, de nager, d'aboyer, de beugler, de
hurler. Je voudrais avoir des ailes, une carapace, une écorce, souffler de la
fumée, porter une trompe, tordre mon corps, me diviser partout, être en tout,
m'émaner avec les odeurs, me développer comme les plantes, couler comme
l'eau, vibrer comme le son, briller comme la lumière, me blottir sur toutes
les formes, pénétrer chaque atome, descendre jusqu'au fond de la matière, —
être la matière" (*Tentation de Saint Antoine* [Paris, 1922], p. 200). Gide's
early fragment offers a much milder version of the same impulse: "Il aurait
voulu être goutte d'eau, se disperser comme une buée subtile, se perdre dans
les rayons, dans les brises, et, le soir, humecter de rosée les pétales des
pervenches" ("Fragment de la 'Nouvelle Education sentimentale,'" *Œuvres
complètes*, I, 4).

ogists examine as a rule, and they only in its advanced stages. This is not, to be sure, the one explicit "subject" of Gide's many and changing self-portraits. It is rather the thread that binds them all: the preoccupation and enduring conflict, sometimes fully conscious but at other times not, which they share in common. The present chapter offers an emphasis which is not always the author's emphasis. It draws together writings far separated in time, notes involuntary recurrences in phrasing, and attends closely to imagery which may have been relatively casual. Here and there it presses for meanings which Gide himself may have "missed," or may have wanted to conceal. Its method is thus, speaking very roughly, psychiatric. And surely the subject matter is psychiatric: this dark struggle of the atavistic id, the uneasy ego, and the tyrannous superego, waged beneath a surface history that was certainly disturbed. All this being so, it is natural to wonder why the short-cut explanations of modern psychology are not applied throughout the following pages. Gide wanted both to isolate the ego and to destroy it. Why not refer, then, to Freud's death wish, or to Rank's trauma of birth? With Jung's help we could cut through Gide's many verbal contradictions in a few pages or even in a sentence: "Gide really longed to recover the timeless vital unconscious, the ghostly saving anima, the peace of the buried mandala." We could, again, distinguish "oral" and "erotic" phases, and weigh the drama of passage through the womb against the drama of anal retentiveness. Or, if we resent such shadowy mythology, we could use Karl Menninger's clinical categories of focal suicide — of self-destructiveness in payment for childhood guilt.

It is easy to ridicule glibly such formulas, and I for one should like to see an expert psychoanalytic study of Gide's autobiographical writings. The great danger of these formulas is that they tend to become, in the hands of the untrained at least, comfortable substitutes for close reading and thought. With Rank on one's desk, it is only too easy to dismiss the most diverse introspections as indiscriminate womb-wishing. The author's very struggle for exact expression, which intensifies his art, immediately disappears. Beyond this — and beyond the fact that Freud, Jung, Rank, and Menninger differ so widely in their explanations — lies the fact that Gide was often conscious of this inward conflict, and sometimes saw it in exactly the terms we shall use. The dramas of Jung and Rank occur far below the level of consciousness and remain unseen to the unaided patient. But Gide's drama, as he described it, occurred near the margins of consciousness. His major and prolonged effort was to push those margins a little further back, to discover and understand what is just out of sight. To apply categories of the unconscious to Gide's exploration of the preconscious would be, for descriptive purposes, more misleading than helpful.

It would be a mistake, on the other hand, to separate Gide's effort from that of the twentieth-century psychologist. Gide formulated the essential conflict as strikingly as Freud, and at about the same time. He thus seems to stand between the probing amateur metapsychologists and moralists of the nineteenth century and the twentieth-century professionals. For the best subjective minds of the nineteenth century also dramatized, after all, this particular inward contradiction. Shelley did not perhaps realize what he was "writing about" in "Alastor," nor Senancour in *Obermann*, nor Poe in "The Island of the Fay." But Maurice de Guérin, Amiel, Baudelaire, and Nietzsche all dimly saw these dual impulses to unify and to dissolve the self; *The Birth of Tragedy from the Spirit of Music*, in this respect, culminates a century's introspection. Gide was more conscious of the struggle, however, than all except perhaps Nietzsche, and he had a more disciplined mind than Nietzsche. His minute effort to understand his own life and inward experience has few parallels in literature — the minuteness consisting sometimes in a reasoned attempt to define or remember, sometimes in the dense struggle to find the right image for a feeling. The definitions are made, of course, in the traditional language of the moralist, but the distinctions are drawn very fine. The reader will miss much who does not respect Gide's respect for nuance. And it may even be that such intensive lay psychol-

ogizing as his, when served by such a scrupulous mastery of
language, will have something new to offer. In literary terms,
at least, the prolonged effort is impressive. It deserves to be
described and explained, not merely "explained away."

Henri Massis, the most intransigent of Gide's Catholic
critics, saw more clearly than anyone else his impulse to
"dissolve the self" but interpreted it narrowly: as an effort to
rationalize "animal" desire, and ultimately as a Satanic effort
to destroy the conception of human nature "on which our
civilization rests." [1] Gide's disintegration equally threatened, as it seemed, the classical concept of an orderly inner
hierarchy of faculties and the Christian concept of the
sacredly inviolate personality, which we should abandon
only at the insistence of God, and that his substituting Presence be admitted. That this was the burden of one of Gide's
messages cannot be denied. What Massis failed to observe
was the dialogue: the perhaps even stronger impulse to concentration of self; to unity, order, and coherence.

We may turn to nearly any of Gide's volumes for illustra-
tion of the two impulses — though remembering of course
that a man does not long for order except when aware of its
absence. Only in the later years, in 1924 for instance, was
Gide able to cut through the tangled problem with a brief
and assured statement: "Some people work over themselves
to obtain the unity of their person. I let myself go." [2] A single
scriptural passage, which for the orthodox runs through
Gide's work as a diabolical refrain, served to justify the
impulse to dissolution:

He who loves his life, his soul — who protects his personality,
who is particular about the figure he cuts in this world — shall
lose it; but he who renounces it shall make it really living, will
assure it eternal life; not eternal life in the future, but will make
it already, right now, live in eternity. [3]

This exegesis was written in 1916. In 1917, however, Gide
described the centrifugal impulse as Satanic, as Baudelaire
had done before him:

That there is — against this cohesive force keeping the individual consistent with himself, and by which (as Spinoza said) he tends "to persist in his own being" — another force, centrifugal and disaggregative, by which the individual tends to divide himself, to strive for dissociation, to risk himself, to gamble himself and to lose himself . . . I won't go so far as to say that Baudelaire anticipated this as clearly as, for instance, Dostoevsky. But I cannot read without a shudder of recognition and terror these few sentences from his intimate diary: *The taste for productive concentration should replace, in a mature man, the taste for deperdition — or, further, the vaporization and the centralization of the ego. Everything is there — or, further, there are in every man at every hour two appeals which are* SIMULTANEOUS (the entire interest of the sentence is in this word): *one toward God, the other toward Satan.*[4]

Removed from the context of Gide's long moral struggle, the two passages hardly seem contradictory; they might serve to illustrate a basic distinction between self-renunciation (*abandon de soi*) and self-indulgence (*abandon à soi*). Gide did not always make this distinction, however, and even in the later works he sometimes preached self-indulgence and complete self-realization as means to the suppression of a factitious self. When Gide went to North Africa in 1893, self-indulgence required a greater effort of will than rejection; this is the first term of the paradox. By 1918, however, a new character had entered the drama: the Devil. Had he appealed to the young puritan's strongest impulse (the impulse to take the harder way) in persuading him to let himself go, or in suggesting that virtue demands its own sacrifice? Gide asks himself these questions in one of his most deliberate efforts to explain his early contradictions:

I began then to seek out which, among the thoughts, opinions, and tendencies of my soul and mind that were most familiar to me, were the ones that I most certainly derived from my ancestors; from my upbringing and puritan formation, which at first had constituted my strength; from that sort of moral atmosphere in which I was beginning to stifle. And doubtless, pushing that relinquishment to the extreme, to the absurd, I should have ended up in complete impoverishment — for "what have you that you have not received?" — but yet it was complete impoverishment that I coveted as the truest possession. Resolved to give up in this manner every personal possession and convinced that I could not hope to dispose of everything except on condition that I possessed nothing in my own right, I repudiated every personal opinion, every habit, every modesty, my very virtue, as one throws off a tunic in order to offer an unveiled body to the contact of the wave, to the passing winds, to the sun. Strengthened by these abnegations, I soon felt my soul only as a loving will (yes, this is the way I defined it to myself), palpitating, open to all comers, like unto everything, impersonal, a naïve confusion of appetites, greeds, desires. And if perhaps I had been frightened by the disorder into which their anarchy led me, was I not able to reassure myself at once by recalling these words of Christ: "Why should you be troubled?" I surrendered then to this provisional disorder, trusting in a more sincere and natural order that would organize itself, I thought, and believing moreover that the disorder itself was less dangerous for my soul than an arbitrary and necessarily artificial order, since I had not invented it. Divine ray! I exclaimed, isn't what is opposed to you above all that false wisdom of men, made up of fear, lack of confidence, and presumption? I resign everything to you. I surrender myself. Drive out all shadow from me. Inspire me.

Considering later on that nothing separates one more from God than pride and that nothing made me prouder than my virtue, I began to detest that very virtue and everything on which I could pride myself, everything that allowed me to say: I am not like you, common run of men! And I am well aware that this excess of renunciation, this repudiation of virtue through the love of virtue itself, would appear as merely an abominable sophistry to the pious soul who reads me. Paradox or sophistry that thenceforth bent my life, whether or not the devil prompted it I shall examine later on. It is enough for me to say, for the moment, that I advanced boldly on this path that was so new. What am I saying: path? Every step I took forward was a venture into the unknown.[5]

Did the solace of confession obtained through *Si le grain ne meurt* virtually end the inward debate? In any event, the promised examination of the Devil's share was never made. The first paragraph of this statement, however diabolic its logic, honestly admits compulsions which are not wholly religious: the desire to escape both a suffocating moral atmosphere and a conscience in some way burdened. The statement is inadequate, for a general picture of the early Gide, only because it fails to record the repeated reactions back toward concentration and unity. Even before the turn of the century Gide recognized how precarious and evanescent were his moments of complete spontaneity. He had scarcely time (as he wrote in 1896) to enjoy a liberating "intoxication" before the self reasserted its claims:

> At such moments I felt, as if in spite of myself, my whole being stretch, stiffen, harden; I became harsh to myself and took delight in treating myself very roughly. At times, convinced as I was that any of my actions would always result in the greater glorification of my life, I dreamed, almost out of spite, of letting myself go, of relaxing my will, of giving myself respite and leisure. I never could, and I realized that in me restraint was more natural than yielding to pleasure is in others, that I was not free not to will; to relax, and to cease resisting; and I realized at the same time that from that very absence of liberty came the beauty of my acts.[6]

Sometimes, however, Gide did achieve this relaxation of will, and too fully for comfort. Even Hylas in *Les Nourritures terrestres* recognizes that we are sometimes enslaved by our desires; that the place vacated by the conquered ego may be occupied by quarreling masters.

This is the theme of *Saül*, which Gide wrote almost immediately after his famous *manuel d'évasion* (though he did not publish it until 1902) and as an antidote to its excesses.[7] A *feuillet* of the same period describes the new freedom and wise passiveness — the tendency of the heart to surrender to every outside influence — as a "reflux of savagery" which undid a long and laboriously accumulated inheritance. Disintegration, however pleasant in theory, however productive of energy, could interfere with both work and sleep. In January 1906, suffering from "restless will and undefined personality," Gide studies his piano "for hygienic reasons." A year later he forces himself to work on his diary with the same

purpose: "I must struggle by every means against the dislocation and frittering of my thought." A few months later he falls
abruptly into "a state of complete anarchy," and the experience is frightening.* In 1912, at Neuchâtel, he is sufficiently
distressed to think (though somewhat ironically) of the comforts of the confessional. But what director of conscience
could understand this irresolution and "impassioned inde-
cisiveness," a depersonalization so voluntary yet with such
great difficulty achieved? "Constant *vagabondance* of desire
— one of the chief causes of deterioration of the personality
. . . Urgent necessity to recover possession of myself." The
penitent makes resolutions: to go out only when he has a
definite purpose, to walk without looking around, to dis-
dain none of the will power's triumphs, however slight. "For-
bid oneself every kind of vacillation."

But can one still make resolutions when one is over forty? I live
according to habits now twenty years old. Did I know what I was
doing at twenty? When I made the resolution to look at everything, never to prefer myself to anything and always to give preference to what differed most from me . . .[8]

The same evening, to be sure, Gide reacted against his reaction, and predicted that everything he had written that
morning would soon seem to him absurd. Yet these were by
no means the last resolutions he would make. Any reader of
the *Journal* knows that some of its most interesting pages
record exercises in discipline of the will. Whatever "position" Gide argued at any moment concerning the problem of
the ego, the energies of his art struggled at every period with
the centrifugal and disintegrative impulse. The early subtle
rhythms and the later classical prose were as vigilant in their
guardianship as the prosody of Baudelaire.

The passages which recommend dissolution of the self, or

* "Une sorte de vertige déconcerta en un instant ma volonté, dont
aussitôt les freins se relâchèrent: me voici livré à toutes les impulsions sans
aveu de la curiosité, de la vanité . . . à tous ces menus ressorts sans nom que
l'on maintient en esclavage et courbés, mais que, parfois, chez moi, une
défaillance nerveuse laisse se redresser . . . bref, un état de complète an-
archie . . ." (*Journal*, May 17, 1907).

which reveal unmistakably the centrifugal impulse, are far more numerous than those which counsel preservation. The commentator is nevertheless embarrassed in various ways. He is faced, for instance, by the lack of English equivalents for minute shades of difference: *Anéantissement du moi, abandon de soi, oubli de soi; dénuement, dépouillement de soi; désagrégation, déperdition, épuisement; dépersonnalisation, dissolution de la personnalité, dissolution du moi.* How many of these can we venture to "translate," reflecting as they do a realm of speculation which, until recently, most English and American moralists have comfortably avoided? The short-cuts of the professional psychologist (*auto-punition, auto-destruction,* et cetera) are easily translatable, but Gide does not use them. Using instead the vocabulary of the classical moralist, he allows his meanings to fluctuate with each restless change in context. What for instance is the self which we must destroy, so that another may attain eternal life? Gide's failure to answer this question unequivocally, in any given passage, lies at the heart of our difficulty. What was the "real self" inhibited by heritage of custom? Late in life Gide referred to Montaigne's "être naïf" and "forme sienne": "Une forme maistresse qui luicte contre l'institution, et contre la tempeste des passions qui luy sont contraires." [9] But even *Les Nouvelles Nourritures* of middle-age agree with *Les Nourritures terrestres* that the passions are necessary to the self's discovery. In the same book Gide argued the existence of still another self which remains loyally unchanged, and which he never tried to find: "Yes, I feel throughout my diversity a constancy; I feel that what is diverse in me is still myself. But for the very reason that I know and feel the existence of this constancy, why should I strive to obtain it? All through my life I have never sought to know myself; that is to say, I have never sought myself." [10] The disclaimer may seem perverse, given the number of the autobiographies. Yet a definition of the nature of the *self* (and not merely "the Freudian ego") must rest, for all but the unwary, on a religious revelation, a metaphysical intuition, a metaphor, or a gratuitous affirmation. And unless we are metaphysicians we seldom doubt its existence — which we may find to be, *en bloc*, as painfully unyielding or as comforting as the stone which Dr. Johnson kicked.

In the first fifty years of his life, Gide often found at least one of the selves painfully unyielding. We may assign various reasons for the prolonged discomfort: solitude, guilt, sexual frustration, a general sense of inadequacy, or even that wholly "unmotivated" inner warfare which a few psychoanalysts assume. And we may reduce Gide's longing to decompose that self, as we may reduce very nearly any human longing, to the ambivalent desire for energy and peace. It should first be useful to draw together, however, Gide's own explanations for the longing; or, perhaps his rationalizations of it. There were at least five of these. To be sure, Gide often gave more emphasis to one than to the others, nor would all five normally appear in the same text. But to present them together, as we do here, is to respect Gide's love of contradiction.

1. *Christian surrender of one's self and one's goods.* Gide's self-destructiveness could nearly always find sanction in Scripture. Ingenious exegesis was made to support the fundamental opposition of St. Paul and Christ, in Whom Gide found neither prohibition nor constrictive rule. To sell all and give to the poor meant to renounce one's comfortable moral heritage, and first of all the teachings of the church. The true Christian must suppress not only all worldly pride, but the very concept of spiritual merit.[11] In 1902 Gide tells of his disgust for his hard-won self-esteem, for the proud virtue of an André Walter. "I strained my ingenuity to lose it, and this was not hard . . . I gave myself up therefore to debauch; and indeed it did not displease me to introduce a bit of system into it; I mean to work hard at it . . . And I did not despise anything in me so much as my self-esteem; I intended to make it impossible and took pleasure in debasing myself."[12] The self's attachment to its possessions — to the family, to inherited teachings, to its own virtue — prevents its immediate entrance into eternal life, whose felicity churchmen have stupidly postponed to a hypothetical future.[13]

2. *The creature's manifestation of Divine plenitude.* We should, so far as possible, manifest the whole of God's creation (by definition good), rather than merely those few aspects of it deemed respectable by bourgeois and church morality. The body and not merely the soul is part of this creation, as Gide "learned" at the age of eighteen from the second part of *Faust.* A note to the quasi-Platonic *Traité du Narcisse* anticipates many of Gide's later views as man and artist. Every phenomenon is the symbol of a Truth, which it is morally obliged to "manifest." The one sin is to prefer the self to this Truth or Idea: "The moral imperative for the artist is not that the Idea he manifest be more or less moral and useful to the greatest number; the imperative is that he manifest it fully. — For everything must be manifested, even the most baneful things: 'Woe unto him by whom the offence cometh,' but 'the offence must come.' " [14]

We have here the ethics of eighteenth-century plenitude and the aesthetics of Oscar Wilde, either of which could justify an anomaly. Any factitious unity of personality is bound to silence some obscure inner voice; an aggregate of separate parts leads to a richer harmony than a moralist's restrictive ordering. The radical optimism of this argument was temporarily corrected by Gide's acknowledgment, much later, that the Devil exists, and that evil is something more real than the absence of good. He never renounced his faith, however, that many seemingly "evil" impulses are either innocent or potentially useful. The Arab boy who steals scissors or the *lycéen* who tries to steal a book at least show vitality, energy, independence.

3. *Denudation for the sake of "original uniqueness."* This conception is diametrically opposed to the preceding one, though both demand Gidean "sincerity" for their realization. We should try to rediscover, beneath the false and acquired self, the self still naïve and pure. But to do this does not mean returning to some hypothetical natural man, similar to all other natural men. Each of the elect has his particular role to play: ". . . his own precisely, and which resembles no other; and thus any effort to submit to a general ethic came

to seem to me a betrayal; yes, a betrayal, and one which I associated with that sin against the Holy Ghost which will not be pardoned; through which the particular being loses his precise irreplaceable meaning, his 'savor' which cannot be restored to him." [15] How can we discover our own "savor"? Not by examining and judging our every act. To escape both inward logic and the constraint of education, we must act as unreflectively as possible; we must seek (permit, rather) the "acte gratuit." "Henceforth acting irresponsibly and without giving myself time to reflect, my slightest acts seem to me more significant because no longer calculated. By the same token I freed myself from worry, perplexity, remorse." [16] To impoverish or denude oneself is, in other words, to avoid every form of constraint; the most spontaneous is also the most genuine. The renunciation preached by Gide is often *difficult*, but seldom very *painful*.

4. *Christian self-effacement for the sake of others.* It is easy enough to discern, behind Gide's Nietzschean attacks on Christian pity, a natural sympathy for the poor and the suffering. On the other hand, he seldom recommended the more obvious forms of humanitarian self-effacement. With the honesty of an intellect that scrutinizes even its seemingly most disinterested motives, he suspected the purity of his wartime labors at the Foyer Franco-Belge. "Who will understand that renunciation may be as attractive as luxury and a submersion in distress as attractive as the exaltation of love?" Lafcadio's analysis of his own impulse toward self-effacement was perhaps even more severe: "This need to bestir myself and to help others, from which gushes the purest well-spring of my happiness, and which causes me always to put others before myself — is it perhaps no more, after all, than a need to escape myself, to lose myself, to meddle in and taste other lives?" [17] Gide's first unequivocal defense of humanitarian self-sacrifice was made only in 1935, when he tried to explain his adherence to a communist discipline which for years had killed any impulse to write.

5. *Depersonalization for the sake of energy and art.* In his early autobiographical works, Gide shows the familiar ro-

mantic longing to establish a vital communion with physical nature. Bathing in the sun or in some hidden stream, he hoped both to lose his burdened consciousness and to absorb energy; to enjoy an "afflux from without." But the same peace and the same fervor could be obtained by allowing oneself to become the crossroads of others' opinions and feelings. And ethics could here subserve art. Gide recognized (though seldom so fully as his critics) his inclination, dangerous for the novelist, to autobiography. "The important thing is being capable of emotions, but to experience only *one's own* would be a sorry limitation." Thus Gide wrote as early as May 12, 1892. But the perduring subjectivity reveals itself in the very next lines: "In any event, egoism is hateful. I am less and less interested in myself and more and more in my work and my thoughts." If Gide failed to overcome this radical subjectivity, it was not through lack of effort: a deliberate and prolonged effort to depersonalize himself, to see things through the eyes of others. By 1923, at least, he felt he had been successful:

> It is certainly easier for me to make a character speak than to speak in my own name; and this the more so as the created character more differs from me. I have written nothing better nor with greater ease than the monologues of Lafcadio or Alissa's diary. Working so, I forget who I am . . . if I so much as ever knew.
> So too in life, I am inhabited by the thoughts and feelings of others; my heart beats only in accord with theirs. This is what makes all discussion so difficult for me. I surrender at once *my* point of view. I leave myself and so be it.
> This is the key to my character and to my writings.[18]

And yet — are not all the characters who differ so radically from the creating self also characters in the *Journal?* Are not both Alissa and Lafcadio suppressed "selves" — the one an "André Walter," longing for purity and salvation; the other the narrator of *Les Nourritures terrestres,* longing to escape consecutiveness? Judging on the one hand by the testimony of his friends and on the other by his books, Gide depersonalized himself more successfully in life than in art. But only this unconquerable literary subjectivity allowed him to complete such a detailed portrait of the personality and its dissolution. The most suspicious reader cannot retouch this portrait, but he may want to reinterpret it.

These are Gide's logical explanations, then, of a proposition which has its own divine logic: *Whosoever shall seek to save his life shall lose it: and whosoever shall lose his life shall preserve it, shall render it truly alive.* But they are also reconstructions after the impulse, sometimes long after. The explanations are interesting and not to be dismissed casually, however rationalized they may seem. We may even concede that the impulse to disintegration was frequently moral in intention. But when we examine the immediate and unordered expressions of that impulse, we find that it ministered also to highly personal needs.

First there is the strong desire, especially in the early works, to *crush out thought*. Gide tells of his love of reasoning at the time he was writing *André Walter*; he spent a good part of his life and creative effort trying to destroy the twenty-year-old Huguenot's stiffness. Nothing more reveals Gide's deep-rooted rationalism than his envious admiration of the most disorganized foreign writers. The Devil, when at last he made his appearance, revealed himself as "the Reasoner." *Cogito ergo Satanas.*[19] In 1917, driving in Normandy, Gide longed for the smiles of the "ferocious" North African natives: "An almost animal sympathy draws toward them the most secret depths of my being, while their rudimentary music voluptuously annihilates my thought." Occasionally Gide suggests that a *few particular thoughts*, rather than the weary tramp of reasoning, prevented harmonious joy. "I live with the inconsecutiveness of a lyric poet, but two or three ideas, across my brain and rigid as bars, crucify all joy; everything that would like to try its wings at random bruises against them."[20]

Confronted by such anxieties, we are naturally tempted to rapid explanation and dismissal. We know the particular adolescent drama of *André Walter*, and knowing it propose our equations: to "crush out thought" is to "crush out a few particular thoughts" (is to "crush out remembered sexual misdeeds"). Yet even this early work has a richer content than such a formula suggests. A more useful equation would identify sleep (or unconsciousness) and sexual indulgence; André Walter's puritan will was strong enough to resist sleep as a shameful dissolution.[21] Gide often regarded *will* as masochistic power of control, and therefore "willed to lose the will." Was the desire to volatilize the self not rather, at times, a longing to satisfy sexual desires with impunity? Here, putting aside for the moment our notions of debts to the superego, it is useful to examine imagery. Sun-bathing seems to have had a large significance for Gide, both as a symbolic act in his writings and as an actual lived experience. To bring together three very different passages on sun-bathing may press some further meaning from such a phrase as "volatilize the self." The first passage, from *Mopsus*, follows almost immediately a description of an Arab boy which strongly conveys sexual longing; the second is from *L'Immoraliste* and concerns Michel at a time when he is well on the way to a discovery of his homosexual impulses. The third passage, from *Si le grain ne meurt*, is Gide's direct rationale of sun-bathing:

I want to stretch out naked on the beach: the sand is warm, yielding, fine . . . Ah! the sun burns and penetrates: *I break in pieces, I melt and evaporate, I volatilize myself in the blue.** Ah! delicious burning! Ah! Ah! May so much absorbed light give new aliment to my fever, more richness to my fervor, more warmth to my embrace.

When I got there, I undressed slowly. The air was almost sharp, but the sun was burning. I exposed my whole body to its flame. I sat down, lay down, turned myself about. I felt the ground hard beneath me; the waving grass brushed me. Though I was sheltered from the wind, I shivered and thrilled at every

---

* The italics are mine in all three passages. Some sexual overtones in the diction of the French originals have unavoidably disappeared from the translations.

breath. Soon a delicious burning enveloped me; *my whole being surged up into my skin.*

For it was not only the bathing I loved but the mythological waiting afterward, for the naked envelopment by the god; and, my body penetrated by rays, I seemed to taste an obscure chemical benefit. *I forgot my clothes, and with them my torments, inhibitions, anxieties, and while all will power volatilized, I let my feelings — as porous within me as a hive — distill secretly that honey which would flow in my Nourritures.*[22]

The desire to dissolve the self may be, again, the closely related desire to escape "inner logic," and consecutiveness: "Oh, to be able to escape from myself! I would overleap the barriers behind which self-respect has confined me . . . My mind boggles at the word 'consequence.' Consequence of our acts. Consequence with ourselves. Am I to expect nothing from myself but a sequel?" [23] To break the links which bind us to our past selves is to become free, to become "available" for anything (*disponible*); and once again, of course, is to free ourselves from self-disgust. Innumerable passages testify to the self-disgust, and to this desire to escape the limitations imposed by a sterile coherence. Gide's many journeys cannot be dissociated from this longing to escape the self. "On these warm days I dream of the flight of nomads. Ah, might I both remain here and flee . . . to some other place! Ah, that I might evaporate and decompose myself; and voyage, dissolved in a breath of air." [24] Did Gide try to accomplish by his many restless journeys what André Walter failed to achieve through meditation in his solitary room? Or was the self identified rather with the moral solitude from which André Walter suffered? "What people call 'withdrawing into oneself' is to me an impossible constraint; I can no longer understand the word 'solitude'; to be alone with myself is to be nobody; I am peopled." [25] This passage, like so many others in *Les Nourritures terrestres*, lays claim to a state of mind which is longed for rather than achieved; or which has already been lost.

Mann's Gustav von Aschenbach and Gide's Michel are

driven, of course, by their latent homosexuality. But both men first suppose in themselves a love of savage life and anarchy for its own sake. Gide's own willed disintegration of self may seem, at times, truly atavistic — the atavism separate, that is, from the particular needs of his own life. "My joy has something untamed, fierce, and in separation from all decency, propriety, law. Through it I return to the babbling of infancy, for it offers my mind nothing but novelty." [26] Yet here again, I suspect, we are thrust back on the original paradox. Did Gide try to destroy the factitious self for the sake of animal freedom, or did he force himself to this animal freedom in order to destroy that self? [27] The question is perhaps unanswerable. One does detect, behind all these veiled torments, a general sense of inadequacy, apathy, and deprivation, as well as strong feelings of guilt. *Could not destruction create?* Perhaps long-stored and buried energy could be released through actual splitting of the hated personality, through fission of the self. Gide's eternal enemy is spiritual inertia and the contented laziness of habit, but he could also long for a peace beyond desire. If he brought no final answer to the paradox it was perhaps because he saw it to be a universal paradox and contradiction, no less than the condition of man:

Ah! thought I, all humanity tosses wearily between thirst for sleep and thirst for pleasure. After the terrifying tension, the ardent concentration, and then the relapsing of the flesh, one's only thought is of sleep. Ah, sleep! Ah, if only we were not wakened into life again by a fresh onslaught of desire!

And all humanity tosses like a sick man who seeks relief from suffering by turning in his bed.[28]

The drama may be universal. We shall have to ask, eventually, whether Gide's novels were enriched or narrowed by their marked autobiographical origin. The works considered in this chapter were frankly autobiographical, however, and more directly concerned with the "metaphysic of the ego." It would be grossly unfair to consider these works fiction which

had failed to become fiction, and to condemn them for a subjectivity which lies at the very heart of their purpose. This
purpose was simply the poetic one of defining mood and feeling, and of recreating inner experience. The form might be
that of a journal, travel diary, play, or symbolist novel, but
behind the form was the desire to instruct, and the over-
powering desire to confess. The tension of concealed confession would seem to have ended at the age of fifty, with the
writing of *Si le grain ne meurt*, though not Gide's desire to
universalize his personal experience. *Si le grain ne meurt* is
one of the literary masterpieces of the century, however inferior the crucial confession of the second part may be to the
still hesitant record of childhood and adolescence. For the
psychologist it throws an invaluable backward light over all
the earlier spiritual autobiographies, and on the secret
urgencies of *André Walter, Le Voyage d'Urien*, and
L'Immoraliste. By comparing Gide's retrospective account of
his sexual troubles with the creative work of the early years,
we can see some of the ways in which preconscious drives
and half-conscious frustrations translate into image and
symbol.

The impulse to dissolve the self (or the contrary fear of
dissolution) may be objectified by explicit analogy, by half-
concealed but unambiguous symbol, or by the use of a
certain kind of imagery. We may quote, by way of reminder,
an early passage which directly links the desire to dissolve the
ego with the desire for an absorbing caress:

> I am obsessed by caresses, whether loving, worshipful, or pas-
> sionate; I want an absorbing embrace, an envelopment, or else
> that forgetting of self which makes ecstasy distraught. And that is
> why I suffer so before the beauty of statues. The self does not
> melt in them, but instead rises in opposition.[29]

Explicit analogy may be worked out at great length, or it may
be compressed to a brief and obvious comparison: for instance, between the mobility of thoughts and the mobility of
waves:

Fluctuating waters, it was you who made my thoughts un-
steady. Nothing can be built upon a wave; it gives beneath the
slightest weight.

Will the quiet haven come at last, after all this wearisome
drifting, these tossings to and fro? Will my soul rest at last on
some solid pier beside a flashing lighthouse, and from there look
at the sea? [30]

The use of personal and half-concealed symbols is even
more instructive and takes us still closer to the original
psychic experience and to the active poetic process. A personal symbol is by no means a private or unintelligible
symbol. The greatest writers, in fact, merely explore the
obvious correspondences offered by nature and experience,
and make them intensely their own. Conrad's use of the
dank and impenetrable jungle as a symbol for the preconscious is scarcely original, yet his intensification of the symbol
corresponds to very personal desires and fears. In the same
way submersion in water was for Gide a highly personal symbolic act, though the obscurely felt symbolic equivalence of
water to unconsciousness and to sexual release (as well as to
time) is surely as old as serious psychic speculation. In *Le
Voyage d'Urien* the symbolism of water seems universal (if
we consult Jung), and particular (if we consult *Si le grain ne
meurt*).

Finally — and here we are close to the actual fears of
dreams, to the raw material of surrealism and of all highly ex-
pressive art — there is the revealingly personal use of images:
images showing directly a desire for dissolution, or a fear of
such dissolution. Gide's preoccupation with shadows and
absorbing shade (his acknowledged "goût de l'ombre" and
"sentiment du clandestin") is perhaps too conscious to be
considered here, though it sometimes produces seemingly
unmotivated imagery.* The more indirect sense of dissolu-

---

* This preoccupation is, at its most explicit level, a desire to be a shadow
among dissolving shadows: "Là parmi tant d'indistinctes blancheurs, parmi
tant d'ombres, ombre moi-même, ivre sans avoir bu, amoureux sans objet,
j'ai marché, me laissant tantôt caresser par la lune, tantôt par l'ombre, y
cachant pleins de larmes mes yeux, et plein de nuit, et souhaitant y dis-
paraître . . . Reconnaître à leur voix ces femmes; à leur appel sourire ou

tion reveals itself in the tendency to see things dissolve:
"Compare the clouds I see pass over the mountain, then melt
and dissolve in the blue, with the caravans which the desert
consumes [que *mange* le désert] . . . or vice versa." We
may realize the personal urgency of such a sentence only after
we have made a prolonged study of Gide's imagery. Yet in
this close relationship between visual imagery and psychic
needs lies one of the secrets of Gide's style, and of the intimate appeal which his autobiographies make.

Les Cahiers d'André Walter and *Le Voyage d'Urien* are
the chief works of what is usually called Gide's "période
d'attente" — of waiting for the North African liberation. It

---

m'arrêter; et, dans l'éclat subit que projettent la lumière et le bruit des
cafés, voir tant de mystère rôdeur se fixer, ces ombres un instant prendre
corps, s'arrêter, puis replonger et se déconsister dans la nuit, où je veux me
fondre avec elles" ("Le Renoncement au voyage," *OC*, IV, 318). An extraordinary description of shadows invading a church and *drowning* the women
there is interesting as pure imagery and reveals the impulse to dissolution through the masterly slow prose rhythm rather than through any concealed analogy: "Par la porte grande ouverte, la nuit entre lentement,
envahit l'abside, coule le long des murs de la nef et creuse une ombre de
mystère dans les trous mous des confessionaux. Les coiffes blanches des
femmes semblent plus blanches encore, comme éclairant les ténèbres; puis
l'ombre épandue monte toujours et les noie. Et, tandis que le jour meurt . . ."
("Notes d'un voyage en Bretagne," *OC*, I, 21). The falling of shadow into
water, as in Poe's *Island of the Fay*, is used in one of the most beautiful
pages of *Le Voyage d'Urien*. The ship passes over a submerged city and as it
passes casts a shadow over the cemetery: "Nous serions, ah! si bien sous l'eau
fraîche, au porche de l'église noyée! Goûter l'ombre et l'humidité. Les sons
des cloches sous la vague. Et la tranquillité . . ." (*OC*, I, 338). But if this
passage suggests merely the death wish, there are many others not so easily
explicable. Why, for instance, does Michel in *L'Immoraliste*, at a crucial
stage in his return to health, feel impelled to adventure into the shadows of
the climbing gardens above Ravello? ". . . on y entre, sans bruit, en voleur.
On rêve, sous cette ombre verte; le feuillage est épais, pesant; pas un rayon
franc ne pénètre; comme des gouttes de cire épaisse, les citrons pendent, par-
fumés; dans l'ombre ils sont blancs et verdâtres; ils sont à portée de la main,
de la soif; ils sont doux, âcres; ils rafraîchissent" (*OC*, IV, 58). Whoever
undertakes to write a *Road to Biskra* will certainly have to take into account
Gide's really abnormal concern with overshadowed places — and he may want
to relate these places to the gardens of Biskra where Gide (*Si le grain ne
meurt*, p. 318) and Michel in *L'Immoraliste* (*OC*, IV, 38–42) watched Arab
boys; and waited for "liberation." But the concern with shadows antedates
the "liberation" and was no doubt associated, at first, with less specific
memories.

would be fairer to consider *André Walter* a formless meditative journal than an unsuccessful first novel. For it admits quite frankly to be what so many first novels are unwittingly: an autobiographical and lyrical celebration of troubled adolescence. The twenty-year-old's conflict between spirit and rebellious flesh fills his universe; the ordinary outer world impinges only rarely. A book which recorded such a unique conflict would certainly be successful: Gide naïvely expected it to win a large public. It is in fact the product of fairly extreme isolation. Gide's only literary friend when he began *André Walter* was the impossible Pierre Loüys,[31] though he was shortly to be adopted by the symbolists. Perhaps the best indication of Gide's immaturity lies in the fact that he had another friend, André Walkenaer, "pose" three hours a day for his book. The "posings" consisted of endless Proustian discussions on all possible subjects. But the finished book has only one character, the adolescent André Gide, and one shadow or double, "Allain."

The form of *André Walter* already anticipates that of *Les Faux-Monnayeurs*; we have the same conflict between real experience and its idealization in fiction. The narrator is writing a novel, *Allain*; he meditates on Allain's spiritual difficulties, but even more on his own. Both creator and hero love an Emmanuèle, both desire a metaphysical and incontaminate union of souls with this highly rational heroine; both are caught in an unending battle of flesh and spirit; both suffer from an undefined malaise. And both long, eventually, for a dissolution of the besieged and tormented self. The identification of novelist and subject increases, and at last becomes a source of anxiety. Not wishing to trouble the purity of his fictional hero, André Walter decides to abstain from "all caresses." In the second part of the book, "The Black Notebook," the impending madness of Allain threatens also his creator. A reading of Taine had led André Walter to induce hallucinations, in order to equip himself to study Allain's mental disorder. The dramatic interest of the book comes down at last to this: will Allain or André Walter go mad first? The book ends with the triumph of art;

André Walter remains sane just long enough to finish his book, and then to wish for death. Nor did Gide see anything amusing in this sacrifice of life to art: he had looked upon *André Walter* as his *Summa.*

It is easy enough to make fun of this extraordinarily naïve book. It is just as unimaginative to see in it all the books that would follow. *André Walter* is obviously the product of a romantic tradition, as well as of a personal dilemma, and belongs in the company of *Werther, Obermann*, and *Joseph Delorme*.[32] (Like Delorme, incidentally, André Walter left a sheaf of posthumous poems.) From the perspective of maturity and hard-won peace, the fifty-year-old Gide objected chiefly to the book's "ejaculatory" tone and its love of indefinite words. The familiar nineteenth-century theme of spiritual isolation appears in the passages on the fatal parallelism of souls in love, which therefore can never meet. The first progress Gide was to make as a writer would remove him from the metaphysics of a Sully-Prudhomme, if no farther than to the salon of Stéphane Mallarmé. *André Walter* nevertheless provided a first exercise in style, and a first debate on the theory of the "pure novel." In a note which describes the novel as a geometrical theorem we are on the track of *Les Faux-Monnayeurs*: "Reduce everything to the ESSENTIAL — no phenomenal life, only the noumena — therefore no more descriptions and the background neutral — to take place anywhere and at any time — to be outside time and space."

The psychological interest of the book is certainly much greater than the literary. It would be impossible to improve on Gide's honest and succinct definition. A puritan education in the evils of the flesh, together with an unrecognized homosexual's aversion, combined to prohibit "the commonly accepted solution": "And yet the state of chastity . . . remained insidious and precarious. Every other escape being denied me, I fell back into the vice of my first childhood, and despaired anew each time I fell. Together with much love, music, metaphysics, and poetry — this was the subject of my book." [33] The struggle between the impulses to concentration and dissolution of self is therefore closely related, in *André Walter*, to the problem of controlling these childish habits. This throws a good deal of light on a romantic malaise which might otherwise seem mere literary convention: "What I wouldn't give to know whether others, even those I love, have suffered from the evil (*du mal*) which torments me. Oh, no! I should have seen it in their faces, I should have detected it in their words . . . They wouldn't speak about these things as they do, with such a casualness." [34]

The impulse to dissolution here takes on several forms. The mind which resists the body regards with disgust the nightly submergence in erotic revery or dream. These dreams encourage indulgence. But there is a contrary desire to obtain purity by allowing the soul to dissolve and commingle with that of the pure Emmanuèle. André regrets that the soul is normally constrained to express its desire to embrace another only through "the caresses of lewd desires." The extraordinary ambivalence of this impulse to dissolution, the simultaneous longing for purity and sexual enjoyment, appears not only in the many passages of nympholeptic longing ("to faint in a kiss," et cetera), but also in one which advises submersion in snow as a hygienic measure. André Walter hopes thereby both to chasten the body and to find "in this icy contact an extraordinary thrill." In the end he longs to dissolve the mind itself, burdened as it is by this terrible conflict, as well as the corrupt body. His very last words are, "The snow is pure."

Without the evidence of *Si le grain ne meurt*, *André Walter* might seem the work of a very talented *lycéen* who had been inspired less by experience than by various nineteenth-century Romantics. The two interesting erotic dreams in the book suggest, however, Gide's latent homosexuality. They seem to be, at a glance, genuine dreams, or the honest records of uncensored revery. In the first André Walter dreams of seeing naked children bathing, and of longing to join them. He awakens early the next morning and runs through a deep forest. "I reveled in my solitude dolorously; I peopled it with those I loved. Before my eyes, at first indis-

tinctly, there wavered the supple bodies of children on a
beach, and whose beauty pursued me. I too should have liked
to bathe, near them, and to feel with my hands the softness
of their brown skins." The second dream is of a woman,
whose coat is removed by a monkey: "Under her dress, there
was nothing. It was black, as black as a hole; I sobbed in
despair. Then she picked up the bottom of her dress with her
two hands and threw it up over her face. She was turned
about like a sack . . . I was so afraid that I woke up." [35]

Le Voyage d'Urien (1893) has had few readers and almost
no commentators; it demands a much fuller analysis than
Gide's other early works. For this earnest prose-poem is one
of the most tantalizing of Gide's works, psychologically, and
its literary and historical interest is much greater than that
of André Walter. One notable advance is that Gide can now
look at his aspirations to purity with an occasional ironic
smile. The twelve pilgrims who resist the seductions of
Queen Haiatalnefus are a little ridiculous, their chastity
somewhat pompous: "Slowly then the twelve of us, in state
and symmetry, hieratic in our sumptuous apparel, descended
toward the sun, even unto the last step where the broken
waves drenched our robes with foam . . . Nobility of spirit
constrained us to make no gesture, to keep silent . . ."*
And the change from the diary of an adolescent in a solitary
room to a symbolist journey to the North Pole and its divine
city already shows some progress toward objectivity. The voyage is a "voyage du rien" (Mallarmé had feared it would be
the account of a real trip), yet contains everything. It is a
Homeric Pilgrim's Progress, replete with sirens and other
perils of the sea: a dream of life as a series of embroidered
and sensuous dreams, and as the puritan rejection of those
dreams. A verse palinode admits that the author might have
resisted all Urien's temptations, but had been subjected to

* All quotations are from the admirable translation of Martha Winburn
England, written for my Harvard seminar on the modern novel, and to be
published soon by New Directions. Mrs. England was helped by Mr. George
Steiner on the first draft of the translation.

none of them. His book nevertheless comes as close to being a novel as anything French symbolism would produce. It represents the extreme limit to which Gide would go to satisfy the symbolists who had adopted him, and writing it perhaps hastened his sharp reaction — to the irony of *Paludes*, to the earthy hedonism of *Les Nourritures terrestres*. Yet even the student of Gide's later style must take *Le Voyage d'Urien* into account: its luxuriant rhythms and exotic descriptive riches, its nebulous appeal to the fringes of the reader's consciousness. These vague harmonies and uninhibited translations of soul into landscape had to be exploited, before the progressive chastening of style could begin.

As a Symbolist novel, *Le Voyage d'Urien* stands somewhere between the occult reality of *Arthur Gordon Pym* and the cloudy philosophizing of Novalis's *Lehrlinge zu Sais*, which Gide had recently read. The voyage of the "Orion" is a dream adventure through desire; an "invitation au voyage" of which the first condition is that the pilgrims leave their pasts and their books behind. These young men, wearied by fruitless studies, set out on an unpremeditated journey. Yet they dimly understand their "valor" will be tested, and vaguely long for heroism. The sirens are encountered early enough in the voyage, and before the first month is out some of the sailors have deserted. To go ashore and there be led astray is of course the obvious temptation. But the obscure temptation to bathe beside the ship or elsewhere soon seems more dangerous. The pilgrims who remain on board, or who watch the others but abstain, eagerly question them concerning the forbidden joys, until these others have a right to say: "Here are bold chevaliers! Are you afraid even to taste the fruit? And does your barren virtue consist only in abstinence and doubt?" After the obvious sensuous enticements and pestilential languors of "The Dolorous Ocean" comes the ennui of "The Sargosso Sea": the ennui which follows not upon surfeit but upon the annihilation of desire. Here the pilgrims casually encounter Ellis (Urien's destined soulmate) or at least a woman who resembles her, and the ship passes over a submerged city. The same day they observe the

first blocks of ice. A few, sick with ennui, must be left behind, but the eight who remain embark on the "Voyage to a
Glacial Sea."

The goal proves to be a disappointing, "apathetic," and
unfrozen little lake. The pilgrims wonder then whether it is
perhaps better not to attain one's goal, but decide that the
joy of effort and satisfied pride is reward enough. What then
has been the voyage's and the book's meaning? That it is impossible to achieve genuine peace without having led the will
through evil, through the temptations of passion and sluggish indifference? "The hard trials are past. Far away are the
gloomy shores where we thought we should die of ennui;
farther still the shores of illicit joys; let us count ourselves
fortunate to have experienced them. One cannot come here
except through them. To the loftiest cities lead the straight-
est ways; we are going to the heavenly city." This statement,
which may be attached so easily to Gide's total meaning,
comes at the beginning not the end of the "Voyage to a
Glacial Sea," and is almost the only one to offer such a comforting explicitness. It is perhaps better to avoid all intellectual paraphase; to admit that any ethical summary of *Le
Voyage d'Urien* falsifies the impression it makes.

For the adventures seem truly gratuitous, unless interpreted psychologically. And here precisely lies the historic interest of *Le Voyage d'Urien*, which has never been fully
recognized: it is a distinct and important episode in the
transition from symbolism to surrealism; from the mysterious but somber soul-voyages of symbolism to the free absurdity of surrealist nightmare. Some of the gratuity reminds us
vaguely of *The Ancient Mariner* and directly of *Arthur
Gordon Pym*. The mysterious ship of the dead which appears
and disappears could have been borrowed from either work,
or borrowed simply from legend. Gide's Paride disintegrates
as easily as Poe's Peters, one losing an arm and the other a
leg. Gide's Eskimo community is more sophisticated and less
cruel than Poe's; at a crucial hour his pilgrims find a warning message written blazingly on ice, as Poe's find a message
in stone. Poe's water gets warmer as we near the South Pole,

and at Gide's North Pole we find an unfrozen lake. The mysterious sheep-woman of *Le Voyage d'Urien* recalls the numerous sheep· lost in Maeterlinck's marshes, but also the
white luminous deity at the end of *Arthur Gordon Pym*.
Most interesting of all, in both works, is the gratuitous menace of water. "I felt a numbness of body and mind," Poe's
narrator tells us, "a dreaminess of sensation . . ." He
watches an animal float by. "I would have picked it up, but
there came over me a sudden listlessness, and I forbore. The
heat of the water still increased, and the hand could no
longer be endured within it. Peters spoke little, and I knew
not what to think of his apathy." *

It takes no psychiatric bias to see that *Arthur Gordon Pym*
also dramatizes preconscious longings and fears. There is
nevertheless a great difference between the two works, which
brings Gide's much closer to surrealism. Except in the final
pages, Poe is as careful to prepare and justify his mysteries
as any Gothic novelist. Gide, on the other hand, does not
even bother to explain how his pilgrims happened to set out.
There is no logic in the connection of events, other than an
inner logic of psychological necessity. Streams may flow backward; the *Orion* may "become" a felucca in an instant; a
monument — "for some unknown reason" — may suddenly
rise out of a plain. The mysterious child of the sixth chapter
is perhaps borrowed from Novalis, but Ellis is borrowed
from no one. The pilgrims' first meeting with her is a midpoint, as is were, between the revery of Poe or Baudelaire
and the dense inconsecutiveness of Roussel's *Impressions
d'Afrique*; the meeting is completely unprepared. We may
even see the transition between the two modes, in successive
paragraphs. The first paragraph is in the symbolist manner,
the second in the surrealist.

The fourth day on the banks some smoke-colored herons
hunted worms in the ooze; beyond them a level lawn extended.
At night beneath reflected clouds pallid in the lingering day, the

* These similarities are not offered as proof that Gide was influenced by
Arthur Gordon Pym, which he may or may not have read by 1892. They
merely help us to "locate" *Le Voyage d'Urien* in a general literary movement.

river appeared to run in a straight line, for the banks were hidden in shadow. The oars of the felucca, as they turned, caught in the reeds of the bank.

The seventh day we met my dear Ellis, who was awaiting us on the lawn seated under an apple tree. She had been there a fortnight, having arrived before us by the overland route. She wore a polka-dot dress and carried a cerise parasol. Behind her was a little valise with toilet articles and some books; a Scotch shawl was over her arm; she was eating a salad of escarole and reading *The Prolegomena to All Future Metaphysics.* We had her climb into the boat.

It is difficult to argue the influence of *Le Voyage d'Urien* or of *Les Chants de Maldoror,* alike unread at the time, against the influence of Rimbaud and Laforgue. But in terms of Gide's own development, the absurdity of the second part of *Le Voyage d'Urien* certainly led to *Paludes, Le Prométhée mal enchaîné,* and *Les Caves du Vatican.* And these, we know, had a real influence on surrealism.

The major interest of *Le Voyage d'Urien* is nevertheless a personal and psychological interest. The "objective psychic content" would be inviting under any circumstances: the transparently homosexual reactions, the accumulated images of dissolution, the unexplained fears of water and submersion in water.* This psychological interest becomes compelling — dangerously compelling — when we consider the circumstances under which the book was written. It is the last of Gide's books to precede his discovery of his homosexual nature, and immediately preceded that discovery. It is therefore only too easy to find — in the increasing homosexual language — a literal and dramatic breaking of submerged forces to the troubled surface of consciousness. The danger is that we should infer too much about the creativity of the preconscious from this single instance, where many instances would be needed for proof. But beyond this we know, from *Si le*

---

* Robert O'Clair, in my seminar on the modern novel, shrewdly observed that "the great difficulty which one finds in trying to apply Rank and Freud to the *Voyage* is that the narrative does not offer sufficient resistance to analysis."

grain ne meurt, that *Le Voyage d'Urien* accompanied that same struggle with masturbation which affected *André Walter*:

At La Roque, the summer before the last, I thought I would go mad. There I spent nearly all my time cloistered in the room where only work should have kept me, trying in vain to work (I was then writing the *Voyage d'Urien*) . . . haunted and obsessed. Hoping perhaps to find some escape through excess itself, and to recover equanimity beyond it; hoping to debilitate my demon (I see there his advice) and debilitating only myself — I spent myself obsessively until exhausted; until there awaited me only imbecility and madness.[36]

Given such a forthright statement, it would be amusing to demonstate that the richer imagery and freer revery of *Le Voyage d'Urien* was due to the fact that it was written during a period of excessive self-indulgence, while *André Walter* was written during a period of attempted self-control. But the fact that *André Walter* was a first book, an exercise in learning to write, makes any such inference dangerous. The biographical background of *Le Voyage d'Urien* is unquestionably significant. But we will lose that significance if we try to define it minutely.

"Souls are landscapes," says Gide's Preface to the second edition, and the landscapes of *Le Voyage d'Urien* are fluid and dissolving. Longing for fixity, the pilgrims travel past transforming shores evanescent as "insincere actions." They explore floating islands, and are lost among shifting dunes and moving knolls. Crossing an ambiguous plain they come upon a valley of mists, and then a prodigious city of hanging gardens and fantastic minarets. But "the voices were dying away; and as they fell, lo! the city faded, evanesced, disintegrated on a strophe; the minarets, the slender palms vanished; the flights of stairs crumbled; sea and sand became visible through gardens on fading terraces." Some of the imagery of dissolution and putrefaction must be discounted as symbolist and decadent commonplace.[37] This is perhaps least true where the dissolving agent is water — warm water, the recurrent menace on this voyage of the Puritan will. In the queen's grotto air and diaphanous water merge, and solid objects seem magically displaced. Icebergs melt in warm water at significant moments in the story. Can we not see in the corpse, imprisoned in a solid ice wall, a wishful image of fixity and unmenaced purity?

If we are to believe *Si le grain ne meurt*, Gide did not yet know where the real menace lay. The homosexual images and reactions, so curiously uncensored, must be accepted as undeliberate too. Like Huxley's noble savage, Angaire fears that even the slightest tenderness will cause women to take off their clothes, and he admits preferring solitary pleasure. The pilgrims walk away from a performance by whirling dervishes when their flowing robes become too revealing. That evening the sailors bathe in the warm water and then lie down on deck, "writhing with desire." But the pilgrims do not bathe, nor do they dare even lie down. On another occasion the sailors return from their sexual exploits, bringing fruits which bleed like wounds. In Queen Haiatalnefus' realm the native men have long since retired to live by themselves. There remain on the streets boys with women's faces, or women with the faces of boys, "admirable creatures." And significantly enough, Ellis must dissolve before Urien can unite either with her or with God.

In one remarkable chapter, we shall see, an almost uncensored homosexual imagery supports the binding symbol of water. More obvious and less interesting is the explicit disgust with normal sexual experience — yet not entirely normal, since through one fevered night the sailors and native women engaged in "incomplete embraces." The equation could not be simpler: those who traffic with the native women vomit, contract the plague, and die, while those who abstain survive. The three crucial expeditions into narrow, sheltered yet dangerous places suggest no such conscious meanings. The queen's grotto is a lovely place, approached through calm canals overhung by creepers and trees; the second grotto is a shadowed place of stagnant waters, where lethargic bats hang from the ceiling. The narrow fiord of the third part is "gloomy" and with somber depths. The invitation is pressing to see in all three only the trauma of birth — yet still more evident seems the imaged fear of normal sexual penetration. The pilgrims find no difficulty leaving these narrow places but great difficulty entering them. In the first grotto they refuse to bathe because of the crabs, sea nettles, and "cruel' lobsters. Ellis contracts swamp fever in the second, and there first causes Urien to doubt her identity. Auks nest on the cliffs of the fiord. Frightened, the females abandon their eggs, which roll down the rocks and shatter in "horrible streaks of white and yellow." Is there not some significance in the fact that Eric's wanton destructiveness, in hurling rocks at the birds, occurs at this particular point in the story?

The water, in any event, is "polluted" by the eggs — and we may want to take the actual consistencies of water into account when we consider the pilgrims' attitude toward bathing.* Only "water born of ice" seems wholly pure and invigorating. Yet the saffron-skinned men who bring snow from the icehouses of the original port have "bloody loincloths," and the blue water of the harbor is stained by bales of purple and dissolving dyes. Plague-stricken for their orgies, the sailors and native women "pollute" the water of the washhouses with their "defiled tunics." "With long poles they stirred the slime at the bottom; clouds of sediment arose; bubbles came to the surface and burst. Bent over the rim, they inhaled these odors of the fen without revulsion; they laughed, for they were already stricken." The significance of these sentences derives from the fact that they are wholly gratuitous.

Water is yet the attractive as it is the destructive element, and the temptation to bathe is a more real one than any encountered on land. On the fifth day the pilgrims swim in

* For an interesting psychoanalytic interpretation of water pollution, see Gaston Bachelard, *L'Eau et les rêves* (Paris, 1942), chapter vi. Water is the image of the mother, as the sun of the father; pure water is — for the unconscious — an appeal to pollution. The four volumes of Bachelard's *Essai sur l'imagination de la matière* reveal a wide literary culture and a sensitive critical talent; all four volumes should be translated.

the ocean and are penetrated by the "languor" of the waves.
Later they refuse to bathe out of fear of the sirens whom
their less courageous shipmates have visited. On a third occasion the sailors, bathing after sexual indulgence, are beautiful yet "gleam with unwonted pallor." A single sentence concludes the sixth chapter: "We did not bathe that day." The
effect "is of a statement in code" [38] — and the obvious inference is that bathing is simply equated with sexual indulgence, which is both ruinous and beautiful. A full census of
the baths taken by pilgrims and sailors supports this equation, which may even have been an intentional one. Tepid
water is the property which debilitates, which dissolves will
and energy. But it is also the obscure source of riches and
dreams. The longing to bathe may also be a longing to dissolve the personality, to rejoin the healing depths of the unconscious, to achieve Jungian integration. When Queen
Haiatalnefus drops one of her rings into the sea, Urien refuses to join the other pilgrims in diving after it—"not
through ennui, but on the contrary through a desire too
great, so fascinated had I always been by the mysterious
depths of the waves." His companions remain long under
water, and on their return fall into a deep sleep. "A numbing
torpor at first drugged my senses," Clarion says on awaking,
"and I thought only of the pure slumber I could have in that
cool water, couched on the soft seaweed." * Later, the submarine city beneath their ship is an azured vision of repose;
it fills Urien with a "lyric ecstasy." In unconsciousness and
in death, in water, the miserable self may be dissolved.

The desire to dissolve the self thus seems to take on several
forms in Le Voyage d'Urien, and to have a multiple meaning. A verbalized and conscious longing for fixity is affronted

---

* For Jung, Clarion would have descended to the collective unconscious
(and hence achieved "the restoration of life, the resurrection, and the conquest of death"); and in the same act would have successfully dissolved personality and lost his burdensome identity. "It is the world of water, where
everything floats in suspension; where the kingdom of the sympathetic system, of the soul of everything living, begins; where *I* am inseparably this and
that, and this and that are *I*; where I experience the other person in myself,
and the other, as myself, experiences me" (*The Integration of the Personality*,
translated by Stanley Dell [New York, 1939], pp. 242, 70).

by the spectacle of a dissolving universe. But what does this longing for fixity really signify, and does it not cover a less conscious longing to be one of the dissolving forms? And what would dissolution itself bring, if accomplished in these tepid waters: escape from the "miserable personality," or the riches of restored energy, or sexual release and expense? A passage from the *Lehrlinge zu Sais* suggests that these impulses may be, at a given moment, inextricably connected: "He felt his miserable personality melt, submerged beneath waves of pleasure, and that nothing remained but a home for the incommensurable genetic force — a whirlpool in which everything is swallowed by the vast ocean. What does the flame ubiquitously offer? An intimate embrace, from which the sweet liquid trickles in voluptuous drops." *

Compared with the diffuse *Lehrlinge zu Sais*, *Le Voyage d'Urien* has the density and economy of the most conscious

---

* This reminder of the *Lehrlinge zu Sais* (which Gide had read, and which he virtually paraphrased on one page of *Le Voyage d'Urien*) raises an old but important question. In weighing the psychological significance of a text, how much must we discount as mere literary imitation? Certainly Novalis treated more consciously than the Gide of 1892 both *Auflösung* (the dissolution of the soul in nature) and *Einfühlung* (the projection of the self into nature). *Le Voyage d'Urien* seems, on the other hand, a much less metaphysical and a much more personal document. It is reasonable to suppose that Novalis' novel may have suggested the frame of a pilgrimage to the divine city ("every new road traverses new countries, and leads us at last to these dwellings we dream of, to the sacred homeland"), and that his turbulent images of dissolution may have encouraged in Gide an already existing area of feeling. Beyond this it would be unwise to go. A much more obvious "source" is Maeterlinck's *Serres Chaudes* (1891). Some two-thirds of the poems deal with lassitude and ennui, and sixteen out of thirty-three have hospitals or gratuitously sick people. "Cloche à plongeur" in particular may have suggested much to Gide. We find, in thirty-three Whitmanesque lines, a gulf-stream specifically linked with "ennui"; ice-ships; whales encountered on the way to the pole; snow applied to the foreheads of the fevered; obscure grottos; flames on the sea; sailing-ships passing over submarine forests. A few sentences are still more suggestive: "Ils arrivent comme des vierges qui ont fait une longue promenade au soleil, un jour de jeûne . . . Et fermez bien vos yeux en restant sourd aux suggestions de l'eau tiède . . . Et tout attouchement à jamais interdit!" It seems undeniable that Gide "echoed" Maeterlinck. But what does this prove? Perhaps no more than that we may arrive at highly personalized imagery — the imagery which expresses our most intimate conflicts — through the reading of innocent texts. No one would argue, I think, after a comparison with *Le Voyage d'Urien*, that "Cloche à plongeur" is more than a "literary" or "innocent" text.

art. Yet the fifth chapter of the first part — which conveys both the latent homosexuality and the fear of dissolution — must certainly have escaped any rational "intention" and all but the most rudimentary of unconscious censorship. It forces upon us not merely the equivalence of water, indulgence and dissolution, but also the very physical terms of the homosexual embrace. The pilgrims go to a coral islet, and there watch fishermen dive for coral, sponges, and pearls. "The men had saffron-colored skin; they were naked, but around their necks hung bags to be filled with shells." They must cut away with knives the tentacles which attach to their bodies; when they come to the surface their lungs contract, and a thread of blood — "sumptuous on their golden skin" — almost makes them faint. The pilgrims are "diverted" by seeing the ocean floor and the blood of these men. They then bathe themselves in pools which are too warm and in which children are playing. At the bottom of a pool are mosaic figures and two statues that spout perfume into basins. The pilgrims allow the perfume to flow over their arms and hips. And soon a torpor comes over them, as they breathe "this tepid mist — immobile, floating, abandoned; in vain swooning in the marvelous water, green and blue, where glowed only the dimmest light, where the arms of the slender children were tinted blue by the light, and drops falling from the ceiling plashed in monotone." That evening the sailors and the weaker of the pilgrims go on shore in search of women, and those who remain on board are tormented by the thought of their embraces. There is an enormous red moon; there are fires on shore; the night is unbearably hot over the phosphorescent sea. And now we learn, abruptly, that the pilgrims have been watching the sleeping fishermen: "And out of the forest wide-winged vampires, prowling near the sleeping fishermen, sucked the life from their naked feet, from their lips, and overwhelmed them with slumber by the silent beating of their wings."

All this is conveyed in a little more than five hundred words. It should be emphasized that there are no logical connections between the four "episodes": the observation of the fishermen, the swim in the magic pool and subsequent torpor, the evening restlessness on the ship, the coming of the vampires. There are no transitional phrases, yet not a single word breaks the prevailing and complex mood. Mere revery — which normally results in such diffuseness — has here imposed rather than destroyed unity by the very urgency of its demand: by its longing for a nevertheless dreaded relaxation, by its "selection" of particular and revealing imagery. However florid some of its pages, *Le Voyage d'Urien* already shows Gide's ability to record feelings exactly; to penetrate — more successfully than he knew — beneath the level of full consciousness.

Between *Le Voyage d'Urien* and *Paludes*, finished during the winter of 1894–95, lies the partial self-discovery of Gide's first voyage to North Africa; his sickness and his attempt to "normalize" himself, his crucial confession to his mother that he had escaped her control. His first impulse was to preach the gospel of liberation; to persuade others to break their bonds. He was already planning *Les Nourritures terrestres.* Returning to France, he was astonished to find the literary salons unchanged — and that none of his friends, bound by their miserable and routine lives, suspected the importance of his message. How could he save these friends from a misery of which they were wholly unaware? Even a partial liberation had alienated him completely. "Such a state of *estrangement* (which I felt especially when with those closest to me) could well have led me to suicide, had it not been for the escape I found in describing it ironically in *Paludes.*" [39] Gide's own escape from routine and habit would not come until the second trip to North Africa in 1895, and perhaps not even then. *Paludes* is not merely the satire of comfortable and resigned stagnation. It is also self-satire: the ironic portrait of a convention-bound writer who preaches against conventions. It could even be described as a satire on the seriousness of the existential revolt against seriousness, half a century before literary existentialism. It could also be called a satire on the books Gide would later write, and on his famous "attitude": on the desire to rescue readers from complacency by disturbing them.

Paludes is another book within a book. Gide is writing a *Paludes*, but so too is his ridiculous hero. (This double, incidentally, has already thought of the "acte gratuit" — which a philosopher quickly reduces to absurdity.) * By describing the monotony of Tityrus, staring at his marshes, the apostle of freedom hopes to demonstrate to his friends the vanity of their lives. He preaches against comfortable resignation and habit, against routine and bourgeois complacency, against a timid refusal to live, against everything that reduces the individual to a function or social role. "If one knew he was imprisoned, he would at least have the desire to get out." Who is Bernard? The person one sees Thursdays at Octave's. Who is Octave? The person who receives Bernard on Thursdays. Our personalities have been reduced to the masks society compels us to wear. What will such men have accomplished in the only life that is given them? "They will have fulfilled their role." The author of "Paludes" is asked why he complains, since everyone is content in his servitude. "But precisely because nobody complains! The acceptance of the evil aggravates it. It becomes a vice, gentlemen, since one ends by enjoying it." One charm of *Paludes* (Gide's and not the story of Tityrus) lies in the fact that its rebel is more bound by habit, memoranda, and convention than anyone else. He argues the necessity of deracination, and finally takes a one-day trip outside Paris with the sensible Angèle. But only the unrebellious Hubert and Roland have the courage to go to Biskra. (The one-day trip fell by ill-chance on a Saturday, and of course one had to return to Paris for Sunday-morning worship.) The author of "Paludes" is also trapped by the "revolutionary" book he is writing; it stands between him and the enjoyment of "life," from which he is compelled as

* "Il me semble, Monsieur, que ce que vous appelez acte libre, ce serait, d'après vous, un acte ne dépendant de rien; suivez-moi: détachable — remarquez ma progression: supprimable, — et ma conclusion: sans valeur. Rattachez-vous à tout, Monsieur, et ne demandez pas la contingence; d'abord vous ne l'obtiendriez pas — et puis: à quoi ça vous servirait-il?" ("Paludes," *OC*, I, 408).

a writer to profit. His function is to be the person who writes "Paludes"; after finishing it, he begins at once on "Polders." The *saugrenu* of *Paludes* derives from the second part of *Le Voyage d'Urien*; Ellis has become Angèle. The calculated formlessness and sprightly playing with ideas take us much closer to *Le Prométhée mal enchaîné*, however; souls are no longer landscapes, except for purposes of ridicule. Even *Les Caves du Vatican* would be no freer of sensuous detail and surface subjectivity. The liveliness of the satire and coolness of the humor almost totally conceal the personal compulsion under which *Paludes* was written. The fact remains that though Gide makes fun of the unliberated liberator, he fully approves his doctrine. The self which we must now dissolve is no longer the frustrating and unseen superego, nor the perceived sense of guilt. It is rather the self formed by habit and custom, by inertia, by the docile logic of everyday civilized living. But this impulse to awaken from a complacent somnambulism is not treated subjectively at all. Sartre would dramatize these problems more massively in *L'Age de raison*, and *Paludes* is beyond doubt an anticipation of literary existentialism — though the revolt preached by Sartre and Camus seems an inevitable and recurrent reaction to a mechanized age, and to a society as conservative and restrictive as the French. In terms of Gide's own development, the self-satire of *Paludes* marks an important progress toward the critical, detached subjectivity of *L'Immoraliste*. It is indeed hard to conceive how Gide could have written, after such a cool book, the uninhibited *Nourritures terrestres*. In many ways *Paludes* seems a more mature work than the famous testament which followed it.

Les Nourritures terrestres (1897) is both the testament and the manual of liberation, a vindication of the long-distrusted senses and a grammar of "dis-instruction." [40] Thirty years later Gide insisted it was an apologia of "dénuement," of disvestment and impoverishment, and not a glorification of instinct. It was, he argued, the book of a convalescent who embraced life the more fervently because he had almost lost

it. Its excesses were retrospective and even pedagogical, since
its author had already surrendered through marriage the
complete liberty it celebrated. [41] And its sensuous hedonism
represented a reaction not only against a personal puritanism
but also against the pallid aestheticism of the day. Literature
was stifled by artificiality, however properly unmoral, and
needed to be brought back to earth. In 1927 Gide could
complain the more bitterly that a later generation should
summarize his attitude only through this book. It had been
ignored by critics when it appeared, and sold only five hundred copies in the first eleven years. Today we can recognize
Gide's natural impulse to artistic discipline and control, yet
still insist that *Les Nourritures terrestres* is both a manual of
undiscipline and a highly undisciplined book. Or we can say,
at the risk of banality, that it shows the fervor of a man to
whom sight has suddenly been restored, and who feels compelled to recognize, fondle, and enumerate things he had
known only by name.

The compulsion was religious, perhaps, but its expression
was very diffuse. The form admitted anything the author
chose to put in it, from the verse "ronde" to the imagist
"feuille de route" or the compact and startling maxim. Inevitably such a canticle to the sun at times invited a prose as
relaxed and luxuriant as Whitman's verse, and therefore as
structurally monotonous. *Le Retour de l'enfant prodigue*
and the late *Thésée* were the only autobiographical medita-
tations to show the self-contained firmness of *L'Immoraliste*.
In *Les Nourritures terrestres*, form and spirit alike bow to
every wind that blows. "Thereafter, each moment of my life
took on the flavor of novelty of an absolutely ineffable gift.
Thus I lived in an almost continuous and passionate stupe-
faction. I could become drunk very quickly, and chose to
walk in a kind of amazement." But nothing tires so quickly
as incessant novelty and indiscriminate enthusiasm; *Les
Nourritures terrestres* must be read in fragments, rather than
at a sitting. As a work of art, it succeeds through its isolated
charms and particular successes, which are to be sure considerable. The intimate and sensuous appeal of the style

could persuade readers of a message which was not, after all, very new. Or is it inaccurate to speak of "a message"? *Les Nourritures terrestres* has had a diversely liberating effect on very different readers over several generations. Intended to destroy comfort and inertia, it appears to have brought comfort to many. It is a book which creates longings; or, perhaps, reveals them. Thus to abstract and summarize one aspect of its meaning, as we must do here, is more than usually misleading.*

The impulse to destroy the self is now no longer a desire to annihilate tormented consciousness and to escape sexual inhibition, not even primarily to destroy habit and routine. The major impulse is instead to "open" the self at every pore, to expand it in every direction, to absorb all nature's energy. The longing is not negative but Protean — as though an intense enjoyment of all the senses and of every moment might fill at last certain vacant places of the body and spirit. Should a man follow a well-marked path across a field bursting with spring, or should he smell every flower, taste every stream . . . and scrupulously avoid the path? Gide's hedonism may be verbally close to Pater's in its insistence on immediate enjoyment, but its willful indiscriminateness and emphasis on physical energy reminds us rather of Whitman's.

The process of depersonalization must precede regeneration. One must first liberate oneself from everything that induces the habit of rejection: family and home, systematic ethics and metaphysics, "ascetic ideals" and the very idea of sin, the "contamination of books." "Happy is the man," Ménalque says, "who is attached to nothing on earth and who carries his fervor unremittingly with him through all the ceaseless mobility of life. I hated homes and families and all the places where a man thinks to find rest; and lasting affections, and the fidelities of love, and attachment to ideas — all that endangers justice; I held that every new thing should always find the whole of us wholly available." [42]

* For a brief analysis of the influence of *Les Nourritures terrestres* see below, Chapter 5, and for a full account see Yvonne Davet's *Autour des Nourritures terrestres* (Paris, 1948).

But this is merely the first step. The soul should be emptied, so that it can be filled with love, a "love" which consists of the fullest enjoyment of the largest possible number of sensuous experiences. *Les Nourritures terrestres* is the celebration of these experiences; natural piety consists of a refusal to choose between them. For all the specific sensual longings, Gide here shows no renewed impulse to identification with a social group, and his conquest of egotism is therefore more truly primitive than Whitman's. Solitude is overcome rather by energy, by the realization of all physical potentialities, by the satisfaction of every desire. "True it is that I have done my best to arrest the cruel expense of my soul; but it was only by an expense of my senses that I was able to distract it from its God. It was busied with him night and day; it ingeniously invented difficult prayers; it wore itself out with fervor." [43]

Only the soul which no longer worries about its relationship with God can be exposed to the living God; that is, to the plenitude of His creation. Through the first seven books of *Les Nourritures terrestres* this receptivity to light and energy is offered as an end-in-itself, but in the final book it becomes a wise provisional passiveness. If we succumb to the senses' *every* suasion, if we assume or realize *all* human potentialities, we may finally stumble upon those destined only for us. We reach ultimate individuality through ubiquity. "Every being is capable of nudity; every emotion of plenitude." But the end is neither nudity nor plenitude nor annihilation: "Care for nothing in yourself but what you feel exists nowhere else, and out of yourself create, impatiently or patiently, ah, Nathanael, the most irreplaceable of beings."

In the same year Gide published the first of his witty attacks on Maurice Barrès, "A Propos des Déracinés," [44] arguing that arboriculture as well as psychology demands uprooting and transplanting. The coincidence of Gide's hard-won personal escape and of Barrès plea for closer moral and national roots may have made *Les Nourritures terrestres* a more extreme argument than it would otherwise have been, though the antagonism was to become still sharper in the later Dreyfus years. While in some ways far in advance of its time, the book unmistakably belongs to that time. It is the last of Gide's nonpolitical books to date itself in this way. In terms of the author's personal history, it represents a culmination and a new beginning, the extreme point not of immoralism but of amoralism.

Les Nourritures terrestres was complete, and required no further restatement. For all the sanction which he was to find in the reading of Nietzsche, Gide had already begun to examine critically the dangers of total relaxation. To consolidate the advance required an honest valuation of all possible dangers. *Saül* — conceived at about the same time — would show the dangers to the individual of extreme hedonism. And *L'Immoraliste*, however understanding of Michel, would dramatize tragically the suffering which freedom could inflict on others. For more than twenty years Gide tried to legitimize his liberation and his "individualism." But even by 1897 the dialogue with guilt had resumed, though on a very different plane.

"What am I to say? *Things that are true.* OTHER PEOPLE — the importance of *their* lives. Let me speak to them . . ." These cryptic words at the end of *Les Nourritures terrestres* announce the close of Gide's purely introspective period, and look forward to his career as a novelist. The desire to confess remained compelling during the next twenty years, but the personal dilemma was objectified with singular success — with such success, at least, that we are more interested in the anguish of Michel and Jérôme than in the anguish of Gide. *Saül*, which depersonalizes the problem of enslavement by desire, completes the transition from the diarist of *André Walter* or *Les Nourritures terrestres* to the novelist of *L'Immoraliste*. Never were the demands of the stage (which required not only a story but even the translation of desires into physical "demons") of greater personal service: Gide's use of the "supernatural" in this play opened a final window on the natural, outside world. Hereafter most of his studies of the ego and its schisms would be dramatized — dramatized in the novels. He continued to write symbolic prose monologues, a form in which he had no rival. But these frankly autobiographical pieces are less interesting, psychologically, than the novels. We cannot hope to follow in detail all the nuances of feeling they describe.

Mopsus (1899), for instance, does little more than define exactly a feeling of relaxation beyond satisfied desire. No doubt, it is just as truly a concealed confession as *L'Immoraliste*, but lacks all of the novel's tension. The pages on the "sentiment du clandestin" or on the native child would scarcely be intelligible to the unprepared reader; the entire monologue now reads like an exercise in style, in a prose combining purity and variety of syntax, richness and calm. An occasional lapse reminds us how carefully Gide avoided the usual decadent excesses.* *El Hadj* (1899) seems to have been a very deliberate experiment in abnormal lengthening of the sentence, and in systematic baffling of the ear.† The historian of expressionism may find some resemblance between the curious journey of the prince, the false prophet, and the tribe, and the ambiguous journeys described by Kafka and others; he could as well look back for an analogue to Vigny's "Moise." The play *Philoctète* (1899), with its distant allusion to the Dreyfus case, has still less personal urgency; Philoctetes' solitary admiration of his own unexercised virtue at most echoes the satire of *Paludes*, or anticipates that of *Le Prométhée mal enchaîné*.[45]

This rollicking "sotie," which also appeared in 1899, now appears even more experimental than *Les Caves du Vatican*, though less disturbingly subversive. Too deliberate and too intellectual to satisfy the purist, it yet seems at a first reading authentically surrealist in form. A second reading is likely to insist on its heavily hammered moral. Critics have differed

---

* For instance: "La volupté qu'elles vendent est grave, forte et secrète comme la mort" (*OC*, III, 5).

† "A cela durant le jour je songeai; une ferveur soutint ma marche, et le désir de cette nuit me la faisait lente à venir, que j'allais emplir de mon chant" (*OC*, III, 73).

notoriously as to what this moral is, though the eagle who descends to a café on the Boulevard des Capucines and begins to feed on his master's liver is surely Prometheus' conscience. As one of the customers at the café observes, every man has his eagle: " 'But we don't wear them in Paris,' he continued. 'In Paris it's very incorrect. The eagle is troublesome. Just take a look at all he has done! If it amuses you to feed him your liver, go ahead. But I assure you it's unpleasant for those who see you do it . . . Keep out of sight when you feed him.' " [46]

Le Prométhée mal enchaîné is in one sense an expanded version of *Paludes*, but all connections with realistic satire are now broken. The arguments concerning the "action gratuite" malign God (the playful "Miglionnaire") rather than the laws of cause and effect; they seem to be introduced for a comic rather than intellectual purpose. The degree of self-satire is hard to determine, and certainly Prometheus is a less pathetic figure than the author of *Paludes*. Did Gide feel that he had already carried spiritual autobiography, the tortured *examen de conscience,* to an absurd length? Had he merely dramatized compunctions from which everyone suffers? Were all eagles as splendidly weather-beaten as his own? Prometheus' retelling of the story of Tityrus suggests this interpretation. The time has come for Tityrus to detach himself even from his dear oak tree; to abandon conscience and self-analysis. And so too the time has come for Prometheus to kill his eagle; he and Cocles share it for dinner. The final lines of the "sotie," obvious though they are, seem to have escaped most readers:

"Then he has served no purpose?"
"Don't say that, Cocles!"
"His flesh has nourished us."
"When I questioned him, he never answered . . . But I eat him without malice. If he had made me suffer less, he would not be as fat as he is. Less fat, he would have been less tasty."
"And what remains of his beauty of yesterday?"
"I have kept all his feathers." [47]

The introspective torments and analysis of ten years, the puritan conscience itself, had not been in vain; they had trained the psychologist and sharpened his prose style. Gide now felt he could yield up moral questions with a smile; and go on, conscience free, to write wholly objective novels and to enjoy life as it came. But he was of course mistaken.

The *Journal* for November 1904 records that Gide had done no serious writing since finishing *L'Immoraliste* in October 1901. The creative sterility was accompanied by a constant ennui which seems to have been much like Conrad's: an agonizing blend of apathy and disquiet, a "dismal torpor of mind." Conrad's deep reticence makes diagnosis impossible; we know only that he suffered acutely from gout, and that he was financially obliged to go on writing even on the worst days of depression. Gide, with an independent income, could afford to spend most of his time gardening at Cuverville, or reading, or trying by repeated voyages to stir the sluggish spirit. He was patiently aware that a few months of successful writing must be preceded by months or even years of germination, while the unconscious does its silent and shaping work. He did no serious writing. Yet during these "sterile" years he was going through the experiences on which *Les Faux-Monnayeurs* would draw, and *La Porte étroite* (begun in 1905) had been conceived long since. [48] It would be hard to exaggerate the lonely effort of intelligence and will which *L'Immoraliste* must have cost. The very success of the definition may have necessitated a period of recovery; a writer cannot with impunity project and reshape himself so ruthlessly. But there are many passages in the *Journal* which suggest a still unappeased conscience: the need to justify both the experiences of 1893–1895 and the delinquencies of the years that followed. The mind tramped within the anguished circle of contagion, symptom, and attempted cure: "I indicted my morals (and how could my utterly stagnant mind have triumphed over my body?). The fact is that I was becoming brutalized — without enthusiasm or joy." [49]

The debate between Cuverville and Biskra continued through these uneasy years. Gide's wife, the placid and retiring "Em," proved as difficult an antagonist as the more dominating Huguenot mother. Longing to return to Biskra for the sixth time, Gide could not feel free to go until she agreed that he *ought* to: "I almost killed myself in efforts to justify my conduct. To leave was not enough for me. In addition Em. had to approve my going. I hurled myself against a disheartening wall of indifference." [50]

Yet every voyage — as an effort to escape the self — seemed destined to partial failure. The sadness of this failure underlines the various travel diaries, and gives them their particular accent. It is as though the beauty of every new landscape were overshadowed by the remembered gardens of Biskra, or made pallid by the memory of a healing North African sun. And even in Biskra itself, it was impossible to recapture the past. The saddest return of all was this sixth one in 1903, described in *Le Renoncement au voyage*. "Softness of transparent shadows, murmurings in gardens, odours — I recognize all, recognize trees and things . . . the only thing unrecognizable is myself."

Le Renoncement au voyage traces, though Gide hardly realized this at the time, the homeward steps of his Prodigal Son. He can still enjoy an occasional mood of happy indolence, or a sense of fusing the self with its surroundings so successfully that the subject-object antagonism is destroyed. More often, however, he feels himself a stranger. The adventurous "sentiment du clandestin" has been replaced by a weary desire for anonymity; the dark doorways and mysterious gardens attract him with their illusion of peace and consciousness extinguished, rather than as a promise of forbidden joys. The charming native children whom he had watched at play ten years before have grown into tradesmen or thieves, and even Athman must be treated with the considerateness of a former mistress, and given legal advice. Gide now feels the blankness and desolation of the desert, rather than its healing energy; one morning he reads Virgil while crossing it, and longs to visit the Louvre and to reread La

Fontaine. The final lines of the book throw a backward glance of loneliness over its scattered impressions. But there is no distance of spirit from the solitude of Biskra to the solitude of Cuverville, and memories of bathing in a warm *oued* or of sunlight on the caravans near Touggourt are really memories of a much earlier time. "Companion, companion! Friend! In the Normandy autumn I dream of springtime in the desert." [51]

Le Renoncement du voyage is the last work of this period to reveal the impulse to dissolve the self. A notable change of tone appears in the *Journal* for 1906 and 1907. The self has been only too successfully disintegrated, and Gide now longs for restored coherence. To shatter the logic of personality and deny one's moral heritage permitted actions which those austere guardians forbade. But it left one at the mercy of his own individualism, and sharply aggravated isolation. The discomfort of Gide in these years is that of a man who recognizes no limits except those he has set himself, and who yet has a natural liking for boundaries. He had trained himself rigorously to act and think inconsecutively, and found himself incapacitated for writing by "the dislocation and scattering of thought." The contrast between "concentration" and "dissipation" is now a contrast between periods of centralized energy and the aimless waste of time. He who had so long tried to destroy the ego complained of "dispossession of myself." [52] And the author of *Les Nourritures terrestres* sharply criticized the naturalism of Léon Blum's *Du mariage*, its failure to recognize the value of resignation and restraint. [53] The sadness of naturalism is that it leaves one in a restless vacuum. And the great problem for the modern spirit is not, as Michel discovered, to acquire freedom, but rather how to endure it. In such a frame of mind, and now actually tempted to conversion, Gide wrote *Le Retour de l'enfant prodigue*, the most compact and perhaps the most moving of his works.

Especially remarkable is the achievement in prose of an exactness usually confined to poetry: exactness in the definition of feeling and mood. Seeming simplicity of style has

seldom been carried to such an extreme, but the simplicity
is that of mastered complexity: of overtone and nuance minutely explored and controlled. The prose has the full range
of a speaking voice; the voice betrays not merely the weariness and joy of the returned Prodigal, but also the particular
maturity of his disenchantment. It is the voice of a docile
and humbled child, who will hereafter ask no questions. But
the child is a grown man, and he has been humbled by life
itself, by the failure of an honorable dream. The act of
renunciation is complex only if the penitent still carries some
taste in his mouth of what he has renounced. The Prodigal's
encouragement of his younger brother to follow in his own
footsteps is not the diabolic palinode which some of Gide's
Catholic critics have seen. It was perhaps intended to say —
and particularly to Claudel — that its author was not ready
for actual conversion. But even in 1906, as certainly today,
Gide's parable transcends a specifically religious reference.
The Prodigal is equally sincere when he promises to remain
in his father's house, and when he applauds his brother's departure and hopes he will never return. It seems difficult to
question the sincerity of Gide's effort to concentrate and
dominate the self during 1906 and 1907, though in later
years he would more than once wish again for dispossession.

However personal his interpretation of the parable, Gide
is never irreverent; the telling of the story is so natural that
we accept unquestioningly the addition of a younger brother.
Only the jealous elder brother (the Catholic who is orthodox
for pragmatic reasons, a Barrès or Paul Bourget) is treated
severely. The Father is still the charitable God of *Les Nourritures terrestres*, who waits for the wanderer not merely in
His house, but at the end of every long road. The mother
stands, but much less definitely, for wife and family and
friends: for all those who cannot understand the significance
of the Prodigal's heterodox wanderings, but who long to give
him comfort and rest. The younger brother suggests a generation younger than Gide's; his "disciples," who can begin
the adventure of individualism unencumbered by inherited
conceptions, habits and faiths. "You know very well that I,

the younger brother, have no share in the inheritance. I leave without anything." Will this younger generation be able to work out an ethic of freedom, and endure that freedom? Or will it too, suffering from isolation and ennui, return to some restrictive but comfortable home? "Be strong," the Prodigal says in farewell, "forget us; forget me. May you not have to return . . ."

Le Retour de l'enfant prodigue is another recapitulation of Gide's spiritual adventure, and a comment on its apparent failure. In the four interviews the Prodigal tells why he left home, and why he was drawn back. It is no accident that his explanations to the four listeners should differ slightly; whether or not truth is relative, human needs most certainly are, and the needs of one's "disciples" and one's public. The great single motive for leaving home was still the desire to discover and realize the true and hidden self. This self could be brought to life only by denuding it; by ruthlessly casting aside everything factitious and acquired, by sacrificing its moral and intellectual heritage. Thus far the Prodigal's argument is simply that of *Les Nourritures terrestres*. He now recognizes, however, the great part which rationalization had played. He had sought happiness, but finding happiness unattainable, had sought drunken fervor in its place. And worst of all, he had submitted to servitude. Assailed by doubt and moral isolation, he had served masters who mistreated his body, exacerbated his pride, and gave him scarcely enough to eat. And in the end the impulse to identification had driven him home. Fatigue, cowardice, and moral isolation determine our need for a roof over our head; the roof of home at least promised the enjoyment of one's heritage, or what remained of it.

It seems probable that the symbolic action of writing *Le Retour de l'enfant prodigue* helped save Gide from actual conversion in 1906 and 1907. *Les Caves du Vatican* (1914) represents, in any event, another swing of the pendulum; it is a major effort to present human motives as they are, rather than as Christian-classical psychology supposes them to be, and to dispense with the idea of sin. But meanwhile the religious and moral crisis which would become most severe in 1916 was slowly developing. In January 1912 Gide asks whether the time has not come to consolidate his far-flung boundaries, and even to return to the center. He makes resolutions to concentrate his attention and will. A month later he observes that he feels himself profoundly Christian, though Catholicism is "inadmissible" and Protestantism intolerable. The actual crisis of 1916 which drew him close to the Church was a product of the collective anguish and demoralization of that terrible year, but also of an intense physical struggle and a strong sense of guilt. The Devil had become a personal adversary, tempting him once more to his solitary habits; or tempting him to a futile resistance.[54] "It is always foolish to begin a conversation with the Devil. For, no matter how you snare him, he always wants to have the last word." Abominable imaginings threatened sanity itself; it was necessary to organize the struggle against them. The inner debate between the centripetal and the centrifugal impulses had resumed, and virtue now demanded a conservation and concentration of the self; it was comforting to discover passages in Pascal and Baudelaire which recognized the terms of the debate. The worst hour of the struggle, and the closest approach to conversion, seems to have come in October of 1916:

Slow decrease of ardor. Yesterday, abominable relapse, which leaves my body and mind in a state bordering on despair, on suicide, on madness . . .
What does it matter that it is to escape yielding to sin that I yield to the Church! I yield. Oh! untie the bonds that hold me. Deliver me from the frightful weight of this body.[55]

The cry echoes, at a distance of twenty-six years, the longing for purity of the adolescent André Walter. But the circle was not quite closed. "I have no less trouble in reviving in myself the idea of sin than I once had in weakening it."
The distilled record of the religious crisis is to be found in a brief "Feuillet" on the existence of the Devil, and in

the famous twenty-fourth or "green" cahier, *Numquid et tu . . . ?* written almost entirely in 1916. In the "Feuillet" the Devil is the Reasoner who had dictated the paradoxes of Gide's early hedonism; who had persuaded him that the honorable way was the harder one of conquering puritan restraint. When Gide heard Riverat discuss the Devil in 1910, he did not yet recognize that evil was an active force, rather than the mere absence of good. The fact that the "Devil" is of our own creation — a name we give to our inadequacy as well as to our discontent — does not reduce his efficacy. In *Numquid et tu . . . ?* and in the regular diary for 1916 the Devil is again the Reasoner who dictated Gide's earlier "attitude," though the argument is slightly different. Wrongly supposed to be romantic, he can present himself in a classical guise. And so he preached the Goethean doctrine of equilibrium, and that any form of harmony is good. "I did not understand that a certain equilibrium could be maintained, for a time at least, in the worst." Thus Gide wrote on September 19, 1916, in his regular diary. For October and November there are a few brief entries in *Numquid et tu . . . ?* expressing complete humility and abnegation, words of prayer which would not have been out of place in Alissa's journal.

At this point, however, the *Journal* lapses for seven months. When it is resumed on June 20, 1917, Gide is "himself again." He realizes that only fatigue, cowardice, and the longing to satisfy friends had tempted him to surrender his personal ideal and submit to conventional rule. "It was when my thought was boldest that it was truest." In the end those who had tried to convert him actually alienated him by their lack of charity. "I thank Monsieur Massis for having shown me that his religion could not be mine. There can be no further doubt in regard to that, thank God." Thus wrote Gide in 1926, thinking back on his wartime crisis. And this crisis was, apparently, the last religious one he would experience. *Les Nouvelles Nourritures*, written between 1919 and 1935, is merely a restatement of his naturalistic humanism; of the old paradox that we must destroy the conventional and moral self to render our truest self alive; of the individualist faith that we can sacrifice all "useful illusions" and provisional hypotheses without surrendering to despair; that we can endure the loneliness of freedom. There is, to be sure, some change in emphasis; the desire to destroy intellectual constraint (inner logic and "consecutiveness") is now stronger than the desire to destroy puritan heritage and stifling family tie. And the later work shows much less sexual strain; the praise of sensual pleasure as a means to spiritual wholeness seems pedagogical rather than compulsive. This late collection of meditations is an untroubled sermon against asceticism and fear, by a man who no longer suffers from either. Thus on the problem of sexual guilt, at least, Gide seems to have been relatively at peace after 1919, the year he wrote the crucial chapters of *Si le grain ne meurt.*

Sir Edmund Gosse was only one of his friends to protest the publication of this book, surely one of the most sensitive and most beautiful of all autobiographies. "Perhaps I owe it to my protestant upbringing," Gide wrote in reply to Gosse's anxious letter. "Dear friend, I have a horror of lies . . . I wrote this book because I would rather be hated than loved for what I am not." [56] *Si le grain ne meurt* is the final and complete act of confession, toward which all the autobiographical meditations had been pointing. The dramatization of the personal dilemma in *L'Immoraliste*, the half-revelations of *Les Nourritures terrestres* and *Le Renoncement au voyage*, the theoretical defense of homosexuality in *Corydon* * — any of these should have been enough to reveal to

* Paris, 1924, and in *Œuvres complètes*, IX. Anonymous editions had been published in Bruges under the title *C.R.D.N.* in 1911 and as *Corydon* in 1920. These four Socratic dialogues are not among Gide's happiest writings. For all his effort at fairness, Gide makes the skeptical interlocutor both rude and ignorant. He seeks to prove at great length that homosexuality is "natural" (i.e., "good"), while heterosexuality often represents a triumph of civilization over nature ("Troisième dialogue"). Indeed, only the absence of a strong heterosexual instinct among animals explains the extraordinary number of supernumerary males ("Deuxième dialogue"). Uranism is indispensable, furthermore, to the peaceful ordering of society, and protects the family. The social taboo works harm by forcing the homosexual into degrad-

Gide's friends his anomaly, though a few of them long persisted in regarding him as a model of ascetic restraint, merely because he was indifferent to the usual temptations. Could he not have arranged to have the book published after his death? As he explained to Gosse, he was determined to give an example of frankness, as well as to force public opinion to take the social problem into account. Posthumous publications are frequently doctored by relatives. Without the bravado of Rousseau but in all humility he was determined that his public should know him as he was . . . and not merely the public of his own time.[57] And he was determined, perhaps less consciously, at last to know himself. To define his personal situation exactly would be the only way to lay the ghost of his guilt.

As many of the early books point to *Si le grain ne meurt* and seem to be nervous and incomplete confessions, so the entire first part of this book points to the North African confession. While writing these memories of childhood Gide was acutely conscious that he was deferring once again the single chapter he had to write; this may account, in fact, for their dramatic tension and very marked superiority. The childhood is not recreated so much as explored: for minute signs of the artist to be, for psychological and physiological clues to the sexual anomaly; and, even, for personal sources of the contradictory attitude. However carefully selected, the memories are recorded with great simplicity, and only the attentive reader discerns how frequently memory becomes symbolic. The child's fascinated playing with a kaleidoscope, for instance, forecasts in detail the novelist's and psychologist's temperamental curiosity.[58]

The portrait of the nervous and protected childhood shows an understanding so complete as to render interpreta-

---

ing hypocrisy ("Quatrième dialogue"). The intelligent pederast can do the sensitive adolescent much more good than a mistress: "Que cet amant, jalousement, l'entoure, le surveille, et lui-même exalté, purifié par cet amour, le guide vers ces radieux sommets que l'on n'atteint point sans l'amour. Que si tout au contraire cet adolescent tombe entre les mains d'une femme, cela peut lui être funeste; hélas! on n'a que trop d'exemples de cela" ("Quatrième dialogue").

tion irrelevant. Many children experience the idealizing love which the young Gide felt for his cousin. But circumstance permits few of them to marry this first love, and it is perhaps better so. Gide was conscious of his mother's puritanism to the day of his marriage, and thereafter of his wife's. The two forces in his relationship with these two women — his veneration of their purity, and his effort to escape their spoken or silent constraint — may go far to explain both his anomaly and his determined rebellion. The rough-and-tumble of ordinary school life might have counteracted these forces, but the sickly child was tutored at home during the crucial boyhood years; the experience at the Ecole Alsacienne ended disastrously. It seems no wonder that these years were spent, in spite of a rich cultural environment, in a half-sleep of apparent imbecility and fear.

We can well imagine the retrospective anger of the grown man, but his resentment of his mother's dominance is withheld until the final pages of the book. The artistic control of the first part owes much to the desire to be scrupulously fair, to the refusal to liquidate anger. The magic discoveries of the child's wonder, his gradual awakening, the delighted hours of botanizing or playing with animals — these are recorded too. By contrast, the section dealing with the twenty-year-old's literary debut suffers from a lack of detail.[59] It is as though Gide had become impatient on the threshold of confession and could pause only long enough for a few anecdotes. And even the final part, for all its frankness and shrewd analysis, lacks the concentrated and reticent intensity of the first. If these pages on North Africa live as long as the childhood recollections, it will be in spite of their much more relaxed manner.

The difference tells us a great deal about the place of memory in art. In the first section Gide explored half-forgotten years, and by an intense effort of imagination and intelligence selected the few incidents which could stand for all the rest, which could be made to signify. And as he wrote he was constantly aware of what was being suppressed, concealed, postponed. The controlled effort to explore memory, and to conceal yet approach what was still to come, created an intense nervous pressure. And it is this nervous pressure — precisely the pressure under which Michel's plight in *L'Immoraliste* is gradually revealed — that strengthens both structure and style. Its intensity could not be more different from the specious excitement which occurs when a writer "lets himself go."

In the confessional part Gide did let himself go as far as was possible to such a controlled writer. The imaginative shaping of the experience had occurred too long before the moment of writing; had been going on, in fact, through half-a-dozen books and more than twenty-five years. To retell the experiences of 1893–1895, but this time without obliquity, required courage but no imagination. The experiences so long pondered merely told themselves. In the very last pages, in the long-delayed effort to come to a balanced judgment on his mother, Gide recovers some of his initial energy. The conscious anguish and half-conscious joy which occurred with her death led to an exalted and strange "thirst for impoverishment": a desire to rid himself of his most precious material possessions.[60] And now there remained no attachment to his past and moral heritage, except his love for Madeleine. The autobiography stops short at the moment of their engagement.

The spiritual crisis of Gide's brief communist adventure was an intense and highly significant one, and revealed still another effort to affirm the self by renouncing it. But this crisis left no mark on his subsequent literary work. After 1919 and 1920, the tone of a hidden personal urgency largely disappears from his books. The anxiety of guilt had been cured by a determination to avoid excessive resistance to the flesh.[61] All the later novels reveal this equanimity. The conquest of guilt could permit Gide to look on ethical problems with a much greater detachment, and to survey impersonally the consequences of his philosophy, or the moral dilemma of the postwar generation. No doubt this tranquillity must be blamed for the cold unreality of *L'Ecole des femmes* and its sequels; *Geneviève* is both the most objective and the worst of Gide's nondramatic works. But the play *Œdipe* and the monologue *Thésée* show a remarkable recovery of energy and style, however calm their evaluations. The first may reflect an earlier personal crisis. But *Thésée* is a coolly ironic summation of the whole adventure, and an assured restatement of faith.

In retrospect, there seemed to be several different solutions to the anxious situation of the modern individualist who had lost his ancient certitudes. He could abandon himself to a pure hedonism, a complete relativism, a wholly selfish individualism — either because "everything was permitted," or because human nature was unequivocally good:

> *J'ay vécu sans nul pensement,*
> *Me laissant aller doucement,*
> *A la bonne loy naturelle . . .*[62]

Few were long satisfied with such freedom, and many went as far as possible in the other direction. Fearful of social and moral anarchy, they posited, and submitted to, useful substitutes for faith: a pragmatist "belief" in national and church authority, or in the existence of "original sin." Gide went so far with the pragmatists as to imagine a morally convenient Devil, but he was never able to enjoy the literal and genuine recovery of faith of Maritain or Claudel. Still another solution — the social ethics of communism — seemed to him only relatively justifiable. He was briefly willing that communism should destroy individualism (including his own), but only until the economic fight was won. His ideal communist was a rebel against all received ideas and authority, including that of the communist state.

Gide's lasting solution was a puritan modification of the first one: a difficult and self-disciplined individualism, a hedonism founded on self-restraint. In later years Gide argued that he had never wavered from this difficult individualism. But any reader can see that the self-mastery of *Œdipe* is far more arduous than that of *Les Nourritures terrestres*. What Gide did come to admit, with no little

dismay, was that the readers of his books might draw from
them only those parts of his doctrine which were comfortable
or flattering to vanity. This problem, the misuse of one's
ideas by lazy disciplines, furnishes the most interesting pages
of Œdipe (1931). Polynices repeats the common-places of
modern skepticism as unreflectively as any provincial reader
of the Nouvelle Revue française, while Eteocles writes a mal
du siècle of the 1920 vintage, subtitled "Notre Inquiétude." [63] Before leaving Thebes, Oedipus says: "I freely leave
them, for their undoing, a kingdom they neither conquered
nor deserved. But from my example they have taken only
what they find comforting — the justifications and the license
— overlooking the constraint; overlooking the difficult and
the best." [64]

The play Œdipe, though inviting many interpretations,
no doubt dramatizes some of the anguish of 1916 and 1917.
Oedipus is still an antagonist of Barrès as well as of Creon
and Tiresias, and still believes in progress. He argues that
the moral problem presents itself to every man early in his
life (the enigma of the Sphinx), but that this problem is
never the same. Each individual must solve the ethical question in his own particular way. Oedipus does admit, however,
that he has committed a crime in killing his father, and he
refuses the happiness of pretended ignorance and the comfort of impunity. He tears out his eyes not merely to seek
interior light from darkness, but because self-mutilation is
the only way by which he can surpass himself again. He is
an individualist and rebel to the last, but a self-tormenter as
well.

It would be dangerous to relate Œdipe too closely to any
stage in Gide's long adventure. His books repeatedly reflect
crises which he had already mastered, or which he had not
yet squarely faced. Oedipus appears again in Thésée, but
this time to be refuted by the even more Gidean Theseus.
Oedipus, in so far as he now represents his creator at all, recalls his closest approach to a supernatural religion and to a
belief in original sin.[65] But Theseus replies that, however
much he admires Oedipus' superhuman wisdom, he cannot

follow him on that road: "I remain a child of this earth, and I believe that man — such as he is and however stained you judge him to be — must play his game out with the cards he has." The destiny of man is difficult. But it can be accomplished only through self-mastery and through a minute exploration of the labyrinth within, not through self-mutilation.

Œdipe is the culmination of Gide's long effort to purify and simplify his style. *Thésée*, finished in 1944, shows the same extreme concentration of meaning and symbol, but a slightly more enriched phrase. If it is Gide's most impressive book since *Les Faux-Monnayeurs*, this is only partly due to the fact that it was planned many years before.[66] It has none of the characteristics of a book forcibly pieced together from scattered and ancient notes. Any reader can work out, to his amusement, the witty parallels between Theseus' adventure and Gide's own. Theseus too went through a period of relaxed hedonism; then recognized, in sharp reaction, the value of discipline and effort. As a youth he too was timid in society. But he was sufficiently assured to see that he owed something to himself, as well as to Ariadne. His sexual preferences run counter to the accepted ethics of the time; convention demanded a homosexual affair with Glaucos. But he takes Phaedra instead, disguised in Glaucos' clothes. He is strengthened by his belief in progress but also by discipline; he realizes that after the time for adventure and self-discovery must come the time for rule.

The most important adventure is, of course, the exploration of the labyrinth. Before entering it Theseus profits by interviews with Icarus (who in egotistical solitude poses himself unanswerable metaphysical questions) and with Daedalus, who gives much useful advice. The complexity of the labyrinth is in ourselves; though we cannot avoid some intoxication, we should try to remain master of our steps at all times. And the guiding thread attaches one not merely to the past, but to an essential *self*. The actual adventure passes off easily, though Theseus is honest enough to admit that he does not know exactly how he slew the monster. The

Minotaur — at the farthest point in distance and ethical significance from the starting point of Theseus' education — proves to be a young and graceful beast. Theseus remains immobile, transfixed by the Minotaur's physical charm . . . until the beast opens an eye. "I saw that he was wholly without intelligence . . ." At the dead end of pure sensuous experience there is no alternative than to retrace one's steps. On the way out of the labyrinth Theseus passes the room where his companions are indulging in a drunken feast; he has to use force to drive them from the table and from the labyrinth. At first they even regret their drunken forgetfulness, regret returning to the prison of consciousness.

These then are the crucial adventures which the aging Theseus describes, in measured and ironic tones. The style combines the most colloquial and personal accent with an extraordinary purity of syntax and language, and its overtones are unfailingly rich. In the last pages, however, the prose takes on eloquence. The moment was after all a serious one, signed as it was in exile and at the age of seventy-five: both a restatement of the humanistic individualism, and a confident assertion that this philosophy was wholesome and would live:

Behind me I leave the city of Athens. Even more than my wife and my son I have loved it. I have made my city. My thought after me will know to inhabit it immortally. I approach consenting solitary death. I have tasted the good things of the earth. It is pleasing to me to think that after me, because of me, men would know themselves happier, better, and more free. For the good of humanity to come, I have done my work. I have lived.[67]

3   THE EARLY NOVELS

ANDRE GIDE HAS PROBABLY HAD A WIDER influence on the twentieth-century French novel than any writer of his time, and certainly a more diverse influence than Proust.* He was at the start of the two roads which the contemporary French novel has taken. His short novels reinvigorated the traditional "récit" by giving it a new psychological complexity and seemed to save realism by teaching it economy. *Les Caves du Vatican* and *Les Faux-Monnayeurs*, on the other hand, led the movement away from realism, and posed technical problems which novelists are still trying to solve. Yet to judge by most of the many books written about him, Gide is only incidentally a novelist. Most of his critics have given the novels casual and very high praise as works of art, then passed on to what seemed more pressing matters: the fascinating image of a mind always in movement, the ruinous or saving doctrine. The novels have been dissected endlessly for their ideas and attitudes. But only a very few critics — Jean Hytier and Claude-Edmonde Magny most notably [1] — have examined structure and strategy in detail. Thus the great technical influence on other

---

* See below, Chapter 5, for a discussion of Gide's influence on the novel.

novelists has been exerted without much aid from criticism. One curious result is that the novels are often supposed to be fairly uniform in quality, as those of Hardy and Conrad were once supposed to be. Another is that Gide — who dedicated himself at twenty to an exclusively artistic career which would shun all moral and social concerns — was thought of, in the last three decades of his life, as a living philosophy, the hero or scapegoat of modernism.

Any reader of the *Journal* must nevertheless recognize that Gide thought of himself as a novelist, and that the years of literary discipline and most of the shorter works looked forward to *Les Faux-Monnayeurs,* as well as to *Si le grain ne meurt.* Gide felt the obligation to write at least one true "novel" such an august one that he diffidently called his earlier works of fiction "récits" or "soties." And he defined the novel as the very kind of multiform, comprehensive, and decentralized impression of life which he would find hardest to achieve.[2] The "récits" he saw as concentrated critical studies of a single character or a single problem. They vary in length from fifteen to fifty thousand words, and in English would be called short novels or novelettes: *L'Immoraliste* (1902), *La Porte étroite* (1909), *Isabelle* (1911), *La Symphonie pastorale* (1919), *L'Ecole des femmes* (1929), *Robert* (1929), and *Geneviève* (1936). The "soties" by contrast are ironic adventures in the absurd, pre-surrealist fantasies. These are not merely stories of "sots" or fools; the word has some of its medieval connotation of irresponsibility. Of the "soties," *Paludes* (1895) and *Le Prométhée mal enchaîné* (1899) might resist certain academic definitions, but *Les Caves du Vatican* (1914) is as truly a novel as *Antic Hay.* To these we could at most add *Les Cahiers d'André Walter* (1891), *Le Voyage d'Urien* (1893) and *Thésée* (1946).

A half-million words more or less, for nearly six decades of writing. This is indeed a small body of fiction, though unfaded reputations have been made on less; Conrad might have produced no more had he too been freed from the obligation to write for a living. Few novelists have written more slowly than Gide, or allowed their books to germinate over so many years. *L'Immoraliste, La Porte étroite, Isabelle, Les Caves du Vatican,* and *La Symphonie pastorale* were all conceived before the turn of the century. *La Porte étroite* is largely based on experiences which occurred in 1882 and 1884; the first plan for a "récit" dramatizing the lonely death of Anna Shackleton was made in 1890. But the book was begun only fifteen years later, and its fifty thousand words took three years to write. Some of the personal experiences which went into *Les Faux-Monnayeurs* date from as early as 1891. Gide began his diary of the book's composition in June 1919. But he did not write the first thirty pages of the final version until 1922, and finished the novel in June 1925. The brief *Ecole des femmes,* which appeared in 1929, was planned by 1914, and perhaps much earlier. And the thirty thousand words of *Geneviève* (vaguely projected by 1919) were written painfully between 1930 and 1935. We must assume, while allowing for the most severe artistic scruples, that Gide's purely creative gift was both intermittent and slight.*

Gide's admiration for Stendhal and for Dostoevsky, whom he considered the greatest of all novelists, may therefore seem surprising — unless we recall that many writers (like many moralists) prefer and defend the virtues they lack themselves. *La Chartreuse de Parme,* chosen over *Le Rouge et le noir* after some hesitation, comes first on the list of French novels Gide would take with him to a desert island.[3] He admired Stendhal's eagerness to explore the "special case" and to ferret out the hidden or ambiguous in human behavior.[4] But he envied especially Stendhal's uninhibited creative energy and the bright sharpness of his style. Stendhal's prose was the hard bone on which he could "sharpen his beak"; he returned repeatedly to the *Correspondance* "for hygienic reasons."[5] He was drawn to Dostoevsky by that very torment and haunted disorder which so repelled Conrad.[6] Gide frankly admits that his lectures on Dostoevsky offer a highly selective portrait, even a self-portrait.[7] He finds in the Russian novelist his own central argument: that the individual affirms him-

---

* For Gide's comment on an earlier but similar version of these remarks, see his letter of May 16, 1947, at the end of this book.

self through renunciation, and that only through this renunciation can he enter into "eternal life" here and now. Unlike
Western novelists who dramatize man as a social animal,
Dostoevsky explores the individual's relationship with himself and with God. And he knows that man's inner life cannot
be reduced to an orderly combat between such general forces
as "will" and "passion." Gide attacked more than once the
oversimplified psychology of Balzac and the oversimplified
ethics of Dickens. Unlike theirs, the characters of Dostoevsky
are illogical, inconsecutive, contradictory. They are *simultaneously* impelled in opposite directions, and so achieve a
richer anxiety than the neurotic whose two personalities alternately prevail. And where the French realist tends to
throw an equally strong light on all his characters, Dostoevsky
wisely allows some of his to remain shadowed and incomplete.

Gide's ideas on fiction reveal the familiar reaction of the
French intellectual — strongly impelled to logic, order, and
moralism — against rationalism in ethics and art. Gide overlooked Conrad's conservativism, just as he overlooked Dostoevsky's, and was interested especially in the "inconsecutiveness" of Lord Jim's and Razumov's crimes.[8] He was repelled
by the constantly revealed "intention" of *Jean Christophe* [9]
and praised Proust's seeming lack of intention, his refusal
to prove anything.[10] He found Henry James's characters
entirely too rational: "They are winged busts; all the weight
of the flesh is absent; all the fleshly and leafy element; all of
the shadowed savage." [11] He missed in James what only very
recent critics have found: the obscure personal urgency and
therapeutic act of confession which helped give Stendhal and
Dostoevsky their tension and complexity. He was willing to
acknowledge the value of James to the disorderly English
novel, but felt he had nothing to offer to the French: "So
much adroitness and distinction — I have had enough before
I begin. He refines on our own faults." [12] Of the many foreign
writers Gide has praised, only Goethe can be attached easily
to the classical French tradition. It is not surprising that Gide
should have chiefly admired, among American novelists of
today, Faulkner, Hemingway, Steinbeck, Caldwell . . . and

Dashiell Hammett.[13] He had long since argued that the French tradition needed constant revitalizing through the importation of violent and demonic energy from abroad. Gide borrowed several proverbs from *The Marriage of Heaven and Hell* to explain the mysterious Stavrogin. The same proverbs — insisting on the value of energy and on the importance of cultivating contradictions — could also serve as the heart of Gide's aesthetic. To them he added two of his own: "Fine sentiments make bad writing," and "there is no work of art without collaboration of the demon." [14] The long drama of his career as a novelist was sharpened by his struggle to avoid fine sentiments and by his repeated effort to arouse a sometimes sluggish demon. The further problem was to enlist the services of this demon (who must come of course from inside) without reverting to autobiography. The novel should deal with the inner life rather than with society. And it should carry the tension of some unresolved personal difficulty. But it should not be a mere record of one's actual life. In most of the "récits," at least, Gide hardly considered the alternative of imagining lives wholly unrelated to his own. The false novelist, he said, reproduces his own image and experience. The true novelist isolates some frustrated or unrealized potentiality and gives it vicarious life. The distinction is not between objectivity and subjectivity, but between two kinds of subjectivity: that of autobiography and that of symbolic action. And the distinction is always precarious: the problem for the writer of *L'Immoraliste* was to avoid another *André Walter.* As the years passed and the various "récits" fulfilled their therapeutic function, Gide determined to escape spiritual autobiography altogether. Thus *Les Faux-Monnayeurs* was intended to realize at last the parting promise of *Les Nourritures terrestres* — to talk of others' lives. Gide protested repeatedly against the common accusation that his novels were disguised self-portraits. But the total abandonment of himself and of his point of view which he called the key to his character and his work could more properly be called the key to his aesthetic aim.

At the personal level, then, Gide's paradoxical ambition was to overcome the isolating subjectivity of *André Walter* while preserving the urgency of an individualized demon's symbolic action. But also he wanted to revitalize the tired realistic novel, even go beyond it entirely. French realism, based on a grossly oversimplified conception of human nature, merely imitated the conventional masks men wore. And the most mishandled and fantastic epic description was preferable to the dreary photographic detail of the naturalists.[15] Gide was alternately attracted by the sensuous fantasy of the *Arabian Nights* and by the economy of classical drama, which knew the importance of what is left out; naturalism was both diffuse and drab. By the time he began *Les Faux-Monnayeurs*, Gide felt the one thing to avoid was the "simple impersonal récit." [16] André Walter had conceived, many years before, the idea of the "pure novel" stripped of all unessentials: "no more description and the background neutral."

It is nevertheless significant that André Walter's pure novel was to be a morality play: a dramatized struggle between the abstracted forces of good and evil. Gide had to combat his natural impulse to the moralizing "roman-à-thèse," just as he had to combat his impulse to write responsible and realistic autobiography in severely ordered form. The various "projects" for novels which he never wrote show that he usually conceived the human situations in terms of a "problem" — and a problem involving some poorly disguised shadow of himself. In 1898 Gide confessed to the always useful Angèle that he would, if he did not restrain himself, write a book of ethics every three months.[17] Later, and no doubt once again protesting too much, he insisted that he was never for or against his heroes and that his books had no moral intention. A book should neither come to a direct geometric conclusion nor reflect too recognizably its age. "Woe unto the books which 'conclude.' They are the ones which satisfy the public at first. But twenty years later the conclusion demolishes the book." [18]

Gide succeeded in achieving impartiality to such an extent that his first critics completely misinterpreted his books. They understood *La Porte étroite* to be a sympathetic portrait of a religious woman, a penitent palinode to the hedonist individualism of *L'Immoraliste*. But *La Porte étroite*, he replied, was a study of futile religious mysticism, and *L'Immoraliste* a study of individualism become futile anarchy. *And the two books were conceived at the same time.* By insisting on this, Gide hoped to prove that his novels were not bare expressions of his prevailing states of mind. And neither were they "spiritual histories" of a decade, of a collective state of mind. More than once, especially in *Les Faux-Monnayeurs*, Gide was tempted to write such spiritual history. But here once again he preferred to rest his case with posterity, and to dramatize the eternally contemporary anxieties of youth.

The novels, nevertheless, reflect the moral crisis of the early twentieth century: the problem of moral isolation, the dilemma of individualist ethics. And Gide's final theory of the novel belongs also to the twentieth century — its restless impatience with coherent psychology, with leisurely realism, with ethical intention, with rigidly imposed form. Gide more and more consciously struggled against these natural impulses of orthodox French realism. The struggle was of particular intensity because he was himself, by natural inclination and talent, an orthodox French realist.

L'Immoraliste, finished in 1901, is the first, the most autobiographical, and the best of Gide's "récits." Certainly it is the most frequently misunderstood of his novels, partly because its deceptive simplicity of surface invites casual and very literal reading. Like the unread *Voyage d'Urien*, the misread *Immoraliste* demands a fuller analysis than books as well or better known. Historically, it is an important moment in the development of the French psychological novel — which threatened to become, in the hands of Bourget, a lucid pondering of abstract problems and a vehicle for transparent instruction. *L'Immoraliste* brought to the French novel all the seriousness and much of the complexity of Dostoevsky's short novels — and did so first of all through its successful use of the "imperceptive" or self-deluded narratoɪ as subject of the story he tells. *L'Immoraliste* is not, to be sure, *The Possessed*, or even *Crime and Punishment*. But it exists as a touchstone for shorter and less ambitious fiction. It helps us to define a level of achievement which autobiographical and subjective fiction can rarely hope to surpass: fiction which concentrates on one man's destiny (a shadow of the author's own) and which offers no comprehensive understanding of society. Michel's revolt reflects his age (the age of Nietzschean hopes and destructions) but reflects even more the timeless conflict of the unconscious life and the conscious. Already the psychological realism of *L'Immoraliste* seems more important than its critique of individualism; its anticipation of Freud more valid than its oblique reflection of Nietzsche. Its more personal triumph lies in the successful avoidance of lyricism, of confused or angry self-justification, of special pleading — of all the evasions, in fact, to which autobiographical fiction is tempted. The precarious balance of the author's sympathy and detachment remains to the end under minute control.

Gide readily admitted the part which symbolic action played. He told Francis Jammes he had spent four years on the book, not writing but living it. He had struggled through the novel as through a disease, in order "to go beyond." [19] In a letter to Scheffer he reduces such symbolic action to an aesthetic principle:

That a germ of Michel exists in me goes without saying . . . How many germs we carry in us, which will burgeon only in our books! They are what the botanists call "sleeping eyes." But if, by an act of will, you suppress them, *all but one* — how it springs up at once and grows! How it seizes at once upon the sap! My recipe for creating a hero is simple enough. Take one of these germs; put it in the pot by itself — and you soon obtain an admirable individual. Advice: choose preferably (if it's true one can choose) the germ that most disturbs you. By doing so you rid yourself of it at once. Perhaps that is what Aristotle meant by the purgation of the passions. Purge ourselves, Scheffer, purge ourselves! There will always be passions enough. [20]

However, the process was not as simple as this letter implies. A fragment on Ménalque preceded *Les Nourritures terrestres*, and in the completed book only Ménalque has a personal history of any significance. Was Gide long determined to fix the lesson and personality of Oscar Wilde for posterity, or did he imagine once again a fictional blend of Wilde and himself? *L'Immoraliste*, in any event, appears to have been planned as a "life of Ménalque," to be told from the outside.[21] But Gide could not, in 1897 or later, tell a detailed story of subjective torment except in the first person and from the inside. For this or for some other reason a separation occurred. The Ménalque of *L'Immoraliste* is no longer a blend of Wilde and Gide, but a walking manual of hedonism who recalls only too obviously the recorded personality and recorded epigrams of Wilde. He is as sprightly and as unreal as the Protos of *Les Caves du Vatican*, and is therefore out of place in a somber realistic novel. But Michel, transposed to a plane and life of tragic failure, is a potential or suppressed self, a refashioned image of the young André Gide.

There are differences, such differences as made the writing of *L'Immoraliste* possible. The fictional Michel is a latent and frustrated homosexual even after his marriage with Marceline, and is paralyzed by the freedom he has won. The freedom is of course incomplete, since to the very end he does not satisfy his pederast inclinations. Otherwise, the resemblances between the hero and his creator are striking and too obvious to insist on: the double oppression of childhood Huguenot teachings and an isolated bookish adolescence; an ill-advised marriage and the first fascinated observation of the children in Biskra; tuberculosis, convalescence, and the fierce egoism which accompanies it. Later, the dual impulses to concentration and dissolution of the self; the sense of estrangement on returning to the artificial Paris salons; the crucial meeting with a notorious hedonist. And at last the reckless unrest of the journeys to Switzerland and Italy, in roundabout obedience to the ineluctable pull of North Africa, where the last discoveries must be made. Gide thus "used"

extensively his first two trips to North Africa and their surrounding moral complication, though the poachers of the
second part derive from much older memories.[22]

Not everything was so retrospective, however. Gide also
used certain more recent events: memories of ice-skating in
St. Moritz on his honeymoon, of his wife's illnesses in Switzerland and North Africa in 1897 and 1898, of her carriage
accident in 1900.[23] A brief 1897 letter to Jammes from Switzerland — mentioning both his wife's illness and Athman —
reminds us of the very dilemma which Michel could not
define.[24] Weighed against such living forces and memories,
the influence of Nietzsche on the novel scarcely seems worth
mentioning. This other "source" was in any event negative.
The translation of Nietzsche's books into French freed Gide
from the obligation to theorize on individualism at length.[25]
We can only regret that he did not feel free to dispense with
Ménalque as well. But this is perhaps the hardest thing for
any novelist to do: to cut away all traces of what he had once
(and wrongly) supposed to be his real subject.

In personal terms, *L'Immoraliste* was a symbolic act of dissociation from Michel. Had Gide not discovered himself so
fully, he too might have been driven to such a harsh and
aimless individualism. This is the book's "personal" subject.
L'Immoraliste is also, of course, a critique (not rejection) of
Nietzschean individualism. But most of all it is a study of
latent homosexuality, of repression and compensation, of the
effect preconscious energies may have on a man's acts, feelings, and ideas. It is no wonder, since the book was all these
things, that it was little read and little understood at first.
A very few early readers — and readers as different as Madame
Rachilde and Francis Jammes — saw that the conflict was a
sexual one. Yet Lilian Neguloa's valuable census shows that
a large majority of the book's critics (including some very
recent ones) have considered *L'Immoraliste* to be a novel
"about individualism" and have not seen Michel's homosexuality at all.[26] Some, to be sure, may have simply refused
to acknowledge what they saw. Thus Charles du Bos candidly
admits that he could not take up "le problème Wilde" with

the particular audience of his early lecture on the book.[27] Unlike French biography, French criticism has long resisted the influence of psychology and has also remained curiously discreet.

There is the further fact that Michel's revolt against repression and conformity may be transferred to any plane of experience, and so may invite the sympathy of a critic differently repressed. But the strongest obstacle to understanding has probably been the inveterate tendency of critics to take a narrative told in the first person at its face value and to confuse the narrator's consciousness with the author's. It is nevertheless hard to understand why so few critics (including those who return constantly to "intention") have referred to Gide's statement that Michel was an unconscious homosexual.[28] Miss Neguloa's article reminds us that nearly all readers are casual readers, and that most criticism of fiction is inexpert to an unsuspected and scandalous degree. It also suggests that any new commentary on *L'Immoraliste* must, to counteract established misconception, provide an old-fashioned summary of plot.

Michel, a precocious and withdrawn archaeologist of twenty-four, marries Marceline to please his dying father. At first he hardly realizes that she is a human being, with an inner life of her own. He feels at most tenderness and pity, and the honeymoon is loveless in every sense. Michel's long accumulated fatigue brings on tuberculosis. He begins to spit blood while crossing the desert and arrives at Biskra more dead than alive. His first surrender to sickness is followed by a violent craving to live. To consider as "right" only what contributes to health is the first phase of his "immoralism." And as health returns he begins to suspect that life has unexplored joys, that he carries within him a precious and unrealized self. He determines to discover this self by a ruthless elimination of everything factitious and acquired.*

* Michel's sickness and convalescence recalls Nietzsche's as well as Gide's, as this striking parallel shows: "After that touch from the wing of Death, what seemed important is so no longer; other things become so which had at first seemed unimportant, or which one did not even know existed. The miscellaneous mass of acquired knowledge of every kind that has overlain

The self is a palimpsest. All the false superscriptions of education and moral training must be erased before he can discover the "occult text."

Marceline unwittingly takes the first important step toward revelation. She brings Bachir, a handsome native child, to Michel's sickroom. Michel interprets his affection for the boy as a love of animal health. But when he is able to go outside and watch the children at play, he is irritated by his wife's presence. He is "frightened" by the weak, sickly, and well-behaved boys she brings to their rooms but fascinated by the unruly Moktir. He says nothing when he sees Moktir steal a pair of scissors. And now he invents various pretexts for seeing the boys alone: Ashour, Lassif, and Lachmi with his "golden nudity." He wanders into one particular enchanted garden which will haunt his memory, and perhaps account for the attraction shaded places are to hold for him in Ravello and Normandy. But as the hot days approach they leave Biskra and the children behind. Michel feels that his love for Marceline is increasing, yet he takes pleasure in concealing from her his sense of a hidden, undefined self. In Italy, on the way back to France and a resumption of his studies, he has a fight with a drunken coachman. That night he possesses Marceline for the first time.

Michel leads a curiously divided life during the months that follow. On the one hand he tries to impose order on La Morinière, his Norman estate. He guards against "vagabond inclination" by tying himself down to an expensive

the mind gets pulled off in places like a mask of paint, exposing the bare skin — the very flesh of the authentic creature that had lain beneath it" (*The Immoralist* [New York, 1930], p. 64). "Illness likewise gave me the right to a complete reversal of my mode of life; it not only allowed, it actually ordered me to forget; it enforced the necessity of repose, of idleness, of waiting, of patience . . . And all that meant thinking! . . . The state of my eyes was enough to stop all book-wormishness, or, in plain English, philology: I was delivered from books; for years I read nothing — the greatest boon I have ever conferred upon myself! That essential self, which had been buried, as it were, which had lost its voice under the pressure of being forced to listen to other selves continually (which is what reading means!), awakened slowly, timidly, doubtfully — but at last it *spoke again*" ("Ecce Homo," translated by Clifton Fadiman, *The Philosophy of Nietzsche* [Modern Library edition], pp. 84–85).

Paris apartment, and by accepting a lectureship at the College de France. But he is attracted in his studies only by barbarism and indiscipline; by such figures as the fifteen-year-old Athalaric, in revolt against his mother and his Latin education. His lectures become an "apology and eulogy of nonculture." His friend Ménalque (who had visited Biskra after him and had heard of his liking for the native children) demands an explanation of these contradictions. Is Michel one of those who, out of a fear of isolation, refuse to be themselves? Before leaving on another of his fabulous journeys, Ménalque preaches the joys of dangerous living; that is, of the acceptance of life as it comes.

The balance between anarchy and discipline wavers during the months which separate the two visits to La Morinière. Something, seemingly Ménalque's lessons, tips it sharply toward anarchy. On the first visit Michel had spent his days supervising his estate with the prudent and orderly Charles, the caretaker's seventeen-year-old son. But now he is fascinated by the most primitive and irresponsible of the farmhands; feels an "evil curiosity" concerning them. He takes up with Bute, a demoralized army veteran, and listens avidly to his stories of the incestuous Heurtevents. He catches the boy Alcide poaching, and joins him in poaching on his own estate. He now feels a strange urge to destroy the harmony and order he had helped establish. He tries in vain to spend more time with his wife, who had lost a child, and who has begun to show tubercular symptoms. His pity struggles against a deepening sense that she is tainted by this illness. Her weakness seems contemptible.

Michel sells La Morinière and takes Marceline to St. Moritz. But he is intolerably bored by the honest mediocrity of the Swiss. His "reverence" for his wife increases simultaneously with a now demonic urge to spend all his money; to move always farther to the south; to seek out and observe, in each Italian city, the "lowest dregs of humanity." In Taormina he feels an irresistible attraction for a coachman — a Sicilian boy "as beautiful as a line of Theocritus" — and kisses him. A few days later they leave for Syracuse, and here too

Michel neglects his dying wife to seek out the sailors and
vagabonds in the port cafés. But Syracuse is only a last and
futile detour. Their destination is Biskra. This time when
they arrive it is Marceline who is more dead than alive.
In the two years, the native children have changed horribly.
Only Moktir, just out of prison, remains "superb." In his
vague restlessness Michel drags his wife on to Touggourt,
taking Moktir with them. On the first night there he sleeps
with Moktir's mistress in the boy's presence, seeking peace
in highly cerebral perversion. He returns to the hotel in
time to see Marceline die. Only then, freed from conscious
restraint yet still restless, he sends for the three friends to
whom he tells his story. Can they advise him? Tell him what
to do with his objectless freedom? Even Michel is aware that
this freedom is not truly complete. "Sometimes I am afraid
that what I have suppressed will avenge itself." In the months
since Marceline's death he has spent an occasional night with
an Ouled Naïl prostitute. But the girl suspects it is really her
little brother Ali he desires. "Perhaps she is not altogether
wrong. . ."

   L'Immoraliste is one of the first modern novels to deal at
all seriously with homosexuality. But it is most important
to keep in mind that Michel never participates in a homosexual act. The reader who assumes that such acts occur but
are not mentioned, for reasons of discretion, is likely to mis-
interpret everything else. One can imagine Gide's exasperation when Paul Bourget asked him, as late as 1915 (and as
soon as Edith Wharton had left the room) whether Michel
was a "practicing pederast." [29] Through many pages of a first
reading we have every right to share Michel's bewilderment.
We explore him with the same curiosity that he explores
himself. And how much would be lost if the last revealing
lines of the novel were its first ones! But on second and subsequent readings the ambiguities should dissolve. Not till
then, perhaps, does the reader notice that Michel possesses
Marceline only after fighting with the drunken coachman;
that he felt "obliged" (in an hour of frustration) to caress a
strangely textured shrub; that his period of tranquillity at

La Morinière ends abruptly with the coming of the boy Charles; that he longs to sleep in the barn because the boy Alcide sleeps there; that, in fact, he never proceeds beyond the stage of longing for these boys. The important fact about Michel is not that he is a homosexual, but that he is a latent homosexual, a homosexual without knowing it. Thus *L'Immoraliste* is not a case study of a particular and manifest neurosis, but a story of unconscious repression. In the light of this, but only in this light, various unexplained ritual acts take on meaning: the shaving of the beard, or the ceremonial undressing, sun-bathing, and immersion in the pool near Ravello. The vengeance of what has been suppressed touches every fiber of Michel's intellectual and moral life; determines his self-destructiveness and his anti-intellectualism alike. Restrained from sexual satisfaction and even from self-discovery by an unconscious force, Michel rebels in other ways. The outburst may be sudden and specific, as when he leaps into the draining lake and takes a savage excitement in catching eels with Charles. More generally, Michel rebels against his early intellectual training in his philosophical defense of barbarism; against his inherited Norman prudence in trying to destroy the harmony and order of his farm. *L'Immoraliste* dramatizes as clearly as Dostoevsky's *Gambler* the compulsion to risk — and lose. Payment must eventually be made to the internalized parental authority. But the first impulse is to destroy not appease this superego. The harshness of Michel's individualism — and this, in general terms, is no less than the "subject" of the novel — is determined by the harshness of the repression.

The hidden victim of this hidden restraint reveals itself in a curious hostility toward the convention-bound and in an abnormal sympathy for the free. Michel's acts seemed to many early readers (and even at times to himself) unmotivated and "Satanic." Like *The Secret Sharer, Heart of Darkness*, and parts of *Lord Jim*, *L'Immoraliste* dramatizes unconscious or half-conscious identification.[30] The lawless buried self is attracted to all whom the superego and the waking conscience deem guilty, and repelled by all the well-behaved. Even when

he is most determined to lead a regulated life, Michel's affections go out to the unmoral, the corrupt, the unrestrained.
He has a "horror of honest folk," but is paralyzed by "joy"
when he sees Moktir steal the scissors, when he learns that
Alcide is a poacher — or when he uncovers, in the lifeless
pages of his research, the youthful savagery of Athalaric. He
envies Pierre's drunken brutality as he envies Ménalque's
refined selfishness. The movement toward discovery is not,
to be sure, uninterrupted. The alternating and sometimes
simultaneous impulses to concentrate and to destroy the ego
— to use Baudelaire's terminology rather than Freud's — increase or weaken according to the self at the moment dominant and the self at the moment suppressed. The frustrated
Huguenot as well as the frustrated homosexual may demand
satisfaction. In the final chapters, however, the inward aggressions become frenzied as the "authentic self" nears the surface.

Not all of Michel's feelings may be so simply explained.
Does he resent the dying Marceline because he fears a return
of his own tuberculosis, or because he has equated weakness
and virtue, or simply because he longs to be rid of her? One
strength of L'Immoraliste lies in its awareness of the close
interdependence of Michel's health, his degree of sexual ad-
justment, his moral heritage, and his intellectual interests.
The novel's over-all "meaning" is reducible to the barest
Freudian terms, but Michel as a character is not. His intelligence and will, however weak, do play some part. His tenderness toward Marceline develops into love at the same time
as his cruelty toward her — and at the same time as his homosexual impulses. And if his ideas are determined by unconscious needs, his arguments still demand attention. The
problem of individualism, though provoked in this instance
by a specific sexual situation, nevertheless transcends neurosis.

For Gide knew that the problem of the emancipated individualist goes on, even after sexual adjustments have been
made. Must one choose between a refusal to live and an
individualism which makes others suffer? Marceline justly
observes that Michel's doctrine may be a "fine one," but that
it threatens to suppress the weak. And can the individualist

cut himself off to be free, yet live in that rarefied air? "To know how to free oneself is nothing; the arduous thing is to know what to do with one's freedom." It is here, in its critique of Nietzschean individualism, that *L'Immoraliste* is necessarily imperfect — and first of all because Michel is an imperfect Nietzschean. Gide agreed with Michel and Nietzsche that the world is divided into the strong and the weak, and many of Michel's arguments are transcribed from *Les Nourritures terrestres*. But Michel was incapable of the solution Gide elsewhere proposed: to become fully conscious of the inner dialogue between order and anarchy, and to suppress by an act of will whichever voice threatens to become too strong. The very fact that makes Michel so interesting dramatically and psychologically — his imperfect understanding of himself — makes him a poor vehicle for Gidean and Nietzschean ideas. His story could not answer the question raised in the Prologue: how is society to use the energies of the free man? "I fear the failures of individualism," Gide wrote in 1898.* Michel is such a failure; he is not a free man.

Thus the aspect of *L'Immoraliste* most emphasized by critics is in fact unsatisfactory. The novel's strength lies rather in its art and psychological understanding, and in its controlled transposition of personal experience. For it is a "fruit filled with bitter ashes," [31] a novel written severely from memory, but also out of mind and nerve. The triumph of intelligence reveals itself in the close pressure of form. Not a single irrelevant memory has survived this pressure, other than the memory of Wilde's epigrams. This required a con-

---

* For Gide's intellectual conclusions at this time, we must look to the "Lettres à Angèle" (*OC*, III, 222–241). In 1898 Gide failed to distinguish clearly between the final affirmation of Nietzsche and the final renunciation of Dostoevsky, and brought them too close together by verbal legerdemain. If the individualist's energies are stifled, they may break out in some violent antisocial way. A universally accepted individualism, on the other hand, would ruin both the strong and the weak. The true "exceptional" man would be lost in the crowd of "meaningless eccentrics." There is no rule of thumb, Gide observes, by which we may distinguish the successes from the failures, the Nietzsches from the Stirners. We should therefore repudiate "individualism," out of respect for the individualist. Gide argued in much the same terms during his communist period.

scious separation of the author's consciousness from Michel's, and a careful use of the "imperceptive" narrator as a technical device. We shall see in Rivière's *Aimée* and Chardonne's *Eva* (two books possibly derived from *L'Immoraliste*) to what diffuseness and incoherence this device may lead (see Chapter 5). Yet it remains one of the few ways of saving psychological fiction from pedagogical abstractness, and perhaps the best way to convey (rather than "explain") a conflict between conscious and unconscious energies. The problem for the novelist is to keep his narrator (or Jamesian "fool" and observer) self-deluded, imperceptive, blind; incapable of accurate self-analysis — yet have that narrator supply all the evidence necessary to the reader's understanding. He must say enough to convey his daily suffering and betray his true difficulties, but not say too much more.

Critics have more and more come to realize that a novelist's "technique" has some intimate relationship with his understanding of his characters, as well as a more obvious bearing on the mobility, energy, and persuasiveness of his books. But it is nearly impossible to demonstrate these relationships specifically, and even discussions of "point of view" are often disappointingly vague. The device of the obtuse narrator or observer is, however, a particular and definable one, and Gide's major success in using it deserves close analysis. *L'Immoraliste* also demands extensive comparison with other novels, short novels especially. *Great Expectations* prolongs a central imperceptiveness over many hundreds of pages, but does so primarily for dramatic suspense. The technique (which demands unusual and continued alertness on the reader's part) seems particularly suited to the short novel. To measure Gide's success in exploiting this "point of view" we should look to certain familiar short novels of Melville and of Joseph Conrad and Thomas Mann. How did they, faced by such a problem as Gide's, exploit the resources of this technique? The comparisons may seem digressive, but only such comparisons can establish *L'Immoraliste* in its proper place as one of the formal triumphs of the modern novel.

Melville's *Benito Cereno* is certainly one of the more conspicuous successes. Captain Delano is literally a "fool," wholly incapable of interpreting experience or of seeing evil, because of his benign temperament and Emersonian optimism. But for various reasons his story had to be more diffuse than Michel's. Melville wanted to involve the reader in Delano's error, and not merely for the sake of suspense or melodramatic surprise. "You too, optimistic and complacent reader," he might have said; "this is the way you too would have calumniated innocence and rationalized evil!" Following such an intention, and conceiving such a drama of appearance and reality, Melville had to provide much misleading or irrelevant appearance. His grave prose rhythms and mortuary similes promise tragedy, but the reader has little opportunity to detect what this tragedy will be. Only the long legal deposition fully corrects Delano's distortions and reconstructs the events in detail. It provides a retrospective irony and horror, and ultimately proves that even the truth cannot shatter Delano's optimism. The deposition is very effective in its cold phraseology and abstract summation of death; only the lazy reader would want to see it go. But it suggests one of the ways in which the technique of the obtuse narrator or observer may thwart economy.

Dostoevsky, of course, provides several close analogues. *The Gambler* is as autobiographical as *L'Immoraliste*, but offers a much slighter separation of the character's consciousness from that of the author — who, incidentally, returned to his compulsive gambling immediately after finishing his book. *The Double*, however, dramatizes an unconscious conflict with great care, and anticipates the Freudian categories astoundingly: Golyadkin, Sr., as the menaced ego, while Golyadkin, Jr., acts out in turn the obscene id, the successful ego-ideal and the accusing superego. *The Double* is nevertheless the story of a neurotic descending into psychosis, as the early visit to the doctor warns us. Thus an alert reader separates himself from the character almost at once and accepts no evidence at face value. But in *Notes from Underground* Dostoevsky undertook a formal task very similar to

Gide's. Like Gide, he understood that his narrator was neurotic, yet he shared some of his feelings and attitudes: his
hatred of deterministic psychology and his longing to act
gratuitously, his disgust with positivist ethics. The problem
was to write a psychological novel which would yet raise
certain ideas provocatively. But Dostoevsky's blending of the
two interests was less satisfactory than Gide's. The isolated
and self-destructive "underground mouse," compelled to
reënact a few experiences of childhood and adolescent rejection, does not understand why he acts as he does. He long
bemuses us with his circular diatribe against determinism,
but this essay is really irrelevant.

Five pages — and five pages more clearly dissociating author
and subject — would have sufficed. For it is the body of the
novel that proves man can act against his own interests, and
does so not freely but compulsively. In this second part too,
the formal difference from *L'Immoraliste* is enormous. Dostoevsky offers us not only obtuseness but the "original,"
chaotic, diffuse experience of the neurotic. He gives the full
stenographic report of a patient's confession — from which
we may, if we are sufficiently alert, deduce our clear conclusions. And there is much evidence that Dostoevsky knew he
was doing just this. The narrator is diffuse only when what
he says is irrelevant. He reveals the important facts of his
story (his schoolboy experiences, for instance, or his onanism)
in begrudging, bitter, and very brief asides. Thus *Notes from
Underground* is in one sense a more authentic "report" than
L'Immoraliste, and certainly takes us closer to the lived experience of neurotic suffering, the actual impression of hourly
damnation. But for these very reasons it may offer less psychological understanding and achieve a rarer impression of
tragedy. Tragedy is not mere suffering, but suffering delimited
and ordered, understood with finality.

Conrad's *Heart of Darkness* has much of *Benito Cereno's*
density of atmosphere and calculated ambiguity of appearance, and at times it may recall the evasiveness of *Notes from
Underground.* The author's purpose here as in his longer
novels was to involve the reader minutely, and at whatever

tiring of his patience. But other short novels by Conrad, told in the first person or seen by an obtuse observer, show an economy as impressive as Gide's. Conrad's general impulse was the same: to dramatize compulsive inward journeys, the very processes of self-exploration and self-discovery. And he too dramatizes unconscious identification — Marlow allying himself with the atavistic Kurtz, or the young captain of *The Secret Sharer* with the fugitive from the "Sephora," or the crew of the "Narcissus" with the malingering James Wait. But only *The Smile of Fortune* presents the kind of sexual self-delusion which would have interested Gide, and did interest him in *Isabelle*. Conrad's usual practice was to universalize such particulars and to see the conflict with the unconscious or preconscious in large symbolic terms. A few very slight changes could give *The Secret Sharer* a localized and even homosexual meaning. But the story as it stands has no such primary meaning. The captain's double is instead the whole of the unconscious, to be explored and recognized — including that area of the unconscious which may provoke unreflective action and unpremeditated crime. Technically, *The Secret Sharer* shows the same formal control as *L'Immoraliste*. The narrator describes an experience of extreme incoherence, and even manages to convey a state of mind bordering on madness. Yet his cool report, like Michel's, contains very little that is irrelevant. It seems to move with the casualness and waste of unselective realism, but nearly every word counts. Much of Conrad's success here, and in the still more generalized *Shadow-Line*, lies in his full evocation of a plausible speaking voice. This is also one of the reasons for Gide's success with Michel. Extreme economy of narrative is masked by these calm and casual tones.

The closest approach to Gide's novel, in subject and technique, is Thomas Mann's *Death in Venice*, which was written a few years later. It is essentially the same story of latent and unrecognized homosexuality leading to self-destruction — though the reader who finds only theorizing on individualism in Gide may find only theorizing on the artist in Mann. Like Michel, Gustav von Aschenbach goes on a journey, not real-

izing that it is a journey within nor understanding the reasons
for his restlessness. He too pays severely for his years of
discipline and excessive restraint. The same alternating impulses to concentrate and to dissolve the self control these
two destinies, and both men — frightened by their new anarchy — make one last strong effort to recover self-control.
Both rationalize their aggressive inward drives in philosophical terms. But their real objective is the restraining superego,
which must be destroyed before Tadzio and Ali can be enjoyed. Gustav von Aschenbach's homosexual reactions are
fewer than Michel's, though Mann had read Freud and Gide
had not. Mann's hero is repelled by the old and painted
homosexual on the boat from Pola to Venice, that exact image
of his future self, as Michel is repelled for a time by Ménalque. But his most characteristic pederast reaction — a delighted recognition that Tadzio will die young *and therefore
never be a mature man* — comes later in the story than
Michel's resentment of Charles's growing-up. The two men
are most strikingly alike in the way they externalize their
inward conflicts. Michel's frenzied effort to probe and uncover
the secrets of the Heurtevents is a symbolic attempt to uncover his own secret. In precisely the same way Gustav von
Aschenbach, only dimly aware of his inner plague, combats
the efforts of the Venetian authorities to conceal the cholera
epidemic (after a brief period of pleased complicity). These
things, all things, must be brought to the surface.

We have thus the same minute drama of self-delusion and
self-discovery, and roughly the same separation between the
author's consciousness and his character's. The great initial
difference is that Michel is an obtuse narrator and Gustav
von Aschenbach an obtuse observer, whose observations are
rephrased by the author's ironic detachment. But the separation is at first unclear. How much of this sophisticated weary
irony (and how many of these reflections on the "artist") are
shared by Mann and Gustav von Aschenbach? Mann's technique most closely resembles Gide's after Tadzio has entered
the story. At this point we are offered ample evidence of the
latent homosexuality. But Mann does not "explain" why

Gustav von Aschenbach acts as he does until the victim can explain it himself. Both stories, incidentally, show the same technical flaw. These wholly inward stories need no outside pressures to achieve their tragic ends. Yet Mann brings in an outside force — the misdirection of the baggage — to "tip the scales toward anarchy," as Gide brings in Ménalque. Of the two, Gide's mistake is the more serious one. For it suggests that Michel's inward debate needed pedagogical support from without.

These are some of the resemblances. But there are differences in conception, which are reflected closely in structure and technique. *L'Immoraliste* is the purer Freudian drama of the two, since both the homosexual urge and the tyrannical repressive force long remain unconscious. But in *Death in Venice* the restraining force is often conscious — a conscious longing for dignity and order — and the hero is not merely an intellectual but himself a psychological novelist. No doubt he too could interpret his love of the ocean as a yearning "for the unorganized, the immeasurable, the eternal — in short, for nothingness." His more conscious struggle therefore demands more explicit analysis than Michel's — even though much of that analysis may be deliberately misleading.

Beyond this, Mann offers a grand over-all "explanation" which Gustav von Aschenbach could not have made. This is the four-part equation of homosexuality, plague, unconsciousness, and death; the hero approaching one is approaching them all. Thus the daydream in Munich anticipates that atavistic dream in Venice which "left the whole cultural structure of a lifetime trampled on, ravaged, and destroyed." And the tiger in the bamboo thicket of the daydream is a real tiger in the "primeval island-jungle" of the Ganges Delta where the cholera epidemic began. Here already the author has "added something" to nature, for the sake of explanation and for dramatic effect. But how much more he adds in the occult appearance of the three strangers: the man standing near the funeral hall in Munich; the lawless gondolier with his gondola black as a coffin; the entertainer with his homosexual gestures, his unprovoked hysteria, and his heavy car-bolic smell.[32] For Gustav von Aschenbach does not see what author and reader see — that they are the same man, with the same facial characteristics, alike beckoning the hero to self-discovery, unconsciousness, and death. They are, simply, his destiny.

The texture of *Death in Venice* is realistic — and Mann, like Melville and Dostoevsky, offers a great deal of irrelevant detail (the description of Tadzio's sisters, for instance) to make his story more plausible. But the over-all structure is symbolist in a manner as traditional as Chaucer's in *The Pardoner's Tale*. *L'Immoraliste* confines itself, instead, to our only too natural world. Against the ingenious symbolist connections of *Death in Venice* it offers the structural firmness and inward connections of a fully dramatized psychic situation. Most obvious are the falling then rising line of Michel's health, as Marceline's line rises and declines; the balance of the two visits to La Morinière as Michel preserves then destroys his estate, and the vast circular movement from Biskra back to Biskra. Even these unities (if we accept the common view that tuberculosis is often a neurotic illness) seem psychologically necessary. More specifically, each step in Michel's journey looks forward to some future step: the fight with the drunken coachman near Positano to the kissing of the coachman in Taormina; the gardens of Biskra to the gardens of Ravello; the daylight rides with Charles to the nighttime poaching with Alcide. Yet these anticipations are never fortuitous, as the gondolier's anticipation of the entertainer is fortuitous. The changed Michel is compelled to return to the same places and experiences, if only to discover how he has changed.

Still more challenging, to the student of realism, is the fact that nearly everything Michel says and nearly everything he sees has a direct bearing on his sexual problem. He keeps Moktir's theft secret not merely because he sees in it an acting-out of his own longing to rebel against accepted decencies, but because he here enters into a first clandestine relationship with a child. A large psychological situation is thus perfectly dramatized in the action or inaction of a moment; the "gratuitous act" of sympathetic identification is in no sense gratuitous. Yet Michel's prolonged compulsive need to spend all his money is, to the reader of Menninger and Freud, fully as convincing. The novel offers very little "neutral" or innocent imagery. Lassif's canals and Lachmi's gourd for collecting the sap from palm trees are images as primary, for this latent homosexual, as the eels he caught with Charles; clay and shrub alike have a fleshy texture. How could Gide, using so much significant imagery, yet contrive to give an impression of real life, of unselected experience? The question poses itself when we recall the amount of "wasted" imagery in Mann and Dostoevsky, wasted for the sake of realism. One answer is that Gide's significant images also serve as casual images — *and so serve because never explained*. No single image or experience, but the cumulative effect of them all, drives us very slowly to an awareness of Michel's trouble. Everything in Michel's story leads to his revelation in the last line, yet no particular page seems to lead there in an obvious way. The minutiae of style and technique thus disguise an economy as extreme as any in modern fiction. Could Gide achieve a latent homosexual's vision of experience so exactly and so economically only because he had been, himself, a latent homosexual? To ask this is to take a very naïve view of the art of fiction — and to forget the imperfections of certain earlier books. In *L'Immoraliste* he reduced a most confused personal experience to an order which even the best-adjusted writers rarely achieve.

It is hardly the intention of this book to defend realism as such, and the anti-realism of *Les Faux-Monnayeurs* may have done more for the modern novel. But *L'Immoraliste* is a great realistic novel, and perhaps the best novel Gide would write. It demanded a fairly extended analysis because it shows us, at the outset, the characteristic tactics and strategy of Gide's other "récits." Beyond this it proves that even the realistic and subjective psychological novel may be economical. The neurotic experience of a Michel can be more than neurotic experience; it can reflect a universal conflict. And it requires, to be told, neither the diffuseness of *Notes from*

Underground, nor the confusion of *The Double,* nor the superimposed intellectualism of *Death in Venice.* These are great works, and perhaps more astonishing at a first reading than *L'Immoraliste.* But Gide's novel belongs with them. And, like a great poem, it deserves and can survive repeated readings.*

The intense exploration of self which *L'Immoraliste* involved goes far toward explaining the creative apathy of 1901 to 1905. But the book's total failure also contributed to the sterilizing discouragement of those years. A few loyal friends (some of them uninterested on principle in moral questions) constituted Gide's entire public.[33] It required all the more courage to write a novel which might alienate that only public. *La Porte étroite* (1909) seemed at first glance an entirely new departure: a Christian rejection of hedonism, a classical debate between love and duty. Gide insisted repeatedly, in later years, that he had criticized rather than approved Alissa's puritan asceticism and Jérôme's exquisite sensibility, and that he had not "evolved" since 1902.[34] The book was, he explained, a critique of Christian abnegation, of useless heroism, of a "certain mystical tendency." [35] But love as well as irony had gone into the shaping of his heroine, and for most early readers sympathy outweighed detachment. Jules Renard was only one of many to consider the book "clerical," though the Protestant press remained shrewdly silent.[36] The general public, finding itself in a familiar moral universe and recognizing the orthodox tangled skein of sacrifice and sentiment, read the novel widely. After a false start Gide had "fallen into line," the profoundly French

* After reading an earlier but roughly similar study of *L'Immoraliste,* Gide commended my analysis of its "freudisme latent et précurseur," but felt I exaggerated its value as compared with that of his other short novels. "Quant à moi-même, je ne parviens à considérer mon *Immoraliste* comme supérieur aux autres sous aucun rapport, littéraire, moral, psychologique . . ." (See Gide's letter, at end of this book). Authors are, to be sure, imperfect judges of their own books, and *L'Immoraliste* has been a great favorite among my Harvard students, even among those who had read no criticism and heard no lectures on the novel. On the other hand, no published criticism has valued the book as highly as mine.

line of Madame de Lafayette. He thus found himself a partial success, and one of the large company of writers who have won their public through an inferior or misunderstood book. Just so Conrad, exploiting the conventional pathos of love and abnegation, at last made his way with *Chance*.

"The book is furiously, deplorably Protestant," Gide wrote Claudel in October 1908. His intention at one time was, it appears, to draw the portrait of a "Protestant soul" and its unmotivated asceticism. "But I was afraid that the drama — freed from all exterior motivation — would seem paradoxical, almost monstrous, inhuman: hence the invention of the double plot, the fear of buying one's happiness at the expense of others — and hence above all the "fault" of the mother and the consequent vague need for expiation. Etc." [37] This letter to Claudel, published forty years after the novel, reveals that its most modern psychological aspect was an afterthought. But also it helps account for certain contradictions in the book itself: the discrepancy between the self-destructive Alissa of Jérôme's portrait and the Alissa whose heroism is either religious or purely gratuitous.

The published novel, in any event, has the same double interest as *L'Immoraliste*. It is both the critique of an impulse and a psychological account of its development. Alissa may progress no further than Michel in self-knowledge. But she wavers much less than he, scarcely hesitates on her chosen and stony path. Jérôme is only fourteen when the story opens, and his cousin Alissa sixteen; the two serious little puritans are already much in love. Jérôme often plays with Juliette, Alissa's gay sister, but he shares his dreams with the more wistful and quieter girl. One day he discovers the reason for her sadness. He sees his Aunt Lucile flirt with a strange young man, and then goes up to Alissa's room to find her kneeling and in tears. A few days later Lucile runs away. Still horrified by these first encounters with evil, the children hear a stern sermon on the text: "Enter ye in at the strait gate."

The coinciding force of the two experiences makes Jérôme determine to protect Alissa "from fear, from evil, from life," and to earn her hand in marriage by the purity of his own conduct. But the impact on Alissa is much more severe. To Jérôme's astonishment, she postpones their marriage year after year, and insists on long exhausting separations. First she hesitates because of Juliette's love for Jérôme, then because her father needs her, then because she is too old. Embittered but faithful, and always strangely resigned, Jérôme watches her move toward an ever harsher puritanism. Only after her death, when he reads her diary, does he realize that she loved him to the end. She had deliberately sacrificed their love to the love of God. Like Clarissa Harlowe, she had willed her own death, and like Clarissa made the necessary provisions. A few lines at the very end of the diary tell us that the self-impoverishment was in vain. Alissa found herself not with God but alone. In the shadows of both the story and the diary are Juliette's unhappy marriage and her unchanged love for Jérôme.

The great threat to such a story of frustration and unrelieved suffering was sentimentality. It was at least partly forestalled by extreme economy of narrative and by the long sifting of remembered experience. *La Porte étroite* is a short novel of less than forty thousand words, but at least twenty years went into its making.[38] Gide was about thirteen when he discovered his cousin Madeleine kneeling and in tears and resolved to devote his life to comforting her. And he was fifteen when Anna Shackleton died alone in a nursing-home, to provide the final pages of the novel. About 1890 he planned an edifying "récit" of Anna's death, to be entitled "l'essai de bien mourir," and which would bring the most errant back to God. The present novel germinated together with *L'Immoraliste*, certainly before the turn of the century. In spite of a number of reminiscences used virtually unchanged,[39] *La Porte étroite* was the product of hard work, not easy recollection, and the actual writing took more than three years. The sharpest memory may be the most difficult to dramatize; Gide had unusual difficulty with Jérôme's discovery of Alissa's distress.[40] It was no easy task to observe,

with a sufficiently detached scrutiny, one of the central experiences of his own and Emmanuèle's life.

The effect of Lucile Bucolin's infidelity on Alissa is
necessarily lost on the hasty reader. To mislead the hasty is
the price one must pay for using an imperceptive narrator;
or perhaps, it is the reward one obtains. Jérôme stares
blankly at the spectacle of Alissa's steady withdrawal from
the world, and until he reads her diary is wholly unaware of
her fear of physical love. Even in the diary itself there is only
one unambiguous entry. Disturbed one evening by Jérôme
leaning over her shoulder as she read, aware "of the warmth
and pulsation of his body," Alissa experiences "a perturba-
tion so strange" that she is obliged to get up from her chair
and leave the room. Later in the evening she thinks of her
mother: "I slept very badly last night; I was disturbed,
oppressed, miserable, haunted by the recollection of the past,
which came over me like a wave of remorse. Lord, teach me
the horror of all that has any appearance of evil."

This (with Jérôme's suggestion that Lucile Bucolin's behavior had caused her great distress) is the only explicit clue
to Alissa's withdrawal; even Henry James was seldom more
reticent in motivating the negativism which so many of his
characters exhibit. Seen through Jérôme's eyes, it is a steadily
increasing but baffling asceticism. So long as there remains
some good reason for not marrying, Alissa is reasonably
cheerful. But her letters show an increasing love for anything
arduous. She keeps him at a distance, and time after time invents plausible excuses for postponing a meeting; the meeting, when at last it occurs, is very awkward. Alissa finally
admits she has elected "holiness" and expects their marriage
to occur only in the next world. She dresses more and more
plainly, and gives up her cherished classics for vulgar books
of piety. A curious masochism seems to have worn all her
love and all her small geniality away.

Jérôme's part is very like that of Longmore in James's
Madame de Mauves. He remains throughout a curiously
passive sufferer; a little normal aggressiveness might have
changed everything. This lack of aggressiveness — which

flickers occasionally across the reader's mind — was in fact supposed to explain the tragedy: "Without such a hero, the tragedy would not have been possible," Gide wrote in 1909.[41] Jérôme's passivity called forth Alissa's useless "heroism"; everything associated with him remained "stained by virtue." [42] But the novel itself is infinitely more evasive than this. Gide allows Jérôme to admit only once, and then most casually, that he never felt any sexual desire for Alissa. The suggestion that Lucile Bucolin had once frightened him by reaching under his shirt is never followed up. Should not an actual fear of sex have revealed itself somewhere else in such a personal narrative? Hardy was probably incapable of understanding the reticence of his own heroes, but Gide understood the reticence of his. Jérôme represents an entirely too sucessful example of Gidean compression; of his determination to let the reader complete the portrait. It was important to avoid the obviousness which *La Symphonie pastorale* would show. But *L'Immoraliste* had proved that even an obtuse narrator may supply the evidence we need.

Gide himself disliked the figure of Jérôme intensely, and held his flabby character responsible for a certain flabbiness of style. But he considered Alissa's diary one of the best things he had written.[43] Gide was a subjective moralist who longed to be an objective creator. To picture the self-destructive mysticism of a woman must have seemed to him a high achievement of creative imagination, and a genuine escape from self. The achievement was a very real one, though any reader of Gide's uneasy diary for 1905 and 1906 will see that the self has not been left so very far behind. Alissa's diary was at least sufficiently convincing to its readers to persuade them that the author had worked into it not only his sympathy but a recovered faith. The diary is a Protestant or Jansenist "carte du tendre"; the picture of a very feminine sensibility caged and isolated by endless introspection; the diary of a mind annihilating its own desires. From the first confusion of virtue with difficulty everything else proceeds, until at last the humiliated penitent fears pride in her own humility. Only at the very end does Alissa acknowledge she has lost the God to whom she had sacrificed everything else. "I should like to die now, quickly, before again realising that I am alone."

The diary is a remarkable document on religious torment, faith and humility, whatever great or little importance we give to the traumatic explanation of Alissa's withdrawal. The form permitted Gide to write in the first person once again, and the spectacle of Madeleine's self-denials helped him achieve both sympathy and detachment. So too, as in *Le Retour de l'enfant prodigue*, a deep lingering piety balances the author's anticlericalism, and gives his pages their authentic accent. The diary nevertheless fails in two ways. It is no wonder many readers did not see Alissa's quest was futile, that she was entering an empty heaven. A few lines of bitter skepticism can hardly erase the impression left by twenty-five pages of tormented devotion. More important still: the diary's revelation that Alissa had continued to love Jérôme as much as ever, that she was merely dissembling, sharply discredits the very fine portrait of the first section. What had seemed to be a moving account of the death of the heart, of love stifled by fear and separation, becomes in retrospect a record of deceptive appearance.

Without the diary, *La Porte étroite* is a small and impressive portrait in the manner of Mauriac, or of James's and Edith Wharton's shorter novels — or, to cite a distinguished recent example, of Josephine Johnson's *Wildwood*. But the novel as a whole is imperfect, if we compare it with *L'Immoraliste*, and not merely because Gide failed to reconcile his psychological understanding of chronic self-destructiveness with his sympathetic understanding of piety and religious self-sacrifice. He also carried reticence too far; not only refused to explain but refused to supply sufficient evidence. The lesson of reticence was especially valuable in 1909, when novelists liked to explain everything, and the lesson of economy is fully as valuable now. Gide was justly proud of everything he had "left out" in the scene in Alissa's bedroom. "I think at length of the virtue which 'reserve strength' may become for a writer. But who would understand that today?" [44] Nevertheless *La Porte étroite* seems to be — and it is difficult to admit such a thing — a novel which was written too slowly over too long a period, which had been allowed to germinate over too many years, and from which too much was finally left out.

Except for the prudence of a few friends, *Isabelle* (1911) might not have been written at all, and certainly not at this time. Gide had read aloud to his friends the beginning of *Corydon*. They were so appalled by his Socratic defense of homosexuality that they persuaded him to put it aside. He turned to write instead this polished short novel, both the least personal and the least "disturbing" of his early books. There is no paradox in the fact that this highly impersonal book closely followed actual remembered experience. The tragic events which occurred on a neighboring estate in Normandy were much farther from home than even the most casual conversation in a remote North African town. The M. Floche of Isabelle was an actual M. Floquet, also a Bossuet scholar; the Bossuet Bible of the story was really sold for the sum of seventy francs; Francis Jammes did accompany Gide on his visit to the ruined property.[45] These facts are irrelevant, unless to make us wonder that the novel is as good as it is. The saving circumstance is that the story is not about Isabelle, but about Gérard Lascase, the naïve young scholar who weaves so many romantic illusions around her name, and who penitently tells the story. But here once again many readers failed to realize that a narrator can be the unconscious subject of his own narrative. Gide later regretted not using his original title, which would have made his intention clear to the careless — "L'Illusion pathétique." [46]

In this book at least Gide remained impersonal, while dealing with a frankly subjective theme: a young man's romantic illusions and distortions of reality. Gérard Lascase is obtuse enough — as obtuse and as cruel as the scholar of *The Aspern Papers* — but he suffers from neither Michel's latent homosexuality nor Jérôme's abnormal passivity. He be-

longs with the narrators of Conrad's *Smile of Fortune* and
Wescott's *The Pilgrim Hawk*. All three propose to tell the
story of a woman's frustrations and inadequacies, but end by
revealing their own. The contrast is not simply one of innocence and experience or of appearance and reality. In each of
these stories the moral isolation of the narrator breeds a
curiosity which overleaps all moral scruple. "Was I subtle?
— That was what I wished to be sure of." The fascination
with ambiguity drives the prying imagination on, until the
pitied sufferer becomes a victim of the observing benevolence. The reticent Conrad, strangely enough, gave this self-
deluded curiosity the most directly sexual turn; he saw in it
the perverse desire for a slovenly and backward girl. The
narrator of *The Pilgrim Hawk* is more complex and more
oblique. Identifying himself with all the other characters
and even with the captive hawk, he is the impotent victim of
his own subtlety.*

Gide's Gérard Lascase, on the other hand, is a fairly ordinary young dreamer, and scarcely seems to involve the author
at all. He would like to be a novelist; he would like to be
subtle. But his restless solitude and frustration are those of
innumerable young men of his age. He is only half-wrong in
describing the cause of his curiosity as "ennui":

The word *ennui* is doubtless too weak to describe the fits of
intolerable depression to which I have been subject ever since I
can remember; they overcome one suddenly; something indefinable in the air starts them; a second before, all was smiling, all
was enjoyable; suddenly a murky vapor rises from the depths
of the soul and interposes itself between desire and life; it forms
a kind of livid screen that separates us from the rest of the world,
whose warmth, love, color, and harmony can now only reach us
as a refracted, warped, transposed abstraction; we are aware of
things, but they fail to move us, and the desperate effort to break
through the screen that thus isolates our soul, might well lead us
into any sort of crime — murder or suicide, or madness . . .[47]

* And, though Wescott may have intended no such bitter personal expression, a commentator on his author's creative difficulties. Wescott may
even have considered the Cullens to be the "subject" of his novel. So far
even a very scrupulous art can escape rational intention.

Such is Gérard's state of mind when he makes his first important discovery. Out of sheer boredom he begins to hack at a rotting panel with his knife and finds Isabelle's faded letter, written to her lover on the night she was to run away from home. From the beginning, however, Gérard had been looking for romantic adventure. He went to La˙ Quartfourche as a scholar writing a thesis on Bossuet's sermons, but with a novelist's heart: determined to study the people living there and uncover their every secret. He found only stylized fossils and Dickensian caricatures. He was desperately ready to imagine anything when the child Casimir showed him a miniature of his mother Isabelle. He falls in love with her at its sight, and postpones his return to Paris.

This "love" for a woman he may never see makes him interpret charitably his subsequent and startling discoveries: that Casimir is an illegitimate child, that Isabelle is somehow responsible for the isolation and poverty of the family, that she has stolen family jewels and begged others, that she is now living in some wretched and ambiguous way. Much later, when the Abbé Santal tells him that Isabelle is living with the creditors' agent and may well have been responsible for the death of the Floches, he still resists disillusionment. He is faithful to his memory of the miniature, and cannot be rid of his obsession until he talks with Isabelle herself. At the extreme point of his pitiless curiosity, he asks her to describe her emotions on the night her lover died, and as she waited for him to carry her away. Isabelle reveals that she herself — afraid of the liberty she longed for — was responsible for his death. Only then can Gérard see her as others see her: still pathetic, but sentimental, corrupt, promiscuous.

This intellectual novel of romantic illusion is obviously the most Jamesian of Gide's books, and therefore the closest to the French analytic tradition. It is also Gide's farthest concession to surface realism. The narrator's attitude, curiosity concerning the reality hidden by appearance, demanded a minute record of appearance. The muslim jabot of the Baron de Saint-Auréol or his eye which remains hermetically closed, the black taffeta hood of the Baroness — this is the kind of

minute vivifying detail which Gide normally rejects altogether and leaves to the reader to imagine. If we exclude the
final chapter, the book is structurally almost perfect, though
in an old-fashioned way. The slow and persuasive establishing
of atmosphere recalls Marlow's purposeful evasions; three
out of the seven chapters are devoted to the first uneventful
day at La Quartfourche. The amusing details of provincial
life, the Abbé's outrageous abuse of his pupil, the slowly
unfolded tragedy of Isabelle — these secondary levels of interest are scrupulously subordinated to the fact of Gérard's
unmoral curiosity. They are made out, dimly, through the
screen of his self-delusion. The same screening of secondary
subjects was to be used, but much less effectively, in *La
Symphonie pastorale.*

The last chapter is therefore all the more disappointing.
Gide did not have this chapter in his original plan, and
almost didn't write it.[48] Later he wondered whether the final
pages hadn't come too easily; whether he hadn't failed to
work into them something he wanted to say.[49] It seems
obvious enough, to the reader, that these pages were un-
necessary . . . or that a great many more were needed.
When Gérard at last has his talk with Isabelle, he ceases to
be the center of interest; perhaps Gide's mistake was to convince even his readers of Isabelle's charm. The final revelations come very quickly: at a speed quite impossible for the
reader who has accepted the slow pace of the earlier chapters.
The hero walks away from Isabelle's bench, wholly disillu-
sioned, before the reader has had time to sit down.

Gide's impatience reveals itself on every page of this
crowded last chapter. Was he, here and in his other drasti-
cally foreshortened endings, afraid of boring? Or did the book
suddenly seem unimportant? It "proved" none of his ideas,
unless that Isabelle's fear of "deracination," her cowardly
refusal to run away from home, caused her lover's death and
all her later misfortunes. Gide predicted *Isabelle* would take
its place in his canon as a "half-frivolous interlude between
two overly serious works." [50] He was most of all impatient,
perhaps, with the delicate hypocrisies and persuasions which

such realistic fiction demands. Less original than *The Aspern Papers*, less urgent than *A Smile of Fortune*, less subtle than *The Pilgrim Hawk, Isabelle* is a slight triumph of orderly fiction. But Gide was now ready to react, once more, against the very principle of order in art. "It is now high time to break with certain habits, certain indulgences in writing. I wish to try at once." [51] His next book of fiction was the experimental *Caves du Vatican*.

Like most of its predecessors, *Les Caves du Vatican* (1914) was intended to be a "demoralizing" book. Gide knew that nothing could be more disturbing than to present a problem — the plight of the deracinated individualist — without also presenting a solution. Bourgeois orthodoxy, even the orthodoxy of bourgeois anticlericalism, could be as sterile as the conservative's pragmatist Catholicism. But the alternative of complete relativism might lead to boredom and crime. To ruffle the complacency of relativist and dogmatist alike was no doubt one of Gide's first intentions, though beyond this he hoped to discredit both the accepted literary psychology and the established patterns of realistic fiction. All this he meant seriously enough. But *Les Caves du Vatican* is also — and this critics are apt to forget — an "entertainment": a riotous blend of the *Arabian Nights, Tom Jones,* and *La Chartreuse de Parme*. One reader may find in it the "agony of an era in progress toward dissolution"; [52] another may consider it a vicious anti-Catholic satire. And critic after critic has been forced into a circular debate on the possibility of gratuitous action. Perhaps only the maligned casual reader sees that *Les Caves du Vatican* is above all a very funny book.

It is hard to say which of the purposes was dominant; we shall find, in any event, that art once again escaped intention. Like *L'Immoraliste* and *La Porte étroite, Les Caves du Vatican* germinated over a period of at least fifteen years.[53] By 1905 Anthime Armand-Dubois had acquired both his name and his obscene wen, though the latter was to change its position slightly.[54] There is perhaps some hint of the novel as it stands in Gide's disapproval of "Gérard" (Paul

Gide), and in his professed curiosity concerning the psychology of the vagabond? [55] His first full reference to the book,
in 1909, argues that there is no essential difference between
the ordinary man and the scoundrel. Lafcadio's history is to
be that of an honest man who, having taken one false step,
becomes a criminal. "In the path of 'sin,' only the first step
is difficult." [56] But by 1910 the desire to experiment with a
new form may have been more urgent than the impulse to
psychological speculation. Then Gide seemed chiefly impatient with the sober limitations of the impersonal realistic
novel, and dreamed of his new book as something entirely
different, written in a "merry" style.[57] His experiences as a
juror on the Rouen Cour d'Assises in 1912 reminded him
once again of the inadequacies of orthodox psychology. But
the first pages of his novel are those of a writer willing to be
seduced into any amusing adventure; and who will allow
nothing, least of all "realism," to interfere with his fun.

The resources of absurdity have no limit, once one has
divided society into the shrewd adventurers and the innocent
or complacent dupes. Lafcadio Wluki is the speculative
picaro of the tale, but the epic adventures belong to the pious
and chaste Amédée Fleurissoire, who sets out from Pau to
deliver the Pope — said to be imprisoned in the Castle St.
Angelo, with a Freemason reigning in his stead. Amédée
(who had promised a friend and disappointed suitor never
to sleep with his wife Arnica) is devoured by bedbugs in
Marseilles, by fleas in Toulon, by mosquitoes in Genoa. He
arrives exhausted in Rome, to make the classical error of
taking a bawdy-house for a hotel, and does not feel qualified
to continue on his mission until absolved by a bogus
cardinal.

The extravagant comedy of Amédée's sufferings is tempered by the more serious satire of his worthy brothers-in-
law. Anthime Armand-Dubois tries to drive God into an
ever-narrowing corner with his experiments on the condi-
tioned reflexes of rats, and expresses his anticlericalism by
desecrating a statue of the Virgin; he would not be out of
place in *Antic Hay*. He is converted by a dream, and ruined

by the Church's ingratitude; then restored to atheism by
rheumatic pains and the rumor that there are two Popes.
But if Gide was disturbed by the easy and boastful conversion of so many of his friends, he still felt the genial Catholic
pragmatist, the conservative moralist with no real religious
conviction, to be the true enemy. (History itself had supplied
the grotesque fact: the Catholic party had found it difficult
to believe that Leo XIII could ask the faithful to support the
Third Republic.) Julius de Baraglioul, who by writing many
bad books had reached the threshold of the French Academy,
is a lesser Bourget. Intelligent enough to see the feebleness
of his Cartesian literary psychology, he adopts Lafcadio's
theory of gratuitous action as the basis for his next book. But
the spectacle of a real and apparently unmotivated crime
(Lafcadio's murder of Amédée) drives him back to orthodoxy
in terror. He has all the proper notions about the moral disorder of the age. But when Lafcadio confesses to him, and
thus confronts him with the most difficult moral choice of
his life, he worries about the breaking of an exquisitely
tailored fingernail.

Obviously, Gide had once again "sharpened his beak" on
Stendhal. Irony and sentiment mingle inextricably, but
neither they nor logic and verisimilitude are allowed to interfere with sheer creative energy. Anything can happen, at
any moment; the suspense swiftly built up in one paragraph
is as swiftly relieved in the next. Each character stumbles on
the traces of the others, and if Lafcadio is always ready for a
new audacity, Amédée is always ready to be duped. Action is
gratuitous, but so too is literary form. Through the nightmare sequence of absurdities, each of the pilgrims clings to
his particular illusions, to his logical and coherent assumptions. Only Lafcadio and Anthime, as fanatical in his orthodoxy as in his anticlericalism, can profit at all from experience. That Lafcadio should profit so far from experience as
to make us take him seriously raises the chief critical problem
of the book. The fact that he gradually becomes a normal
human being, and so invades both a familiar moral universe
and our sympathies, accounts for much of the uneasiness

which the final chapters cause.* Gide was aware that this transformation was taking place in the last months of composition; it greatly complicated his task.[58]

In the early chapters, the characters move back and forth among shifting planes of reality. Constant change in the degree of stylization was one of the book's most interesting innovations, and one of the grounds for its lasting influence.[59] There is nevertheless a general movement from the fantastic to the real which may be more open to question. The sufferings of Anthime and Amédée are too grotesque and too hilarious to arouse sympathy; the reader regrets not Amédée's death but his disappearance from the book. But when Protos sheds the last of his disguises (unless he be the Devil in disguise), we are returned to a harshly real world. Even Carola, strangled so casually, has by then enlisted some sympathy. But the most disturbing change is Lafcadio's. From the beginning he has an amusing stylized reality; he is alive, yet a metaphysical abstraction, exempt from ordinary human vexations. But when he begins to suffer from moral isolation, ennui, and guilt, he loses all abstractness and much of his sprightly interest. He threatens to become a Michel with fewer sexual problems. His difficulties are now those of "his time"; his distance from the reader and author diminishes. Absolutely considered, Gide's failure to preserve his moral impudence and atmosphere of fantasy was a failure of art; it meant return to an already perfected mode. But this very failure also changed the playful toying with a verbal

* The revised stage version, which had its première at the Comédie Française in December 1950, takes Lafcadio fairly seriously from the start. Amédée is pitiful as well as ridiculous. The great problem must have been to put Lafcadio's crime on the stage without destroying all sympathy for the murderer. This was done by insisting from the first on his youthful charm and rigorous sincerity. (The interior monologues — Lafcadio's speculations before he commits the crime, for instance — are conveyed by a deep metallic off-stage voice.) But if the play takes Lafcadio seriously throughout, it also exploits as fully as possible the farcical elements of the early chapters. The first act is worthy of Molière. The speculative second act seems very slow by comparison, perhaps because the discussion of the gratuitous act is both familiar and dated. Dramatic critics insisted on the transformation from "sotie" to "farce." But the play's greatest weakness is its attempt to dramatize nearly all of the novel's important ideas and scenes.

absurdity into a serious human enquiry. So serious, in fact, that the final Lafcadio looks back to Dostoevsky's Kirilov and Raskolnikov, and forward to Camus's Meursault.*

Lafcadio is the true "free man" — so much freer than Julien Sorel, for instance, as to be wholly without ambition. He is a bastard, of uncertain language and nationality, and has been educated by a succession of hedonistic and demoralizing "uncles," each of whom has perhaps contributed to his individualism and reckless charm. But no coherent *self* has been imposed upon him, which he is obliged to imitate; he has no intellectual or moral heritage. He attended one strict school, but stayed there only long enough to acquire some of Protos's contempt for the average respectable man and to learn that life is a game of chance. This being true, the easiest way to make a decision is to throw a pair of dice.

What would such an education produce? At the beginning of the novel Lafcadio is a charming, intelligent, and unconventional boy of twenty, but proud and unusually secretive. He is normal enough to be moved by the discovery that Juste-Agénor de Baraglioul is his father, and that he will soon be wealthy. But he accepts without protest the fact that he will never be recognized. He detests every form of complacent moralism, and is as contemptuous of Julius' stiff respectability as of his artificial and academic novels. Freed from all but self-restraint, he is not above petty theft as a form of amusement, but dislikes purposeful swindling. He is capable of cruelty, but also of impulsive generosity; he flings himself upon life for the immediate pleasure or adventure it may bring. He is a free man; and, as Julius suggests, is "at the mercy of the first opportunity." He boasts that he is an "inconsecutive creature," but has evolved a punitive ethics of his own. He dislikes yielding to anyone, even to himself, and stabs himself carefully with a knife whenever he

* In *L'Etranger*, Meursault's feelings are even more gratuitous than his actions; he comes as close as possible to having no preferences at all. His crime, rather more plausible than Lafcadio's, has even less apparent motivation. There are certain important differences between the two books, though one may well have led to the other. Whereas Lafcadio becomes increasingly human, Meursault becomes increasingly abstract; in the end he is symbolic of man faced by a hostile and incomprehensible destiny.

has acted conventionally or out of false pride. Curiosity concerning himself and others, delight in chance and risk, a child's love of masquerade and an egotist's love of moral independence — these are some of the forces which contribute to his peculiar complexity. He meets an old woman struggling under a load, and thinks himself equally capable of helping or strangling her. And he is capable of throwing Amédée out of the train, though he has never seen him before, and has nothing at all to gain from the murder.

The early Lafcadio is thus the independent "strong man" who had long since evoked Gide's mingled admiration and horror: [60] the "free man" he had wanted to be himself, the symbolic hero of individualism and Prodigal Son's younger brother. The disturbing thing for the reader, here as in *L'Immoraliste*, is less that the hero commits a crime than that he is a spokesman for Gidean ideas. The disturbing thing for Gide, who saw his character escape him, is that Lafcadio is seriously tempted to repent. But it would be wrong to pay too much attention to Lafcadio's belated regrets. *Les Caves du Vatican* does not repudiate individualism or a relativist ethic. It merely defines Gide's awareness that these problems are not simple ones. Lafcadio is a twentieth-century man who has unknowingly inherited much from a few nineteenth-century minds. His arguments are Gide's own:

1. Lafcadio demonstrates the value of deracination and free energy, against the conformist's refusal to live. The pragmatist ethics of Julius are scarcely more productive than Amédée's cloistered impotence. The determinism of family and class have reduced both to automatons; the determinism of an uncritical liberalism has reduced Anthime to a fanatic. In 1913 Gide still believed that human nature could change and "progress." But where was progress to come from, unless from the individualist who questions norms and refuses to be merely a "function"? Possibly it could come only from the energizing force of what society calls "evil." [61]

2. Lafcadio asserts the even more significant revolt against the determinism of self. His boast that he is an "inconsecutive creature" echoes Gide's most familiar longing. Can man

do no more than imitate an ideal conception of himself, supposedly projected into the future but actually inferred from the most obvious consistencies of his past? The bastard is a break in the continuity of society. Cannot the present act be a break in the continuity of the personality itself? The classical French novel, Gide remarked, denies the possibility of "inconséquences." Against it, Lafcadio and Gide insist that man is not the bounded and logical abstraction of Julius' books. He is capable, like the characters of Dostoevsky, of rich antagonisms, of incessant self-contradiction. But until he visualizes the possibility of freedom, he cannot hope to be free.

3. The keystone of the classical arch is the self-interest psychology of La Rochefoucauld. Lafcadio argues, against such a universal determinism, that man can act against his own interest and without an external motive; even, can will his own perdition. Both Lafcadio and Gide persuade us that men can direct sadism inward, and are inhabited by the imp of the perverse. It may seem paradoxical that a man with Lafcadio's horror of choice should risk his skin in order to prove that the will is free. But this is no doubt one of his unacknowledged motives when he throws Amédée out of the train. It is the act of a "free man."

4. And yet, Lafcadio is not really free. He had already felt some of Gide's "horror of liberty," and had taken pleasure both in self-control and in the punitive stabs of his knife. Once the murder is committed, his feelings are drawn steadily back toward those of ordinary and restricted human beings. The first step is a curious "disgust" which prompts him to leave telltale evidence against himself in Julius' room. An interview with Protos quickly proves to him that he is not even independent. Protos, who had discovered the crime in his own miraculous way, welcomes him to the company of criminals: a society with its own rigid laws. Lafcadio refuses his command to blackmail Julius, saying he would prefer the police. When Protos is arrested for the murder of both Carola and Amédée, Lafcadio finds impunity just as intolerable as did his Dostoevskian forbears. He too

cannot endure the loneliness of an unmoral universe, and longs for his brother's friendship, now that he has irretrievably lost it. He is rescued from suicide by the love of Geneviève, and at the very end is ready to fling himself upon life. Unlike Julien Sorel, he is not beheaded; unlike Raskolnikov, he is not converted and does not give himself up; unlike Kirilov, he does not kill himself to square the metaphysical circle. We are not told exactly how much Lafcadio has learned, nor how effective his restraining knife will be in the future. The problem does not end with the book.

Les Caves du Vatican thus resumes the nineteenth-century debate on the possibility of free action. Is there any escape from the determinism of the eighteenth-century "sensationalists" or the nineteenth-century positivists; from Condillac, Littré, and Taine? Ultimately Lafcadio descends from the ambivalent Byronic hero and from the subtler Julien Sorel. But his gratuitous act derives rather from Baudelaire and Dostoevsky — though the poet who threw the vendor's glass out the window and the philosopher who committed suicide to prove his freedom were more careful to draw a moral. Kirilov seems to have fascinated Gide more than any other character in fiction, as he was later to fascinate Albert Camus.* And indeed indebtedness is inevitable, where the terms of a debate are so few. Even the immediate background of the unmotivated act was perhaps suggested by Dostoevsky. Lafcadio recalls a childhood experiment in secrecy immediately before murdering Amédée, just as Raskolnikov and the Stevie of Conrad's *Secret Agent* dream of cruelly beaten horses before committing their relatively gratuitous crimes. But the gratuitous act is not necessarily an act of violence. There is scarcely a character in *The Possessed* who is not "possessed," who does not in the every-

---

* See especially "Lettres à Angèle," *OC*, III, 238–240, and "Dostoïevsky," *OC*, XI, 294–304. "Le suicide de Kirilov est un acte absolument gratuit, je veux dire que sa motivation n'est point extérieure. Tout ce que l'on peut faire entrer d'absurde dans ce monde, à la faveur et à l'abri d'un 'acte gratuit,' c'est ce que nous allons voir" (*OC*, XI, 295). Camus's essay on Kirilov appears in *Le Mythe de Sisyphe* (Paris, 1942), pp. 142–152.

day conduct of life act absurdly against his own interest. The impulse to self-destruction seemed to break at least the cruder forms of materialist logic. Why does an apparently reasonable man go out of his way to light a cigar near a barrel of gunpowder?

. . . to see, to know, to tempt destiny, to force oneself to give a proof of energy, to gamble, to know the pleasures of anxiety; and for nothing, out of caprice, because one has nothing to do.[62]

This explanation, which so aptly fits Lafcadio, is actually that of Baudelaire, who called the impulsion "satanic."

The "acte gratuit," though always associated with *Les Caves du Vatican,* had interested Gide as early as *Paludes.* Endless somber discussions have been devoted to Lafcadio's crime, and even Jean Hytier has felt obliged to prove that an effect must have a cause. But few critics have tried to explain the gratuitous act in modern terms — as the outward flaring of an unconscious self-destructiveness or as the product of unconscious identification — and neither, it must be admitted, did Gide. He dramatized just such processes in *L'Immoraliste* and *La Porte étroite,* and to a certain extent in *Les Caves du Vatican.* But his theoretical explanations, outside the novels, were often made in general and even nineteenth-century terms. Lafcadio's crime (if we look only at these personal comments and afterthoughts) was intended to prove three things. First, the motive for an act may be so remote, so complex, and so obscure that it cannot be discovered by ordinary deduction. "The sources of our slightest acts are as multiple and remote as those of the Nile." Further, these sources may exist only in the personality of the actor, rather than in provocative external causes. Finally, and for Gide this was the most important point: a disinterested act is not necessarily a "good" act. All this is scarcely abstruse, as Gide himself acknowledged. In 1924 at least he was willing to admit that there is no act, "however absurd or prejudicial, which is not the result of converging causes, conjunctions, concomitances."[63] By 1927 he was thoroughly weary of the futile debate and explained himself clearly:

I merely meant that the *disinterested* act could well not always be charitable; but once this is said, you are free, with La Rochefoucauld, not to believe in disinterestedness at all. Perhaps I don't believe in it either, but I claim that the individual's potentialities and his inner meteorology remain a bit more complicated than you ordinarily make them, and that what you call the bad potentialities are not all egocentric.[64]

As intuitive and literary psychologist, dramatizing the role of the unconscious and preconscious, Gide still seems very modern. But his intention in *Les Caves du Vatican* was far more general: to shatter the vulgar conception of man as a creature divided into tidy compartments — passion, will, reason, self-interest, and the like. He was determined as well to shatter the accepted conventions of the realistic well-made novel. *Les Caves du Vatican* is a "sotie" because it treats serious problems lightly, but also because it deliberately violates every rule of plausible, impersonal fiction. "Lafcadio, my friend, you are verging on the commonplace. If you are going to fall in love, do not count on my pen to paint the disturbance of your heart." Few important novelists since the eighteenth century had intruded themselves so willfully, or with such an apparent disregard for illusion.

In *Les Faux-Monnayeurs* we have both an impertinent roving narrator and an "auteur" who intrudes at length to comment on the progress of the book; neither should be exactly identified with André Gide. Here as in other respects *Les Faux-Monnayeurs* carries the innovations of *Les Caves du Vatican* a little further, and hence we may as profitably postpone technical analysis to the later novel.* *Les Caves du Vatican* anticipates especially the lively opening chapters of *Les Faux-Monnayeurs*. The careful building of atmosphere, the dramatic possibilities of the extended scene, the opportunity to suggest motive and the traditional analysis of character are all abandoned at the first beck and call of adventure. The novel virtually begins again with each chapter, sacrificing all acquired momentum (and resist-

---

* Some of these innovations were predicted in Jacques Rivière's essay, "Le Roman d'aventure" (1913). See below, Chapter 5.

ing all reader involvement); each incident is the result of coincidence. The timing of the novel and Lafcadio's quickness of thinking resist every effort on the reader's part to identify himself with the characters or otherwise settle down.* Julius de Baraglioul had been commissioned to interview Lafcadio without revealing his purpose. But in nineteen casual lines Lafcadio has time to discover that Juste-Agénor de Baraglioul is his father, to buy one of Julius' books, and to form an opinion on its dullness. The abused body of Amédée Fleurissoire shuttles back and forth between Rome and Naples as swiftly, both before and after his death. All the demands of realism (and most of all "foreshadowing" and plausible transition) are sacrificed to narrative speed, surprise, entertainment.

The pace slows only when Gide pauses to satirize the realistic or analytic novel directly. Then, in the section on the childhood of Amédée and Blafaphas, the useless details accumulate. We are even told why Albert Lévy (who has no part in the story) changed his name and place of business, and why "Roman Plastic Plaster" is superior to "Marblette." The challenge to the conventional realist of the period was unmistakable; as impertinent as the challenge to a complacent society. Less surrealist than *Le Prométhée mal enchaîné* or than parts of *Le Voyage d'Urien* (since most of the dreamlike coincidences have here an explanation), *Les Caves du Vatican* yet suggested that logic and imposed form have no place in the modern work of art. The book was slow to reach the general public, but was read eagerly in 1918 and 1919 by young writers. Inevitably they saw Lafcadio's independence but not his self-discipline; or saw Gide's recklessness of technique but not his extreme economy. Instead they read into the book everything they themselves were waiting to say.

* For all its multiplicity of scenes, the stage version inevitably fails to capture this pace. Thus a few lines of the novel may require five minutes on the stage. Even a far more anti-realistic play could hardly hope to keep an audience at a distance, or to vary so subtly the distances between author, subject, and audience.

4 THE LATER NOVELS

GIDE'S *CAVES DU VATICAN* THUS HAD NO small part in the Dadaist and other rebellions which broke out toward the end of the First World War. It was a promise of freedom, of willful irresponsibility both in ethics and art. The example of an eminent middle-aged writer conferred the respectability which even revolutionaries cherish. *La Symphonie pastorale* (1919) therefore came as a disappointment and shock, though it placated the readers of Bourget. The Dadaists felt themselves betrayed by this orderly and thoroughly classical "récit," much as the symbolists had felt betrayed by *Les Nourritures terrestres*. At least one young writer complained directly to the author, who saw fit to make public his reply.

La Symphonie pastorale was written, he explained, to liquidate a debt contracted toward himself long since. All of his books had been conceived before his thirtieth year (we know from *Si le grain ne meurt* that this one was germinating as early as 1894),[1] and thus none of them reflected his most recent state of mind. This short novel completed payment of the debt, and he was quite willing to acknowledge the pains it had cost him to return to an outworn manner. He admitted that his correspondent was right in assuming he had written the book with distaste, "that all the time I was writing it I fretted against the 'petit point' work which the nature of the problem demanded; against these half-tones, these nuances . . ."² Later he expressed annoyance that this and *Si le grain ne meurt*, the least original of his books, should have enjoyed the greatest immediate success, and that *La Symphonie pastorale* had given comfort even to a Catholic priest.³

Gide's retrospective comments on his own books are often abstract to a point of unreality, or seem designed to fit in with some theory concerning his "career." His explanation of *La Symphonie pastorale* certainly needs to be qualified. We must also recall his life-long tendency to react sharply, both against the book he has just written and against any aspect of his art which threatened to become fashionable. He insisted that he wanted to escape his admirers, and feared the orthodoxy of the *avant-garde* as much as any other.⁴ Moreover, the undeniable personal overtones of *La Symphonie pastorale* seem closely related to the religious crisis of 1916. The debt contracted long since was also a moral debt. He too, like the frustrated and casuistical pastor, had interpreted Scripture in such a way as to flatter "passionate inclination" and justify its satisfaction. He too had neglected the epistles of St. Paul to find in Christ's words release and not restriction. *La Symphonie pastorale* is nearly as subjective in theme as *L'Immoraliste*, yet as impersonal in judgment as *Isabelle*. It is a lucid demonstration of the evils of romantic sensibility and self-delusion, of the Rousseauistic confusion of "conscience" and "instinct." So methodical a demonstration, in fact, as to bring it perilously close to such a "roman-à-thèse" as *Robert*.

The story is told once again by a self-deluded man. A few irritated comments in his diary are enough to convey his boredom and isolation: the monotony of a small mountain community and the slow wearing-away of all romance by years of poverty and household care. To adopt impulsively a blind orphaned girl of perhaps fifteen seemed an act of pure charity. She had been reduced by neglect to a "soulless lump of flesh," and had nowhere to go. The pastor justifies this added burden on his frayed wife, and the fact that he had never given the same attention to his own children, by the parable of the lost sheep. At first Gertrude merely brings a new interest into the vacancy of his days. He longs to penetrate the "wall of darkness" behind which she lives and is excited by his success in teaching her words, concepts, and even the principles of music. But he carefully skirts, in her religious education, any mention of sadness, sin, and death. Even when he sees that his son Jacques loves Gertrude, he does not understand the reason for his own dissatisfaction. He knows only that he must protect the girl's "purity." He arranges for her to board at a friend's house and imposes on himself the "duty" of visiting her every day.

By the time the pastor begins his second notebook, however, he is fully aware of his own love for Gertrude. His problem thereafter is to justify himself by a careful reading of Scripture. "I search the Gospels, I search in vain for commands, threats, prohibitions . . . All these come from St. Paul." He resents the cold restraint preached by his son; true Christianity speaks from the heart. To be sure, he continues to pretend that his love is spiritual and paternal, but the girl herself cuts through this verbiage. She is already vaguely aware that their companionship distresses his wife, and begins to wonder whether the visible world is really as carefree as Beethoven's symphony would suggest. The pastor reminds her that love cannot be wrong unless we feel it in our hearts to be so.

This still unconsummated love is threatened by an operation which may restore the girl's sight. What will she feel when she sees him as he is, middle-aged and tired? He steals up to her room the night before she leaves for the hospital; she does not resist him. But when she returns with her sight restored, it is to understand at once their sin, and the anguish of Amélie. Jacques, horrified by the complacency of his father's liberal protestantism, has decided to enter the priesthood; Gertrude, also converted, realizes too late she had loved the son, not the father. She throws herself into a river, takes a chill, and lives only long enough to define the full horror of the tragedy, and to repeat St. Paul's words: "For I was alive without the law once; but when the commandment came, sin revived and I died."

Gide's honesty (which should not be confused with the detailed frankness of his confessions) consists in his willingness to dramatize the dangerous consequences of his ideas, if held by weak or self-deluded men. Or perhaps this is merely one of his strongest creative impulses: to separate himself symbolically from an earlier or a doubtful attitude and condemn himself by proxy. It would be difficult to say to what extent *La Symphonie pastorale* condemns "Gidean Christianity," as well as its very obvious abuse. But it would also be hard to imagine a book more accessible to French conservative moralists, or to the American neo-humanists who at about this time took alarm. Atmosphere, dialogue, and plot are subordinated to an extreme concentration on the moral problem. Even Conrad never insisted so strongly on the latent egoism of pity, or on the cruel consequences of sentimental optimism and indiscriminate benevolence.

The device of the imperceptive narrator once again permitted Gide to use the congenial diary form. It may have further seemed, in the abstract, the best way to convey such extremes of self-delusion. The sentimental pastor is, like all sentimentalists, isolated by his vanity and optimism. He is long incapable of seeing the drab suffering of his family or anything so gross as a sexual impulse in himself. His children wander into the story only as casual annoyances, and it is left to the reader to construct the background suffering, the tragedies of Gertrude, Jacques, and Amélie. The obtuse point of view does save the first part of the story from extreme sentimentality; it screens or filters a melodrama and pathos which only very slow realism could have absorbed. Otherwise, the technique operates clumsily. The unconscious irony is too obvious, the self-betrayal too complete and too succinct. "I know that Claude is teething (at least that is what his mother declares every time he sets up a howl) but does it not encourage him to howl, for her or Sarah to run

and pick him up and be forever petting him? I am convinced
he would not howl so often if he were left to howl once or
twice to his heart's content when I am not there." Gide
rarely moves his pastor as transparently or as crudely as this.
These sentences nevertheless show how unconvincing a mis-
directed economy can be in such a story of self-betrayal.

In *L'Immoraliste* too, every sentence was made to count.
The great difference is that *La Symphonie pastorale* is, for
all the sudden flaring of the pastor's sexuality, a drama of
intelligence. The pastor's physical passion is simply a *donnée*
of the problem; it is stated, not lived, imagined, dramatized.
Only his ingenious interpretations of Scripture seem to have
enlisted Gide's creative energies, and these wholly intellectual energies; the pastor is as unreal as the lecturing
Ménalque. Perhaps Voltaire could have told a story of extreme rationalization in the first person and with such extreme economy. Normally, a narrative of imperfect intelligence invites the more diffuse technique of *Benito Cereno*
and of James — the observing or narrating "fool" to betray
himself not in every other sentence but in one out of ten or
twenty. However, Gide's difficulty probably goes deeper
than this, for he would show the same clumsiness in the
slightly less economical "récit" *Robert*. He was apparently
incapable of dramatizing intellectual failure from the inside,
once he had taken the exact measure of that failure. He
could vivify a remembered sexual conflict, but not remembered mental error. The truth may be that such a psychosexual conflict as Michel's never ends; or, at least, that the
author can come to understand it only by writing his book.
But Gide understood his pastor before he wrote the first page
of his novel. There was no Devil's share of creative exploration, no chance for "collaboration with the demon." Thus
the objectivity of *La Symphonie pastorale* — the complete-
ness of the author's dissociation from his hero — suggests that
Gide's earlier subjectivity may have saved his art, whatever
limitations it imposed.

The recent film drawn from the novel shows the advantages of a dense texture and slower movement for such a story

of weak intelligence. It also suggests the advantages of a leisurely realism — of careful transition and casual everyday dialogue, of landscape even — where the plot is frankly melodramatic. Certainly the film underlines, by its excisions as by its slowness, the indecent haste of Gide's last pages. The crime against Gertrude, her operation, her conversion at the hospital as a result of Jacques's revelation of St. Paul, his decision to enter the priesthood, Gertrude's return and her discovery that it was Jacques she really loved, her attempted suicide and her death — all this is hurried over in a dozen very short pages. The determination to have done is even more marked than in *Isabelle*. No doubt Gide's telescoped endings are due in part to the fact that while writing one book he thought actively of the next one. And in 1918 and 1919 he was eager to start *Les Faux-Monnayeurs*, the "first novel" he had postponed so long.

The dreary trilogy of novelettes which followed *Les Faux-Monnayeurs* — *L'Ecole des femmes* (1929), *Robert* (1929) and *Geneviève* (1936) — may be dismissed briefly; it is as well to get them out of the way before turning to that long book. They do provide the American reader with an accurate picture of the extreme conservatism that still prevails in certain bourgeois families; no one could come away from these somber stories with his notions of French frivolity uncorrected. They thus help explain the violence of Gide's attack on cautious and protecting institutions: the church, the family, the home. But their only critical interest is negative. They show how serious the threat of the "roman-à-thèse" had always been for Gide, and how totally he failed when he tried to dramatize from within the feelings of persons very different from himself. In *La Symphonie pastorale* he could at least recreate some of his own rationalizations. But now his "imperceptive narrators" are a long-suffering wife, her Catholic pragmatist husband, and their vaguely rebellious daughter. Gide could bring such persons as Eveline and Geneviève to life if he looked at them from the outside, with pity or mild amusement. He did so with

Pauline and Sarah in *Les Faux-Monnayeurs*. But only the grotesque satire of Anthime Armand-Dubois could have saved Robert. All of Gide's suppleness of intellect vanishes when he tries to convey, seriously and subjectively, the arguments of his opponents. This is one of his greatest differences from Dostoevsky, and the place where Gide seems least aware of his own failings. He cannot, by an act of creative imagination and sympathy, inhabit a mind so alien; he cannot give a fool his due — even his due share of complexity. The three stories further testify to the danger, for a novelist, of trying to write "useful" books. Certainly they show a loss of creative and stylistic energy, and suggest an anticlimax as unfortunate as Conrad's. But Gide caught his breath at least once again, in the remarkable *Thésée*.

Gide had outlined *L'Ecole des femmes* as early as 1914: the story of a girl who marries against the advice of her parents, and whose husband rises in their esteem while he lowers himself in hers.[5] Even before her marriage Eveline begins to suspect some of her husband's hypocrisy (which is only too obvious to the reader), and the first part of her diary shows suspicion making inroads on love. The second part of the diary, written twenty years later, tells of an exasperation so great that life with Robert no longer seems tolerable. But he falls sick and insists he is dying; both Eveline's family and the sinister family confessor persuade her to remain with him. Even if it were true that he be vacuous, dishonest, hypocritical, and a "moral profiteer" — is it not her duty to conceal his weaknesses? And how can she think of leaving him, since he still loves *her*? The present events occur during the first war. While Robert finds himself a safe mission and a shiny uniform, Eveline quietly retires to a special hospital where she is certain to contract an incurable disease. This is *L'Ecole des femmes*, which was once intended to furnish the central plot of *Les Faux-Monnayeurs*,[6] but which was repeatedly postponed and at last finished only at the insistence of *Forum* magazine.[7] The sequel *Robert* was suggested by Ernst Robert Curtius, who thought it would be interesting to know the husband's side of the story.[8] These encouragements were not the greatest services rendered to modern letters by the American magazine and the distinguished German critic.

Eveline's youthful imperceptiveness is not wholly incredible, though her bride's diary offers too many obvious clues. The deliberate and tiresome banality of style, to be carried still further in *Geneviève*,[9] is even more annoying. The unconscious irony of *Robert* at least gives it a certain tightness which the other two short novels lack. *Robert*, written after Eveline's death, is the husband's angry reply to Gide's unfairness in publishing her diary. It is offered as a "defense"; and is, of course, a terrible self-condemnation. Where *L'Ecole des femmes* was a belated answer to such a book as Prévost's *Le Jardin secret* and attacked the concept of indissoluble marriage, *Robert* is a satire on conservative Catholic moralism. Robert had enjoyed a protected and untempted childhood, and had been taught that the best way to combat evil was to look away from it. He has a formulated horror of free thought, and advances all the orthodox humanist arguments. He distrusts the natural man and believes strong conventions are necessary to counteract original sin; he insists that duty (which tends to concentrate and unify the "soul") is far more important than Gidean sincerity. A doctrine of sincerity, he argues, is merely another form of antinomianism and leaves the soul "inconsecutive" and divided. But his conservative pessimism is, on his own showing, a mask for vicious egotism. He believes in the subjugation of women and children, and regrets that a certain note of fear gradually disappeared from his wife's voice as the years passed. He is a spokesman for the ideas of Bourget and Massis, and is also an intolerable scoundrel. Not the least of his villainies is the founding of a Book-of-the-Month Club.

Geneviève is the statement of the daughter, who significantly is more interested in her "ideas" than in her story. So too was Gide, who went on with the distasteful task only for the sake of these ideas; he wanted his book to explore the whole problem of feminism. He had considered the necessity of a sequel as early as 1919; [10] it is distressing to observe him

still at work on it in 1932 and again in 1935.* For the final
version, not more than thirty thousand words long, is a wholly
unreal exposition: as abstract as *L'Ecole des femmes* or
Robert, and more sentimental than either. It dramatizes once
again the conflict of generations. The mother, in spite of her
own sufferings at the hands of the orthodox, jealously protects her daughter from the dubious friendship of an illegitimate Jewish girl (whose father, to make things worse, is a
painter). A certain subtlety of theme distinguishes Geneviève's novel from her parents'. The girl is a lesbian without
realizing it, and thus does not fully understand the motive
of her revolt against marriage. She even wants an illegitimate
child and asks the family doctor to be its father; she objects
on principle to committing herself further. "Thus you believe
that a woman — in order to have children — must consent to
ally her existence with that of a man whom perhaps she cannot continue to love?" [11]

This style is of course that of radio soap opera; it is surprising that critics have not insisted on its coincidence with
Gide's communist adventure. It is more reasonable to cite
his stubborn refusal to give up a subject which would not
come to life, and the willfulness of his attempt to write a
completely objective "roman-à-thèse." But even the commu-
nists of 1936 must have derived cool comfort from the book,
which concludes with an astonishingly orthodox palinode.
Geneviève finally realizes that the doctor's restraint, and his
loyalty to his wife, is far more important than her theoretical
liberty: "Ah how much more worthy of respect than my
selfish resolutions, how much more authentic especially, the
delicate feelings of my mother now seem, or those of Doctor
Marchant and even of my aunt — all those mysterious and
secret wires strung from heart to heart, which I snatched at

* Gide, commenting on these remarks, defines the waste effort eloquently:
". . . ainsi que vous le dites, mon *Ecole des Femmes*, ou du moins la troisième
partie (*Geneviève*), est de tous mes livres le plus péniblement écrit (et de
beaucoup). C'est tout ce qui reste d'un grand naufrage: le nombre des pages
écrites, puis déchirées, eût formé un volume épais, qui sans doute eût été
détestable. J'étais alors empoisonné par la question sociale. N'en parlons
plus" (see Gide's letter of May 16, 1947, at end of this book).

while inconsiderately forging ahead." [12] This is good sense, though banal good sense, and very bad writing. It is a relief to turn back to the livelier art though more insidious doctrine of *Les Faux-Monnayeurs*.

A first novel is usually a formless and scarcely disguised autobiography, lyrical and a little unreal. But Gide's "first novel" was the culmination of a thirty-year effort to escape realism, responsibility, and concentration of form, as well as to escape the self. "I dedicate this, my first novel, to Roger Martin du Gard, in token of profound friendship." Thus Gide defined the central importance of *Les Faux-Monnayeurs* (1926), which he thought would be not only his first novel but very probably his last one. Over the years the *novel* had come to represent for him something both ambitious and irresponsible; "the novel, as I define or imagine it, carries a diversity of points of view subject to the diversity of the characters it brings on the scene; it is, by nature, a deconcentrated work." [13] Neither the "récits" nor the "soties" had given a comprehensive picture of life. The closely structured *L'Immoraliste* had isolated two characters and two problems from the multiplicity of life, was admittedly a subjective, therapeutic book. And *Les Caves du Vatican*, for all its formlessness, scarcely reflected ordinary life. All Gide's fiction had been critical and even ironic; had taken some favorite idea or some unrealized facet of self and magnified it for the purposes of ethics or art. His only "novel" would have to be, like those of Roger Martin du Gard, a resolution of extremes: a balanced, comprehensive picture of a group of very different human beings. It must not be another spiritual autobiography.

The paradoxical aim of the expressionists, carried to its extreme by Joyce, was to abandon "realism" for the sake of a more realistic imitation of life; to disintegrate the form of the novel until form itself expressed the baffling complexity and disorder of experience. Gide refined on this aim by juxtaposing this disorder and the effort of one of his characters (the novelist Edouard) to describe it. But his immediate technical objectives were to describe a series of interpenetrating destinies, and "to avoid at all cost the simple impersonal 'récit.' " * [14] *Les Faux-Monnayeurs*, he resolved, would avoid the narrowness of his earlier books even at the risk of unmanageable excess; it would become a receptacle for everything he observed, for everything he wanted to say.[15] By 1921 Gide felt he had enough material for half-a-dozen books. It took Roger Martin du Gard to bring him back to his original intention; to persuade him to knit together the diverse plots and interests, rather than write a series of separate "récits." [16] Gide's impulse to orderly, consecutive construction was so strong that he set himself a working rule for the achievement of disorder. He resolved, once again, never to profit by what he had already written, and to make an absolutely fresh start with each chapter.[7] Even the most inventive or the most irresponsible novelist would find such a rule difficult to follow.

The *Journal des Faux-Monnayeurs* reflects some of the struggle. This is a brief commonplace book and diary of the novel's composition, running very intermittently from June 17, 1919, to June 8, 1925, the day the book was finished. It consists of random notes on still unresolved difficulties, ideas for scenes or chapters, and general discussions on the art of fiction. Many entries were apparently transferred to the diary which Edouard keeps in the novel itself, but enough remains to make it an invaluable document for young or discouraged writers. It can teach them that the periods of agonizing unproductiveness may be productive in their own occult fashion; that a first or tenth project for a novel may be very far from the final one; that even the best opening chapters regularly recede to the middle of the book; and that often a great deal must be "written" before the pen begins to write. (The first thirty pages of the final version were apparently written as late as November 1922.) [18] As a document

---

* These were among the objectives outlined by Rivière in his 1913 essay on "Le Roman d'aventure." *Les Faux-Monnayeurs* comes even closer than *Les Caves du Vatican* to being the new novel Rivière predicted. See below, Chapter 5.

on Gide's own novel, the *Journal* is disappointingly brief, and perhaps so selective as to be untrustworthy. How much of major relevance has been omitted for one reason or another? It is most immediately interesting, for our purposes, as a record of projects abandoned.

From the very beginning Gide proposed to work into a single novel as much as possible of what life had taught him,[19] but he foresaw two main plots. The first — the story of a woman who discovers her husband's mediocrity too late, and whose family continues to think him a paragon of talent and virtue — was still under consideration as late as June 1921, but was finally abandoned, to be used later in *L'Ecole des femmes* and its sequels.[20] The second was to be the story of a would-be seducer who ends by becoming the "captive of the act he had resolved to accomplish," having exhausted imaginatively its pleasures in advance.[21] Few traces of this plot appear in the novel as we have it. At this time Gide also envisaged dramatizing the eternal conflict between younger and older generations,[22] and this does remain as an undercurrent in the final version. Two days later he resolved not to make his novel an "exact picture of states of mind before the war," since this would eventually date it. But little more than a month later he reconsidered an earlier and even more ambitious idea: to measure the impact of the war on these states of mind. He would show each character only the more firmly rooted in his original convictions — socialist, nationalist, or Christian — as a result of his wartime experience.[23]

This attention to clearly localized spiritual or intellectual history gradually diminished. The political and social problem disappeared almost entirely, to be replaced by the problem of individualist ethics. The "Argonauts" (originally planned as a patriotic boys' club) becomes the title of a literary magazine, and nothing remains of Bernard's conflict with a traditionalist of the Barrès persuasion except his brief excursion with the Angel.[24] Gide rightly saw that his old problem of individualist freedom belonged to the century, not to any particular decade. It is thus impossible to "date" *Les Faux-Monnayeurs* exactly. Its young men are less earnest than those of the Dreyfus generation, and less rebellious and despondent than those of the first postwar years. Gide supplies prewar gold coins, yet cultivates anachronism amusingly. He introduces briefly Alfred Jarry (who died in 1907), but has Armand's literary magazine publish Marcel Duchamp's famous "Tableau Dada" of the Mona Lisa with moustaches.[25]

A few interesting entries suggest that Gide wanted to make *Les Faux-Monnayeurs* his "Life of a Great Sinner" — and, like Dostoevsky, found such a task beyond his powers. In January 1921 he considered having the "nonexistence of the Devil" his central subject. The Devil was to be a character "circulating incognito" through the book, and whose existence would become more real the more it was disbelieved.[26] The great sinner would be Vincent Molinier, the seducer of Laura — gradually penetrated by the diabolic spirit until he believes he has become the Devil. The more firmly he disbelieves in the Devil, the more surely he feels he *belongs* to the Devil, *is* the Devil.[27] Gide was here again indebted to *The Possessed*. Vincent was to prove himself the Devil by much the same logic Kirilov used to prove himself God. What remains of Vincent's history in the novel itself is disappointingly slight. We do see, but still in the *Journal's* undramatized outline form, Vincent's rationalization of his abandonment of Laura;[28] we see him corrupted by Lady Griffith and tempted to betray his brother to the Comte de Passavant. But at this crucial point in his moral history, he disappears from France and from the book. Only a brief letter near the end explains that he has murdered Lady Griffith and come to think himself the Devil.

The loss of Vincent is less regrettable than the loss of the ambulatory Devil. A "demon" does appear from time to time in an expository paragraph, but only as the mildest of figures of speech. The obscure character of Strouvilhou is perhaps all that remains of Gide's plan to present a diabolic and secret force working behind the scenes. But when Strouvilhou appears in the flesh to talk with the Comte de Passavant he seems merely a disappointed disciple of Nietzsche. Gide at least occasionally believed in the Devil; believed, that is, in an occult inner force which not the longest plumb-line of psychology could reach. It would have been no small achievement to distribute this force through a novel; to dramatize a force of evil, circulating incognito, and operating wholly· outside the motivations which a behaviorist or psychiatrist could record. To present such a force without personifying it is by no means impossible. A sense of ever-threatening hysteria animates the novels of Dostoevsky apart from the hysteria of the individual characters; an occult determining or judging force appears in Kafka's *The Castle* and *The Trial*, sometimes distinct from the victims' intuition of that force. And to use an extreme example — extreme because found in the very heart of naturalism — a degrading and contaminating force (the "Golden Fly") exists in *Nana* independent of specific economic and social circumstances. The operation of occult agency was no more than a metaphor to Zola, but to Kafka it was perhaps an article of faith. For Gide the "Devil" existed on a plane which combined faith and metaphor. His failure to dramatize that half-belief (or, at least, to face such an interesting technical problem) is one of the greatest disappointments of *Les Faux-Monnayeurs*.

The novel thus avoided spiritual history and refused to become metaphysical tragedy; was neither *The Magic Mountain* nor *The Possessed*. Momentarily it did promise to become another *Caves du Vatican*. Lafcadio was to appear again, this time as corrupting actor and as Edouard's secretary or private detective, as an ironic observer and further narrator of the story.[29] But once again the "fantoche" took on flesh and blood and assumed an entirely new personality and a new name: Bernard.[30] Bernard is far too independent to be a mere secretary for long, and he so dominates the early chapters that Edouard's appearance as meditative observer comes as an unwelcome intrusion. Bernard is pedagogically the center of a book which could be called a treatise on education and a new *Emile*, were it not so diversely amusing. Like Lafcadio he is a bastard, and therefore need obey no injunction to follow in his father's footsteps; he must find the moral law in himself. Whereas the weaker Vincent and Olivier are easily influenced (the one corrupted by Passavant and Lady Griffith, the other rescued by Edouard), Bernard reacts against any strong influence.[31]

In the last months of composition, Gide conceived Bernard's problem in terms of his own familiar debate. Would the boy be able to master such a difficult attitude? "But will he know to raise himself high enough to accept and assimilate the contradictions of his overly rich nature? High enough to want to feed rather than resolve these contradictions? High enough to understand that the fullness of its vibration and the distance between its ends determine, for the taut string, the power of the tone it will give?" [32] In the novel itself Bernard's dilemma is never presented as explicitly as in this passage from the *Journal des Faux-Monnayeurs*; he remains to the end an undecided character, with an uncertain future. His maxims are, like these of Nietzsche and Blake, the key both to Heaven and to Hell.[33] The reader who pores over *Les Faux-Monnayeurs* for some solution to the ethical problem will find no more categorical answer than Aristotle's. In that uncharted jungle the good disposition will succeed and the bad go wrong. The gift of nature which finally decides the "truly fortunate" does not depend on ourselves. And Gide leaves even this vague summation for the reader himself to make. It is not the author's function to make a final addition and subtraction, and thus be reassuringly conclusive. "To disturb, that is my role." [34]

However interesting and energetically alive, Bernard is not a fully developed character. Nor is his education the novel's "subject." By Gide's definition, the novel should have many subjects as well as many characters. He had repeatedly been told that he lacked imagination and creative energy; *Les Faux-Monnayeurs* is his answer, a dazzling show of inventive force. He proposed to knit together his series of remote destinies in such a way as to bring each character momentarily to the front of the stage.[35] And so too for the diversity of issues raised in turn. The novel should be a "rendezvous of problems"; an elaborate intellectual fugue in which ideas are stated, dropped for a time, and then restated or developed to the reader's greater astonishment.[36] Jean Hytier devoted no less than eighteen pages to a summary of the novel's plot,[37] and Benjamin Crémieux gave a long catalogue of its themes or subjects. On a single page he described *Les Faux-Monnayeurs* as a satire on the family, on education, and on literary mores; an idealization of individual liberty, a study of the relationship of parents and children, a eulogy of perversion contradicted by a defense of self-sacrifice; a Freudian novel, a novel on family hypocrisy, an antiprotestant novel, a homosexual novel, a diabolic novel.[38] To this list one must add at least the existentialist distinction between real and counterfeit personality, and the conflict between appearance and reality which was to be the deeplying subject of Edouard's novel — though fortunately not of Gide's.

First of all, *Les Faux-Monnayeurs* is an impression of life; the counterpoint of contradictory ideas is less striking than the counterpoint of mood. Gide alternately plays all the instruments he had mastered in his shorter books: the comedy and fantasy of the "soties," the complacent unconscious irony of *La Symphonie pastorale*, the satire of *Paludes*, the mystery of *Isabelle*, the tragedy of *L'Immoraliste*, the pathos of *La Porte étroite*. He refused to confine himself to the immemorial subject matter of the novel: the loves and ambitions of men and women in their third and fourth decades. Nothing is lacking to his human comedy but an intelligent and middle-aged "good citizen" and a happily married couple. Otherwise, there is an almost too calculated counterpoint of sex and age — the story moving from the divine imaginativeness and diabolic cruelty of children to the anxiety of adolescent boys and the willfulness of adolescent girls; from the resignation of neglected wives and spinsters to the bewilderment and querulous jealousy of the very old. *Les Faux-Monnayeurs* is also a love story, as most novels are. It was certainly one of Gide's intentions to prove, perhaps in answer to Proust, that homosexual love could be "normal" and happy. Edouard's love for Olivier has its hours of harsh desire and jealousy, but also its hours of idealism and self-sacrifice, of

calm tenderness and intellectual companionship. The argument may seem weighted in Edouard's favor to the reader
who is unbendingly hostile. But Gide is comprehensive
enough to admit the attractiveness of Bernard's idealization
of Laura and the urgency of his desire for Sarah. And honest
enough to admit the existence of a Comte de Passavant, as
unpleasant as any Proustian invert.

Bernard's is essentially a lonely and inward struggle, as
Gide's own had been; neither Edouard nor Laura can "teach"
him to exploit his rich contradictions, rather than cancel
them out. The dramatic center of the novel is instead the
struggle between Edouard and the Comte de Passavant for
the weaker and more docile Olivier Molinier. Passavant can
tempt Olivier with the most flattering offer a young *lycéen*
could receive, the editorship of an experimental literary
magazine. Against this Edouard must rely on an ideal of
artistic integrity and personal honesty — and on love. There
are other dramatic interests. But in this novel at least, Gide
is more concerned with the still undetermined children than
with the adults, who are already the formed and passive
victims of life, of habit, of themselves. All the children in the
book are torn between contradictory forces, sometimes between three or four. Edouard, a psychiatrist, a young girl,
and Strouvilhou fight for the soul of little Boris; Edouard,
his parents, and Strouvilhou for Georges Molinier's; Olivier,
Edouard, and disturbing memories of childhood for Armand
Vedel's. At the end of the book only Olivier seems mildly
saved and only Vincent irrevocably damned. But Armand
can look forward to a life of self-tormenting sadism, and
little Boris is dead. Edouard, as the rescuer not corruptor of
youth, looks forward to knowing Caloub, the young brother
of Edward.

Newspaper clippings furnished Gide with a certain amount
of connective tissue. In 1906 some young Parisian writers,
artists, and students banded together to pass counterfeit
money; in 1909 a few boys formed a club in Clermont-Fer-
rand and succeeded in their object: to persuade a fifteen-
year-old boy to commit suicide.[39] Gide found the technical

problem of relating these two "faits-divers," and of working
them into a convincing and rounded picture of life, an interesting challenge to his skill. Otherwise the seemingly complicated structure of *Les Faux-Monnayeurs* is fairly simple.
To bring each person in turn to the front of the stage demanded a certain amount of ruthless omission, but transferred the problem of structure to the problem of point of
view, and reduced the plot itself to a series of detached and
often fleeting portraits.

Some of these are full-dress portraits or "characteriza-
tions"; others are analytic "case studies," brief but pathetic
"vignettes," or frankly oversimplified "caricatures." The distinction between an imperfect portrait which comes to life
and a perfected one which does not is obvious and basic. It is
sometimes forgotten, however, that a brief and skillful caricature may seem more alive than a contradictory "character"
whose life we know in detail. M. Profitendieu and M. Molinier — very broad caricatures of the respectable middle-class
father; pompous, hypocritical, and blind — are nevertheless
convincing and alive. And so too are the Comte de Passavant and Sarah, though he obviously "represents" the literary
charlatan and she the restless younger woman rebelling
against subjugation. Lady Griffith, on the other hand, has
some of the unreality of Aldous Huxley's minor characters;
her urbanity is too consciously unmoral, her cynicism too obviously motivated. Gide's remark that she *should* remain unreal and as it were outside the book is a concealed admission
of defeat. [40]

The art of caricature depends on a few broad strokes;
except in the hands of a Daumier or a Dickens, it can hardly
hope to accomplish more than a single emphatic impression.
But the brief vignette need be neither slight nor unalive.
Edouard sees Rachel, Pauline, and La Pérouse only occasionally; intrudes briefly on their suffering, helps them as best
he can, and withdraws. The few quiet scenes yet leave a
sense of suffering that began long before Edouard arrived
and that will continue after he has left. Any realist can open
a door, look in, and come away; the difficult thing is to

come away with more than a photograph. The similarity of Edouard's three visits to La Pérouse may help create the effect of a drab and unchanging anguish. The old man has a different complaint to make each time, but his voice remains the same, and so does the dingy squalor of his life. La Pérouse was drawn more closely from life than any other character, and Gide was afraid that memory had impinged too strongly on art.[41] Late in 1923 he wrote that nothing in the book had given him so much trouble. But the memories were of twenty years' standing,[42] and the finished portrait is an exceptional one of helpless old age.

The same pathos appears in the portraits of Rachel and Pauline; they are rescued from sentimentality by their very brevity and by the cool accuracy of Edouard's comments. Gide feels nine out of ten boys should escape their homes, and especially the highly conventional influence of their mothers. But these mothers are never presented unfairly, and even Edouard can sympathize with Pauline's despair as she sees one son after another escape her. Nearly every respectable middle-aged husband in Gide's fiction is scheming, pompous, or stupid; nearly every middle-aged wife is kindly, suffering, and resigned. They remain in the shadows of these stories of emancipation, as do the younger wives and sweethearts: the timid, conservative, and protecting influences on men and on children. These women must be left behind, but are always to be pitied. Does this surprising charity toward women, the sworn enemies of individualism, derive from the curious ambivalence of Gide's feeling for his wife and his mother? Or from his pity for Anna Shackleton? [43] Whatever their sharp differences, these patient women in the background of the novels betray a family likeness.

Rachel and Pauline, known only from the surface of their suffering and vivified chiefly by dialogue, are products of a conventional realistic technique. So too is old La Pérouse, though his self-destructiveness takes on the very special form of "negative hallucination." Little Boris and Armand Vedel, on the other hand, are complex portraits of neurosis. Edouard explores Boris' nervous disorder with the aid of a psychiatrist, and the omniscient narrator goes further still. But Armand's "case" is baffling, shadowy, and incomplete, like that of a minor Dostoevsky neurotic. Something essential is left undiscovered, as it remained undiscovered in the friend — one Armand Bavretel — on whom Armand Vedel's portrait is based.[44] Gide observed the "mal bizarre" of the original Armand in 1891, and soon afterward decided to use him in a novel, together with his father — a grotesquely ugly pastor who gave his family little else than moral apothegms.[45] The striking portrait of Armand in *Si le grain ne meurt* emphasizes the aggressive poverty of the Bavretel household and the young man's curious need to insult the sister he adored. Ashamed of his mother's coy efforts to marry her off, and ashamed of his patched poverty, Armand took delight in exposing everything which the family tried to conceal. All of this remains in *Les Faux-Monnayeurs*, though the fictional Armand does not commit suicide. But a great deal more is suggested. Armand carries this "desire to spoil everything he cares for" so far as to lock Bernard all night in Sarah's bedroom, and thus make her debauch certain. He defines himself to Olivier as a schizoid observer of his own compromising actions, and adds that his puritan childhood and his father's sanctimonious hypocrisy have left him with a horror of virtue. But the strongest feeling he expresses anywhere is disgust with the sister who had been seduced by Vincent. He shows, most of the time, a horror not of "virtue" but of sex.

The most disturbing moment in his history occurs the morning after he locked up Bernard and Sarah, when he goes in to observe them:

A sheet half hides them as they lie with limbs entwined. How beautiful they are! Armand gazes at them and gazes. He would like to be their sleep, their kisses. At first he smiles; then suddenly kneels at the foot of the bed, among the coverings they have flung aside. To what God can he be praying thus with folded hands? An unspeakable emotion shakes him. His lips are trembling . . . *He observes under the pillow a handkerchief* *stained with blood. He rises, picks it up and takes it with him; and, sobbing, presses his lips against the little amber spot.** But on the threshhold of the door, he turns. He wants to wake Bernard so that he may gain his own room before anyone in the house is awake.

A good many textbook explanations might be applied to Armand's original attitude toward Sarah, and to his locking of the bedroom door: infantile *voyeurism*, reënactment of the mother's violation by a hated father, acute self-punishment for undisclosed guilt; or, even, identification with Bernard and the old-fashioned categories of incest. This is, in any event, the self-tormenting Armand who calls Laura a slut. We know little of his childhood, but we know he cannot accept sexual relationships calmly. His first morning reaction of benevolent and calm joy is therefore most puzzling. Does it show that release from tension which comes with the successful acting-out of a neurotic fantasy? Or the calm of momentary escape from a neurotic fear of sex? Such questions soon form a vicious circle of questions — which may mean, only, that Armand has the unformulable complexity of a full fictional portrait, or of a human being. But the pattern of revolt against restricted childhood is a familiar one, to the reader of Gide. Armand not merely triumphs over his parents in helping Sarah triumph over them. He also serves to "prove" that a virtuous and restrictive family childhood is the worst possible one for a child. It is difficult to avoid the suspicion that Gide let his old axioms interfere with his dramatic understanding of Armand. There may be, in other words, not one but two Armands. The first is the authentic neurotic who locks the door on Bernard and Sarah. The second, who kneels at the very moment of symbolic liberation, is merely another of Gide's half-emancipated puritans.†

---

* The lines I have italicized do not appear in the Modern Library translation, p. 289.

† After reading an earlier version of this comment on Armand, Gide wrote: "Mais j'avoue que le long passage à propos du double personnage d'Armand ne me paraît pas très juste; je crois qu'il est et reste le même à travers ses apparentes contradictions" (see letter of May 16, 1947, at end of this book).

Armand proves, in any event, the provocative interest of a "shadowed" characterization. Little Boris, the thirteen-year-old grandson of La Pérouse, offers a much more coherent "case study." Edouard criticizes Mme Sophroniska's psychiatric invasion of the child's mind, describes her as a disguised mystic, and proves that her temporarily successful methods are finally unavailing. Gide nevertheless profits by these methods in describing the child's trouble. Boris shows typical hysterical symptoms which are due to onanistic guilt-feelings: he has various nervous tics, and thinks he contaminates what he touches. Mme Sophroniska learns that Boris had been taught to regard masturbation as "magic"; he had even been given a magic parchment talisman with the words "GAS. TELEPHONE . . . ONE HUNDRED THOUSAND ROUBLES" written on it. The talisman was "the 'Open Sesame' of the shameful Paradise." When Boris' father dies, the child attributes his death to these magic practices; his hysterical behavior is an effort to work off his sense of guilt. He is temporarily cured when Mme Sophroniska penetrates his secret, but Edouard feels that "the malady has simply taken refuge in some deeper recess of his being, as though to escape the doctor's inquisitorial glance." When (thanks to Strouvilhou) one of Boris' Paris schoolmates leaves a copy of the secret talisman on his desk, the child succumbs again to the lure of his magic. He feels there is no escape, and in the agony of his guilt will go to any length to assert his manliness. He agrees to join "The Brotherhood of Strong Men," and though he knows the drawing is dishonest, commits suicide docilely when his name is drawn. Such is Boris' portrait — the only one in Gide's fiction to show a prolonged and *explicit* awareness of contemporary psychological theories. Its effectiveness is more academic than dramatic.

Unlike these minor objects of pity, curiosity, and amusement, Bernard and Olivier achieve an extraordinary illusion of freedom and mobility. Only Edouard, of the main characters, seems fixed and impervious to change, and even he is capable of self-contradiction and suffering. This is no doubt the novel's great technical success: that it takes place in an unrolling yet free present time, that the drama we watch may take an unexpected turn at any moment. Much of this success, we shall see, is owing to the omniscient narrator or "roving conductor" of the opening chapters and of some later ones; to his impertinent curiosity and amusing insistence that the characters *are* free. The manipulations of narrating consciousness are minute and very effective. But there are more general ways to make a character, even "human nature" itself, seem free. The first is that of shadowed characterization, of ambiguous behavior never fully explained. Another, which Gide uses successfully with Olivier Molinier, is to confront a relatively unchanging character with unexpected testing circumstances. Given a certain amiable docility, Olivier seems free because the suasions of circumstance change. A third method is Conrad's (and Gide's in *Isabelle*, or here with Strouvilhou): the underlying human traits remain unchanged, but our knowledge of them increases. Startling contradictions are thus gradually explained; beneath them we discern at last unchanging energies and needs.

Still another method — and Gide admits to it with disarming frankness — is for the author to change his mind about his characters but refuse to go back and correct.[46] Here too *Les Faux-Monnayeurs* becomes a *Kunstlerroman*; or, perhaps, the penultimate draft of a novel. The freedom of Vincent, who starts as a major character and then disappears, or of Georges Molinier, who promises to become a major character but does not, is dubious enough. But no amount of theorizing about the deliberately imperfect novel can justify Laura's transformation from a cringing and stupid girl to an intelligent woman who preaches Gidean deracination. Not Edouard's attitude toward her changes but Gide's. He comes to see her as a vehicle for instruction.

Thus we are confronted, once again, with the problem of subjectivity. Did Gide, in this "first novel," finally escape autobiography? Was he able at last to "invent"? Only the most naïve reader would object to the use of newspaper clippings or of such a well-known event as Alfred Jarry's apparent attempt to shoot Christian Beck at the Taverne du

Panthéon.[47] Olivier, Bernard, Passavant, and Vincent were
probably the most freely imagined of the characters; Gide
said he began to write their dialogue before he knew "who"
they were.[48] But it would be difficult to prove that they are
more intensely created than the remembered Armand and
La Pérouse. The problem is rather this: was Gide once again
constrained to animate his characters with parts of his own
rich diversity? "So too in real life I am inhabited by the
thoughts and feelings of others; my heart beats only in accord
with theirs." [49] Gide dissociated himself from Edouard by
saying that Edouard was too subjective to be able to finish
his novel.[50] Yet Edouard lays claim to the same power of
"decentralization": "My heart beats only by sympathy; I live
only through others . . . and I never feel myself living so
intensely as when I escape from myself to become no matter
who." [51] Over and over the characters of *Les Faux-Monnayeurs* recall familiar Gidean dilemmas and anxieties. When
Armand revolts against the mechanization of life (while re-
maining himself enslaved by routine), he recalls even the
phrasing of *Paludes*.[52] La Pérouse discovers that his conquest
of "vice" has left him, like the author of *André Walter*, the
prisoner of his virtuous pride; Bernard, like the Gide of
1895, sacrifices his liberty to Laura almost as soon as he has
won it. It is scarcely surprising that Boris should inherit
Gide's guilt-feelings concerning masturbation, but startling
to see Strouvilhou inherit his literary opinions. Where Gide
said that he is inhabited by the thoughts and feelings of
others, he should have said that he projects his concerns into
them, distributes his personality among them.

The great difference between *Les Faux-Monnayeurs* and
the "récits" is not that it is less autobiographical in background,* but that it is less subjective in tone and that it

* Consider, for instance, his loss of the key to a suitcase containing his
diary (*The Counterfeiters*, p. 67; *Journal*, July 15, 1905); his fear that "X"
will read the diary he left at Cuverville (*The Counterfeiters*, pp. 76 ff.;
Journal, July 25, 1914); his observation of a schoolboy stealing a book (*The
Counterfeiters*, pp. 78–86; *Journal*, May 3, 1921; and *Journal des Faux-
Monnayeurs*, May 3, 1921). Was Edouard's relationship to Olivier and

does not confine itself to the exploration of one personal difficulty. The problems of Boris, Armand, Bernard, and even La Pérouse are among those Gide had faced. But by 1925 he had solved them. The relative equanimity of Edouard is the equanimity of his middle-aged creator; the struggles are recollected. But these struggles are sufficiently diverse to occupy half-a-dozen characters. Similarly, Gide's tendency to project his own ideas into various characters, which would be fatal in a less intelligent author, is less troubling where the projecting mind is so subtle and varied. *Les Faux-Monnayeurs* is not the manifoldly inventive creation Gide wanted it to be; its author would never be a Dickens or Balzac. But neither was he the prisoner of an imagination as narrow as Montherlant's or Mauriac's. The human comedy of *Les Faux-Monnayeurs* is small but important.

These are the major interests for the reader who is not writing an essay on Gide: his timeless evocation of the anxieties and energies of youth, his posing of certain disturbing problems, his creation of very different characters, his success in providing a wise and witty "entertainment." For such a reader, *Les Faux-Monnayeurs* is a novel among other novels, though somewhat more difficult than most. Its picture of the Quartier Latin may seem less somber than Magnane's in *La Bête à concours*; its panorama of French intellectual life slighter but less tendentious than Sartre's *Chemins de la liberté*. The technique may recall the chronological involutions of *Nostromo*, and almost certainly will recall the fugal structure of *Point Counter Point*. But the reader who passes immediately from *Les Faux-Monnayeurs* to *Point Counter Point* is likely to find Huxley's novel "literary," factitious, dated, and unbearably slow. Gide's world will seem to him by contrast free, energetic, unneurotic. For such a reader Edouard's diary has its initial novelty. But at a second reading all this theorizing on the novel and on appearance and reality may seem irrelevant.

Pauline Molinier suggested by the "Gérard" (Paul Gide) whose education was put into Gide's hands in 1906 by the boy's mother (*Journal*, January 1, 1907)? In 1905 Gide considered writing a study of him (*Journal*, July 1905).

Not so for the literary critic, who has so emphasized
Edouard's diary and novel (the novel Gide didn't write and
Edouard couldn't) as to all but forget Bernard and Olivier.
The structural novelties of *Les Faux-Monnayeurs*, and the
series of interlocking diaries, have offered critics an unusual
opportunity to discuss technique. There is first of all that
extreme Gidean audacity to be described: the diary within
a novel within a diary within a novel within a diary. There
is also the frankly aesthetic subject of Edouard's "Faux-Monnayeurs," which many critics have taken to be the subject
of Gide's: the struggle between the facts presented by reality
and the ideal reality which a novelist achieves through the
stylization of art. But even Gide's own *Faux-Monnayeurs*
offers a "describable complication." The critic may give a
geometric exposition of Gide's success in writing a "fugue,"
and may point to particular structural ingenuities — the
juxtaposition, for instance, of Edouard's speculations on
counterfeit coins and the actual counterfeit coin in Bernard's
hand. Finally, noting Gide's intention to give a slice of life
in depth, he may insist on the importance of divergent points
of view.

Most of this "technical" criticism has been irrelevant. It
has depended too much on Gide's theoretic pages and too
little on the total impression his novel makes. The obvious
fact is that Edouard's reasonings continue to seem important
and central only to the person writing an essay on Gide. We
have no real opportunity to weigh the difference between
actual life and the pattern Edouard makes of it. We have
only four pages of his novel, and these four pages are dull
enough; at most they give Gide the opportunity to indulge
in very conventional psychological analysis. The ingenuities
cease to seem ingenious after a first reading. And does the
completed novel really take the form of a fugue? There seem
to be instead a series of slow, involuntary changes in manner.
The free "roman d'aventure" of the early chapters surrenders
to the comprehensive panorama of society, and this in turn
surrenders to the *Kunstlerroman*. A further change brings in
Edouard the pedagogical moralist, and the last chapters at-

tempt horror, pathos, tragedy. *Les Faux-Monnayeurs* is not one fugal novel but several fairly distinct novels. Critics have indeed been right to insist on point of view. But the most important structural fact about *Les Faux-Monnayeurs* is its failure to preserve the point of view of the opening chapters. Edouard's task was to achieve a higher reality through the stylization of art. But Gide's task was to write a free, spontaneous, anti-realistic novel unclogged by subjectivity. Bringing in Edouard invited the complications and ingenuities; but also it permitted him to revert to an older manner. Put otherwise, the originality and lasting freshness of *Les Faux-Monnayeurs* does not lie in its novel within a novel, or even in its elaborate over-all structure. To prove this we need turn only to *Point Counter Point*, which shows roughly the same innovations. The great difference is that Huxley's is a realistic novel, intolerably retarded by dialogue, atmosphere, and formal psychological analysis. For many chapters, at least, Gide escapes this realism of texture.

The historic importance of *Les Faux-Monnayeurs* in the general drift away from realism is greater than that of many more daring experiments — and not merely because its author paused to explain what he was doing. Lautréamont or Raymond Roussel could be of major profit only to surrealists as extreme as themselves, but Gide proposed ways of making the ordinary novel more entertaining. His most obvious assaults on realism are in fact his least successful ones. He intended to give his opening chapter a "certain element of the fantastic and supernatural" in order to authorize later "unrealities." [53] But little remains of this effort to make the Luxembourg gardens as "mythical" as the Forest of Arden. The ambulatory Devil virtually disappears; Strouvilhou·is more sinister than Protos, but distinctly less occult. Only Bernard's excursion with the Angel promises a frankly supernatural chapter, but his all-night wrestling match returns it to frayed symbolism. The attempt to shatter realistic illusion is too obvious and too willful, yet too modest. The same thing may be said of the famous chapter. "The Author Reviews His Characters," which so baldly announces its eighteenth-century freedom.

Gide's anti-realism is far more successful where it rests on the actual movement of the story: on the "roving conductor's" witty and intruding presence, on startling abruptness of transition and economy of narrative, on an unabashed use of coincidence. The series of events that leads Bernard to Laura's bedroom and to his meeting with Edouard (Chapters X—XIV) depends on a lost cloakroom ticket, and on Bernard's own alert impudence. What would life be if, in order to penetrate others' lives, we had only to make a wish or rub a magic lamp? These chapters distort life only to render life more amusing. Here for once Edouard's diary serves a dramatic purpose, though the vivacity of Bernard's two chapters makes the realism of the intervening diary seem all the more cumbersome. Coincidence, impudence, surprise, humor, speed — these are the novel's immediate properties, when either Bernard or the roving conductor is on the scene. Then *Les Faux-Monnayeurs* becomes, but with more plausible human beings, another *Caves du Vatican*. Its author recovers, after how many years of effort, the theory of fiction of the young Thomas Hardy. He even achieves some of Hardy's freedom from inhibition.

At the farthest extreme from Hardy, however, Gide controls every impulse to describe at length. "Récits," "soties" and "roman" alike share this impatience with surface, visual realism. "Precision in the reader's imagination should be obtained not by accumulating details but by two or three touches put in exactly the right places." [54] However perfect the description, Edouard realized, the reader will substitute his own picture.[55] Gide found pure realism, with its absence of shadow, banal as well as uneconomical. "Study *first of all* the place from which the light comes; all the shadows will depend on it. Each figure rests in and leans upon its shadow." [56] The one thing to avoid was the clear, constant, explanatory light of traditional realism, which destroys all perspective. The contrary danger is that the use of shadow may become an excuse for defective understanding. The obscurity of Strouvilhou, who remains in the deep shadow of frankly incomplete knowledge, is perhaps more justifiable than the final ambiguity of Armand, whose surrounding shadow is much less dark. But the changing source of light and the changing intensity of that light give to the portrait of Boris a pathos, depth, and uncertainty.*

Claude-Edmonde Magny's brilliant essay on *Les Faux-Monnayeurs* finds in it many of the techniques of the modern motion picture,[57] including calculated variations in the distance of the camera. But this matter of distance returns us — as does very nearly everything else that is successful in the novel's technique — to "point of view," to the central problem of narrating consciousness. The lasting novelty and anti-realism of the novel, and the reasons for its vivacity, lie here. But these matters have been described inaccurately so often that it is necessary to look at them very closely. How many narrators in fact are there? Which of them is the most successful? And how much is gained or lost by the intervention of Edouard and his diary?

1. *The alleged author of "Les Faux-Monnayeurs."* This is the personage who speaks in Chapter VII of the second part, "The Author Reviews His Characters" — the hypothetical author who wonders where the story will take him, who is mildly annoyed by Edouard, and has been disappointed by Bernard, Lady Griffith, and Vincent. Some critics have identified Gide with Edouard, many of them with the "roving conductor," and nearly all of them with this "alleged author." Even Claude-Edmonde Magny takes his judgments

* It would require many pages to analyze the varying intensities of light thrown on Boris, and the depth of the resulting shadows. But the varying sources of light can be outlined briefly. Only the suicide itself is observed directly, objectively: (1) La Pérouse tells Edouard about his grandson; (2) Edouard observes Boris at play with Bronja, and notices hysterical symptoms; (3) Madame Sophroniska tells Edouard of Boris' guilt-feelings; (4) She tells Edouard of his confusion of masturbation and magic; (5) La Pérouse tells Edouard of the child's unhappiness in Paris; (6) the omniscient narrator observes Boris' grief on hearing of Bronja's death; (7) the narrator observes Strouvilhou give the fatal talisman to Ghéridanisol, and thus suggests some unknown connection between Strouvilhou and Boris; (8) the narrator observes the machinations of "The Brotherhood of Strong Men," and sees the suicide of Boris.

to be Gide's — and she is of course right when she says that Gide here attempted an extreme degree of stylization.[58]

But is Gide really as ignorant of his characters' destinies as he claims to be in this chapter? The "alleged author" must be separated from Gide, from the actual author of *Les Faux-Monnayeurs* as we have it. It is Gide who conceives of the ambulatory Devil, who carefully conceals the motivation of Strouvilhou, who drops clues and supplies letters, and who (through Vincent and Lady Griffith) slyly offers the book's most direct thematic image:

> Vincent says there are certain kinds of fish which die according as the water becomes more salt or less, and that there are others, on the contrary, which can live in any degree of salt water; and that they swim about on the edge of the currents, where the water becomes less salt, so as to prey on the others when their strength fails them.[59]

The "alleged author" is less subtle than Gide, has a more primitive curiosity concerning his characters. (The complete identification of Edouard and Gide is still less justified. Edouard is a milder person than Gide, even the relatively tranquil Gide of 1925, and a more rational novelist than he. His refusal to use Boris' suicide in his "Faux-Monnayeurs" is not a merely whimsical dissociation. He would indeed want to find a motive for every act he dramatized. It goes without saying that Gide did see much of himself in Edouard, and often spoke through him.)

2. *The omniscient narrator or "roving conductor."* This is the amusing personage who takes us through the first seven chapters and who appears fitfully thereafter. The problem of fictional identification (half-conscious identification by the author as he writes) is here most interesting for anyone willing to read closely. We know that Lafcadio, who was to have been the narrator, became Bernard at some point in the novel's germination, and in the change lost his "conducting" functions. It would therefore be reasonable to assume a tripartite identification, or to suppose that some of Gide's feeling for this new Lafcadio would carry over into his charac-

terizations of both Bernard and the roving conductor. And this is what we actually find. The roving conductor still betrays a kinship with Bernard. Thus he loses much of his sprightliness after the first three chapters, when the plot turns from Bernard to Vincent. Heretofore Gide's sense of Bernard's energy has carried over to the narrator. But now the roving conductor has lost some of his own flesh and blood. In other words, he could profit from Gide's feelings about Bernard as long as Bernard remained on the scene. This is a rather fine point, which no doubt escaped Gide's attention at the time of writing; it is one of the commonest yet least conscious aspects of novel-writing. One can hazard, more generally and more safely, that the roving conductor inherited much of his impertinence and laconic wit from *Les Caves du Vatican* and from the Lafcadio of that book.

On one occasion this personage foresees the future,* and once he makes the serious mistake of referring to "the body of the book" (thus temporarily fusing with the "alleged author"). In the early chapters, however, his position and personality are distinct. He is truly omnipotent, since he can comment on Bernard's dreams and enter into his waking reveries. But on more than one occasion he disclaims omniscience. "I am not very sure how he and Vincent became acquainted." God both knows and watches, yet protests that man is free. The roving conductor is a camera with a personality and a man reading stage-directions aloud: conducting, observing, and listening to a life that unrolls in an eternal present. He is telling the story, as the events occur before him, not writing a book. Until late in the novel — and it would be hard to overemphasize the importance of this — he speaks in the present tense.

Although he gets about Paris with supernatural ease, the roving conductor has a distinct and very human personality. *Nil admirari?* This ambulatory observer is shocked when the characters are shocked and pleased when they are pleased, yet

---

* "We should have nothing to deplore of all that happened later if only Edouard's and Olivier's joy at meeting had been more demonstrative . . ." (*The Counterfeiters*, p. 70).

he can be shocked or pleased by them. He is the unseen guest at every banquet, the shadow walking at one's elbow. One moment he is watching Bernard, and at the next moment is inside him. But usually he remains outside, an amused ghost who can follow any whim. He walks down the Boulevard St. Michel with Bernard and Olivier, listening to their conversation; then sees Georges Molinier and his friends a few steps away, and follows them instead. He may, as the occasion demands, watch, listen, remember, analyze. The saving grace of his omnipotence is that he knows when not to abuse it: "I should be curious to know what Antoine can have told his friend the cook. But it is impossible to listen to everything. This is the hour appointed for Bernard to go to Olivier. I am not sure where he dined that evening — or even whether he dined at all. He has passed the porter's room without hindrance; he gropes his way stealthily up the stairs. . . ." The plausible speaking voice here masks much complexity. For in these few sentences the narrator has defined himself as a person who can be in only one place at one time, as a fatalist who foreknows Bernard's destiny, as a man ignorant of the immediate past, and as the living observer of action only now occurring. The opening chapters of *Les Faux-Monnayeurs* (which may seem the least self-conscious and most traditional of any) are by far the most complex in artistry.

The roving conductor — and it should be clear by now that he conducts the reader not the characters — addresses us directly. Yet he achieves a fuller illusion by convincing us of his physical presence. "Her parents were right when they said to her: 'You never know your own mind.' Let us leave her. . ." "No, it was not to see his mistress that Vincent Molinier went out every evening. Quickly as he walks, let us follow him." Occasionally he permits himself a few lines of conventional psychological analysis. But the brevity and laconic tone always give, as they do in Stendhal, an overtone of irony. Life may be an ironic adventure, but it is still adventure — and an incomplete adventure if known only from the outside. The distance of the roving conductor from the action varies constantly: from cold omniscience to a sympathetic rephrasing of the characters' thoughts and feelings to a full submersion in them.

This impertinent narrator, a personage both sympathetic and *sympathique*, was an ideal vehicle for Gide's attack on conventional realism. He can maintain a pace as swift as that of *Les Caves du Vatican* and can manage a difficult transition in a few lines: "How hot it is going to be in Paris! It is time to return to Bernard. Here he is, just awaking in Olivier's bed." As a rule we look over his shoulder, at the free present. But now and then he glances back at us. He can interrupt the dialogue of his characters to identify someone who has been mentioned, or to supply us with essential background information — not with a feigned casualness but frankly, at the moment we need it. He even permits himself the economical eighteenth-century convention of summarizing dialogue while seeming to report it (by using the third not the first person). He thus interrupts that "deluge of dialogue" to which James and Edith Wharton had already objected. Even interior monologue is sometimes reduced to the economy of shorthand notation, a reduction which very few novelists have been able to manage successfully. The monologues of Bernard sometimes read like Elizabethan soliloquies. At other times the glib summations serve as parodies of this traditional device for psychological revelation.

The roving conductor, violating all the rules of realism, yet achieves a particular kind of realism. The characters seem (and this is a much rarer occurrence than is commonly supposed) to have an existence independent of the reader, the author, the book. This is not a simple matter, and cannot be explained simply. The conductor rarely conceals his intruding presence and rarely loses his ironic detachment. He never stays long in one place or with one character; he offers us little of the surface texture of life and none of its connective ligaments. He leaves few important psychological facts in shadow, but leaves everything else to the reader's imagination: faces, voices, atmospheres. Perhaps Gide's intention was, once again, to involve the reader by making him fill in the details. But the effect is exactly the opposite. Carried at such a swift pace, the reader ceases to care about these details. The result is to repel reader-identification and involvement almost completely, and to conceal the identification and involvement of the author. Thus the classic achievement of the realistic novel, to insert the reader in the action and make him one of the characters, is almost wholly lost. But the characters of the novel — so freed from both reader and author, seen as it were by chance, so integrally keeping their distance — lead lives which are all the more independent. We look at them over the narrator's shoulder, yes. But they go on living after we have looked away. Bernard exists apart from us as palpably and unpredictably as Candide or Trabb's boy. No reader would be satisfied by a steady diet of such "unrealistic" realism. We want, after all, to be involved more intimately in lives which are not our own. But we can rejoice in its occasional appearance — whether in the *Arabian Nights* or Stendhal or Voltaire, or here fitfully in Gide — as perhaps the purest form of fictional *creation*.

3. *Edouard and his diary.* The diary represents, to a degree that has not been sufficiently emphasized, a concession to subjectivity and old-fashioned realism. Admittedly the *Kunstlerroman* asks for some equivalent of Philip Quarles's notebook or of Mark Rampion's didactic harangues. Admittedly too Edouard's diary has a real value for anyone interested in the art of fiction. But the first seven chapters of *Les Faux-Monnayeurs* promised something much more interesting than an intelligent *Kunstlerroman*. Edouard's diary is deplorable precisely because it interrupts the "roman d'aventure" and even threatens to destroy it. How much is gained in compensation? Perhaps the roving conductor could not have achieved some of Edouard's deeper tones: the pathos of Pauline, La Pérouse, and Armand, or the story of his own love for Olivier. We could further defend the diary by saying that Edouard's abstract discussion of "depersonalization" (Chapter VIII) offers a necessary respite, after so much swiftly dramatized action, or that the dark realism of his visits to La Pérouse is a necessary preparation for the tragedies of Armand

and Boris. Finally, we could argue that the didactic Edouard saved the roving conductor from all obligation to moralize and explain. Edouard's digressive impurity as a narrator left the roving conductor's purity intact.

This is a dangerous hypothesis, however — improper because it exists outside the book as we have it. What we do have, in Edouard's diary, is a distinct recession to an older manner and to the devices Gide found easiest: narrative in the first person or through letters and diaries, slow realism, an intelligent brooding on the action. The paradox of Gide's most obvious innovation is that it readmits and even invites the techniques he was trying to avoid. The retrospective diary permitted anything. It invited the conventional realism of minutely described appearance.* It permitted the realism and pathos of Edouard's interview with Pauline (Part III, Chapter VI), a chapter almost wholly written in dialogue. It encouraged the filling in of background and motivation. It permitted incessant recapitulation and the old "flashback" in a novel whose chief charm was its presentness. (Even the roving conductor, reappearing after so many pages of the diary and corrupted as it were by it, talks to us in the past tense.) Finally, it allowed Gide to indulge in prolonged psychological analysis. Edouard was a vehicle through whom he could indulge all his most familiar temptations — the temptations to realism, to careful ordering and elaboration, to the intelligent "roman-à-thèse." The plausible drama of everyday suffering observed by Edouard is interesting and moving; we would have, without him, a less complete impression of life. But is a more ample "impression of life" the achievement that, in this particular book, matters? Many other novelists in our time have attained the sympathy which Edouard conveys, and at least a few have offered refractions of experience as subtle and as intelligent as his. But the first

---

* "La Pérouse opened the door. He was in his shirt sleeves and was wearing a sort of yellowish whitish night-cap on his head, which I finally made out to be an old stocking (Madame de la Pérouse's no doubt) tied in a knot, so that the foot dangled on his cheek like a tassel. He was holding a bent poker in his hand" (*The Counterfeiters*, p. 107).

seven chapters of *Les Faux-Monnayeurs* are unique in their
swiftness and vivacity. There is nothing quite like them in
our century of gloomy fiction. They fulfill at last and though
briefly Gide's old wish — to rival the energy and pure creativity of Stendhal.

Thus Gide did realize, through many pages of *Les Faux-
Monnayeurs* and *Les Caves du Vatican*, one of his major
ambitions as a novelist: to thwart or surmount his natural
creative impulses, and so write the kind of objective irresponsible fiction he was little equipped to write. He did
briefly move as far as possible from the isolated dreamy introspectiveness of *André Walter*, from the therapeutic re-crea-
tion of personal experience, from conventional realism and
explicit psychologizing, from the lucid "roman-à-thèse." As
a novelist too Gide's moral principle was "to follow his slope,
upward"; to exploit his impulses by combating them. We
may choose to call this effort heroic, puritanic, or merely
perverse. But it did directly parallel the political refusal of
easy commitment and the psychic refusal of self-satisfied repose. As a man faced by political and religious choices, as
an autobiographer bent over his own troubled image, and
as a novelist with particular aptitudes, Gide refused to accept
easy or "natural" solutions.

The lesson is an important one, and the example has a
certain austere magnificence. But we cannot judge a work
of art or a career by the amount of difficulty overcome. Gide's
partial awareness of his own limits and temptations did of
course help him. When indulged fully, they led to *André
Walter* and *L'Ecole des femmes*, to confused autobiography,
and the oversimplified problem novel. But *Les Faux-Monnayeurs*, the culmination of Gide's self-denying aesthetic, is
not his greatest book. Like Edouard, he wanted to write a
novel which should be "as particular and at the same time
as general, as human and as fictitious as *Athalie*, as *Tartuffe*
or *Cinna*." [60] He did achieve this universality, but achieved
it in *L'Immoraliste*. This highly subjective book is frankly
devoted to one particular inward destiny, and is so ruthlessly

and classically ordered that it suppresses many aspects of life. And yet it leaves us with the sense of a universal experience exhaustively explored; it is tragedy. It seems to offer, as do the best novels of Conrad and even Hardy, a final vision of human difficulties.

L'Immoraliste is one of the greatest realistic novels of the century; the opening chapters of *Les Faux-Monnayeurs* and parts of *Les Caves du Vatican* are among the triumphs of modern anti-realism. Few writers have succeeded so fully in manners so radically different. Yet the first fact that imposes itself, if we try for an over-all estimate, is the unevenness of Gide's achievement as a novelist. These three novels, but only these three, seem likely to survive on their own merits, in company with *Si le grain ne meurt*, the *Journal*, and a few other autobiographical or quasi-autobiographical works.[*] Prediction is more than usually hazardous where it deals with a writer whose appeal is often to the half-conscious anxieties and longings of his readers. But surely few important novelists have written books as superficial and as dull as *L'Ecole des femmes*, *Robert*, and *Geneviève*. *La Porte étroite* may find the quiet continuing life of *Madame de Mauves*, of *Under the Greenwood Tree*, of *The Shadow-Line*. But the other "récits," *Isabelle* and *La Symphonie pastorale*, are too slight and too easily mastered by even the casual reader. No doubt they will "survive," but only because they were written by Gide.

If we look on Gide in these over-all terms, and as a novelist only, certain limitations become apparent at once. The one specific and glaring formal weakness — the fatal signature, so to speak — was a tendency to hurry or telescope endings. Where other and greater novelists have commonly overextended their last chapters, Gide shortened his to a mere outline. The abrupt endings of *Les Caves du Vatican* and *Les Faux-Monnayeurs* leave us suspended disturbingly, with unsolved problems on our hands. They have some of the effec-

---

[*] *Paludes* and especially *Saül*, two of Gide's personal favorites, have virtually disappeared. *Le Prométhée mal enchaîné*, also little read today, may well be "rediscovered" before them.

tiveness of Elizabeth Bowen's abrupt and frightening endings
— frightening, chiefly, because life obviously goes on after
we close the book. But the final pages of *La Porte étroite*,
Isabelle, and *La Symphonie pastorale* narrow life to undramatized abstraction. Even the ending of *L'Immoraliste* is
truncated — though the defect is covered by a gravity of tone
and a finality of style. Was Gide afraid of boring his readers
through overtreatment? Or, now bored himself, did he long
to get on to the next book? A third possibility is that he knew
too clearly what he wanted to say in these final chapters, and
had fully imagined his climatic scenes too long before coming
to write them.

This is a relatively small matter, though it suggests one of
the dangers to fiction of an excessive thematic lucidity. The
most serious general limitation was a particular kind of subjectivity, an introspectiveness of talent and imagination. This
is a commonplace of Gide criticism, and one which particularly annoyed Gide himself, but it has its large measure of
truth. The commonplace does need to be redefined. In the
first place, a subjective imagination is not necessarily sterile;
the fictional worlds of Melville, Dostoevsky, and Faulkner
are fuller than those of Jane Austen, Trollope, and Arnold
Bennett. It is also a mistake to insist too strongly on the use
of direct personal experience, though this has its symptomatic
importance. Even the frankly autobiographical and therapeutic novel may be a great novel. The two important questions to ask are whether the novelist can universalize his
private situation or dilemma, and whether he can recreate
with intensity a situation or dilemma that no longer seriously
troubles him. Every book after *André Walter* shows the uni-
versalizing power, the ability to present a personal difficulty
in large human terms. Most of all, of course, the "spiritual
autobiographies" show it. They are triumphs of intelligence.
And they remain rich and intense as long as they are directly
autobiographical (*Si le grain ne meurt*) or as long as they
operate in poetic or symbolic terms (*Le Retour de l'enfant
prodigue, Thésée*, et cetera). But the answer to the second
question must be very different. Gide could not, when writing

ordinary unsymbolic fiction, recreate sufferings that were long past. At fifty he could think intelligently about the twenty-year-old he had been. But he could not become again that twenty-year-old. One feels that Dostoevsky and even Thomas Mann never fully solved their youthful maladjustments, and so could refashion them ,endlessly. Or, at least, they had a great power of imaginative memory. But Gide's long psychiatric effort to define his own troubles may have been, for the purposes of the novelist, only too successful.

He could not, then, dramatize with intensity, in ordinary fiction, a self that had long ceased to exist. A kindred and more obvious limitation was his inability to dramatize subjectively persons very different from himself.* He understood the stupid narrators of *La Symphonie pastorale* and *Robert*, but could not share their stupidity imaginatively; could not, for the time of writing, become them. This is, one must repeat, his great difference from Dostoevsky and even Flaubert; he could not give a fool his due. Even the fool, the fool perhaps most of all, has his ample share of complexity, of whimsical longings and vagrant dreams. He can become, in the pages of Dostoevsky, heroic and almost tragic. But Gide, seeing only the mental failings, sums the fool up in bare intellectual terms and through transparent motivations. Great fiction must be intelligent. But *La Symphonie pastorale* and *Robert* are intelligent in a merely demonstrative way. They totally fail to convey the waywardness of every human being, his unpredictable not predictable folly. Dostoevsky could enter into and so create subjectively hundreds of fools, each a little different from the rest; subjectively, Gide could create none.

His only solution was to create them objectively and through economical, classical satire; Anthime Armand-Dubois, Amédée Fleurissoire, and even M. Profitendieu are slight but real successes. No important character in Gide's fiction, however, is thus created wholly from the outside. The most obvious clue to Gide's incorrigibly introspective talent

---

* It is useful to recall here, once again, how much of "self" went into the portrait of Alissa.

is his dependence on the diary or letter or confession as a narrative device. He naïvely argued that to write the diary of a person very different from himself proved his gift for "depersonalization." But the really "depersonalized" creative act is very different; the novelist remains at once within and without and dramatizes subjectively not one character but many. The natural inclination of the introspective novelist is to place himself inside *one* of his characters, and then write in *the first person*. The alternative of *Les Caves du Vatican* and *Les Faux-Monnayeurs* — and for the reader weary of slow realism it was a splendid solution — was the only one open to Gide: to remove from life all its density and texture, to reduce inward confusion to the economy of shorthand or to the objectivity of the motion picture. Gide could say a great deal through this photographic method. But when he wanted to take us inside Olivier, he provided Olivier with the occasion to write a letter.

All this suggests, one must admit, that radical lack of inventive power which most of Gide's critics have observed. For the third of a century between *André Walter* and *Les Faux-Monnayeurs* we have some two hundred thousand words of fiction — and only four characters of any depth: Michel, Jérôme, Alissa, and Lafcadio. Even if we include the minor Gérard and the unconvincing pastor, and such background figures of suffering as Marceline, Juliette, Amélie, and Gertrude, the list remains brief. Ménalque and Protos are not, properly speaking, human beings at all. Only the caricatured "sots" of *Les Caves du Vatican* have some of the brittle yet immediate vitality of innumerable minor figures in Balzac and Dickens. And once we descend to the characters whom Gide himself sees as minor, we are offered only names. Neither the nature of these concentrated novels nor Gide's subjectivity wholly explains the poverty of invention. What novels could be more subjective or more serious than *Notes from Underground* or *The Castle*? Yet life crowds onto their pages — the palpable, swarming, irrepressible lives of innkeepers, bureaucrats, tradesmen, valets, waiters, prostitutes. No doubt Gide's "récits" and psychological tragedies are

purer for their isolation and lack of rich background — and
certainly *L'Immoraliste* would have been weakened by any
fuller treatment of the Moktirs or Alcides. But even the ambitious world of *Les Faux-Monnayeurs* is, compared with the
world of *The Possessed* or that of *Nostromo*, a very small one.
Statistics rarely prove much, but they can prove or disprove
inventiveness. The number of successfully dramatized human
beings, from *André Walter* through *Geneviève*, is extremely
small. Yet some of them (the patient, suffering, and benighted
wife, for instance) appear again and again.

Inventiveness is not, to be sure, the most important of the
novelist's properties — though Gide would seem to have
thought so when he described Simenon as the greatest French
novelist of our time.* Not merely Balzac but also Alexandre
Dumas had infinitely greater inventive powers than Flaubert,
created many more living personages. André Gide does remain, for all his limitations, one of the important novelists
of the century. Much of the importance is a critical or exemplary one; the beginner can learn more from Gide than
he can learn from Proust or Joyce or Kafka. Gide's assault
on realism was relatively moderate, yet more useful to the
fellow novelist than anyone else's — his demonstration, especially, that minute description and painstaking transition
are generally useless.

We find this important lesson in the novels, but also in
the *Journal* and the critical essays. Gide has written more
originally and more lucidly about the problems of his craft
than any novelist since Henry James; the lucubrations of
E. M. Forster are amateurish in comparison. We shall consider Gide's influence briefly in the next chapter. In the direct
terms of his own achievement — Gide raised and solved
problems of "stylization" and anti-realism which still puzzle

* Letter to the author of May 16, 1947: "J'aurais voulu vous parler encore
de bien des choses: de Proust, entre autres, si important sans doute, mais qui
n'a jamais quitté les données fournies par la réalité; n'a pas, que je sache,
inventé, créé, un seul personnage; à mon avis, mémorialiste, à la manière de
Saint-Simon, et non pas précisément romancier.

"J'aurais voulu vous parler aussi de Simenon, à mon avis, notre plus
grand romancier aujourd'hui, *vrai* romancier."

experimental novelists today. And he exploited the technique
of the "imperceptive narrator" more thoughtfully than any
of his contemporaries. He proved that the distorted narrative
— which, because distorted, demands an alert correcting
reader — need be neither diffuse nor confused. He thus gave
new urgency to the old lesson that the novelist must not "explain"; that some obstacle must exist between the creative
understanding of the novelist and the groping understanding
of his reader.

Must we conclude that Gide was, as a novelist, a great
teacher? A subtle critic only, and healthy corrective influence?
Something else obviously exists in his novels, which accounts
for the amount of disturbance they cause. This "something"
is, I suspect, their psychological interest and accuracy. Like
Conrad, the young Gide did not read Freud or his disciples.
He nevertheless dramatized the unending buried struggle
between conscious intention and unconscious need, the forms
which uncalculated self-destructiveness may take, the minute
workings of repression and sublimation, the "gratuitous acts"
of unconscious identification. Intuitive knowledge and successful introspection served Gide better than close study
served others — as the wearied reader of Lawrence's *The Fox*
or Huxley's *Point Counter Point* may verify. The largely fictitious psychology of Faulkner (which posits not merely a
collective unconscious memory but a collective unconscious
foreknowledge) is more amusing and dramatically perhaps
more serviceable. And the old-fashioned introspections and
associations of Proust certainly lend themselves better to
poetic effect. But Gide's "human nature" is the one with
which we must live. He never consciously explored the unconscious, as a few of his contemporaries did. No doubt this
is another limitation. But his intuitive psychology has been
discredited at not a single point. He has been the most accurate of fictional psychologists, though by no means the most
ambitious.

Even this, however, would not account for the lasting
strength of *L'Immoraliste*. Charles Jackson's *The Lost Week-
end* (another intelligent study of self-destructiveness) already

seems dated. Most important of all, in Gide's deceptively simple and "limited" books, is a continued appeal to the "fringes of the reader's consciousness"; an evocation of the reader's preconscious or half-conscious fears, anxieties, longings. The appeal would have been impossible, had Gide condescended to "explain," as nearly all his contemporaries explained. But even more persuasive than this calculated reticence was style: the appeal based on image and the cluster of image, on words and their overtones, on the rhythm of the sentence, on the very movement of syntax. Even the early *Voyage d'Urien* creates complicated feelings, and *L'Immoraliste* has disturbed every serious reader. Gide's abstract conceptions of character and his plots often speak to our waking intellects. But his style acts more personally. The ultimate grounds for Gide's strength lie in subtleties which no English translation can capture; Gide can be paraphrased but not translated.

Where then does the novelist stand? His achievement is more difficult to "locate" than that of more original writers, Kafka or Faulkner for instance. Mauriac and Montherlant show some of Gide's limitations, and they too apply an exquisite art and style to very small though quite different worlds. Certainly their novels maintain a more even level of competence than Gide's. But neither Mauriac or Montherlant begins to show the psychological understanding and tragic energy of *L'Immoraliste*, or the vivacity and intelligence of *Les Faux-Monnayeurs*. E. M. Forster invites comparison — not the conventional Forster of *A Passage to India*, but the sprightly, stylizing anti-realist of the earlier novels. Forster's cool, intelligent stories of half-emancipated puritans offer a very mild version of Gide's hedonism; they handle disturbing problems with the lightness of the "soties." The anti-realism of technique is also similar to Gide's, and deliberately repels reader-involvement in the same ways: through the elimination of realistic texture, through abruptness of transition, through the intrusion of a personalized narrator or author, through the use of extreme coincidence. But everything comparable with Gide is, in Forster, slender, suave, evasive.

Mauriac was incapable of *L'Immoraliste's* tragedy. But Forster was incapable even of *La Porte étroite's* concentrated sympathy and gravity of tone.

One can thus assume, safely enough, that Gide is a more important novelist than Mauriac, Montherlant, and Forster. And we can assume as safely that he does not belong with his masters Dostoevsky and Stendhal. His position lies somewhere between. Already his novels seem timeless compared with the dated "spiritual histories" of Huxley and even Malraux. But they have not vastly widened our sensibilities, as the novels of Joyce, Kafka, and Faulkner have. The novel of the future, the psychological novel especially, may well follow Gide's example, rather than the ponderous embroidery and endless introspections of Proust and Mann. Yet the very bulk of their achievement makes up for the bulkiness of any given page, and no doubt marks their work for survival. And Conrad — who anticipated many of Gide's psychological insights, and who showed at times as perfect a form and style? The most obvious difference is that Conrad (though he too found it difficult to treat subjectively persons very different from himself) created a much larger fictional world. Above all he had a metaphysical strength, and a freedom from speculative inhibition, which Gide usually lacked. His novels of individual destinies are also stories of man's destiny. His very plots follow universal and even mythical patterns. A story of squalid crime and native intrigue, or a story of heroic initiation to the sea, may become (whatever Conrad intended) a drama of the unconscious and half-conscious life. The intelligent Conrad feared that "demon" whom the intelligent Gide tried to raise, but it was Conrad who successfully used him. And here too, as with Mann, the mere weight of a wide and varied achievement must tell. Gide might have written *The Shadow-Line* but could not have written *The Nigger of the Narcissus*; could perhaps have written *Under Western Eyes* but certainly not *Lord Jim* or *Nostromo*.

The conclusion is not one I like to draw, but it seems to me inescapable — that Conrad and Mann will survive as novelists, but Gide as a man of letters who wrote novels: two interesting and amusing novels and one great one. He will also survive (and this imposes a last and difficult inquiry) as a dominant "force" and "influence," as one of those who helped fashion the twentieth-century mind.

5 THE CORRUPTOR OF YOUTH

WE HAVE LOOKED AT GIDE'S WORK IN terms of its intrinsic values and meanings, and with scant attention to the changing demands of readers. But now we must desert criticism for the impressionism of literary history. With Hardy and Conrad, one could confine himself to the achieved works of art and the achieved psychological and moral findings. Both Hardy and Conrad have had some influence on the technique of the modern novel, have perhaps even left some mark on our ways of feeling. But neither of these magnificently old-fashioned moralists has directly affected our understanding of the twentieth century. With André Gide the situation is very different. For here we must reckon with a writer who has modified our ideas and attitudes, and whose energy has been felt by people who care nothing about the art of fiction. Even the personal history, the actual curve of this one man's life, has troubled or comforted many, and for better or worse been "exemplary."

A lesser novelist than either Hardy or Conrad, Gide has had a much greater spiritual influence than either. To weigh him as a novelist and intuitive psychologist only would be comparable to dismissing Voltaire as a storyteller and stylist.

And even the critic interested chiefly in the fortunes of the novel must take this fact of spiritual influence into account. For something has happened to the novel, which Conrad dimly foresaw. Many contemporary novelists have assumed the obligations of the nineteenth-century essayist and poet, the obligations of a Carlyle or Tennyson. They propose to save or corrupt us, and to do so not simply and gently but with the utmost rigor. Even at its most amusing, the best modern fiction is intellectually serious. It is seldom possible, now, to separate a good novelist's mind from his art, as one could still do with Hardy. Such a novelist as Gide affects us not merely because he embodies certain attitudes, but because he offers them in a certain way. Were he a lesser stylist, Gide would have less spiritual influence. To many readers his style composes a voice speaking intimately, seemingly only to them, and so insisting upon a response. We may enjoy Hardy, we may very well be troubled by Conrad. But we are bound to resist Gide, or at least to be much disquieted.

A study of Gide's influence has a further interest. It points to important differences between the cultural life of France and the United States. For an "American Gide" is as difficult to imagine as an American Jeffrey Aspern. There is a time for serious reflection and a time for art and revery; Americans do not like to think of the novelist as a "force," or as anything but a novelist. Henry James was a "man of letters" in the European manner — critic, essayist, and dramatist as well as novelist — and he did write however reticently about his spiritual development. But the American novelist (and reader) of today deeply distrusts such versatility, such intimacy, such intellectual pretension. The novelist should rather be a craftsman, an impersonal and expert storyteller, working preferably in solitude. He should protect himself from critics and professors, and even from vain contacts with his fellow writers. The isolation of Faulkner in Oxford has been far greater than Conrad's isolation in Kent, greater even than Hardy's in Dorchester. Only the writers' projects of the thirties, and only a few universities and writers' conferences in our own day, have brought novelists together or provoked them to public controversy. There have been a very few novelist–men-of-letters, such as Robert Penn Warren and Thornton Wilder. But not even the versatile Warren has published a "journal intime" or taken upon himself the exemplary Gidean role.

Only the subjective and autobiographical Hemingway, in fact, has worked on our intellects and imaginations in the way that Gide and Thomas Mann, through their lives as through their writings, have worked on the European mind. And what has been Hemingway's message and example? A severe anti-intellectualism, a mask of toughness, the incontaminate seclusion of Key West or Cuba, an aesthetic approach to the political crises of our time, the stoicism of a lonely and baffled man. Half-educated and immune to criticism, belonging to no cultural community and in some instances belonging nowhere, the American novelist between the two wars was in no position to present a reasoned *criticism of life* or to incarnate public dilemmas. He was impelled to express, rather, a *tragic vision of life* and to document the alien injustice which surrounded him. He was often closer to the worker than the European novelist could be. But for that very reason he had less to say to an elite — or to a young intellectual of twenty, casting about for a way of life and for a "directeur de conscience."

The very conception of the exemplary role or the exemplary conflict is foreign to our way of thinking — the notion that two writers could, through their private quarrels, sum up public dilemmas and so offer enlightenment. To find an American analogy to certain debates among European intellectuals, we must look to the Hiss-Chambers affair, imagine the trial occurring eight or ten years earlier, and imagine Hiss and Chambers as novelists. Then only can we conceive of that ruthless exploration of private and public motive which sharpens European controversies and makes them "exemplary." Over the terrible hostility and alienation of many years Gide and Paul Claudel yet agreed to publish their correspondence. For they both recognized that their intimate debate had a symbolic and exemplary value which transcended their personalities. Not their individual lives but the representative curves of their lives now mattered. And what French writer of the twentieth century has not, in some sense, been exemplary? Has not, like Claudel and Gide, tried to incarnate and so clarify the moral issues of our time? Péguy, Valéry, Maritain, Maurras, Alain, Breton, Cocteau, Max Jacob — and, among novelists, Romain Rolland, Barrès, Bourget, Proust, Malraux, Bernanos, Mauriac, Aragon, Céline, Julian Green, Giono, Jouhandeau, Montherlant, Saint-Exupéry, Sartre, Camus, and (after all) Maurice Sachs and Jean Genêt — most of these writers have taken us into their confidence, usually with frank self-portraits. Nearly all underwent important crises and changes of attitude, and made their private suasions and resistances matters of public interest. Nearly all have given answers to the question, "How to be?"

They have been, for better or worse, moralists; even the most primitive have been intellectually primitive. Meeting constantly and alike formed by a rigidly intellectualist education, these writers naturally turned to debate, and their debates inevitably became public. The result, it might seem, was a dilution of purely creative talent and energy. Faulkner might never have achieved *Light in August*, had he seen his experiments subjected to the ruthless French irony or had he passed through the Lycée Henri IV. On the other hand, this atmosphere of representative controversy has incomparably enriched French spiritual life. Even the slender Jacques Rivière has, in his one completed novel, something "important to say." The French atmosphere, better for the reader who is not a novelist, may be worse for the highly original artist. But only in such a European atmosphere could André Gide's influence have exerted itself so strongly.

Given this favorable atmosphere — the provocatively close association of writers, and a long tradition of looking to writers for guidance — the extent of Gide's influence still remains puzzling. His influence before the first war was out of all proportion to the small number of books sold, and his subsequent impact far greater than the abstracted message of the books would seem to warrant. The friendly *Hommage à André Gide* (1928) naturally accepts its subject as one of the great forces of French spiritual life. But even the frankly hostile *Latinité*, by devoting one of its 1931 issues to the problem of Gide's influence, testified at least to the strength of a legend. "It would be impossible to imagine the life of European youth in the third and fourth decades of this century without Gide," wrote Erich Ebermeyer, one of the *Latinité* contributors.[1] To Jean Cassou, Gide had accomplished, thanks to his "representative character and the universality of each of his experiences," a revolution comparable to those of Montaigne, Nietzsche, Rousseau, and Rimbaud.[2] The *Latinité* survey, which published in good faith even such embarrassing answers as these, was conducted among creative writers and professional critics. Still more surprising has been the response of unprofessional readers, many of whom sought out Gide to confess to him and ask advice. More books and more articles have been written about Gide than about almost any modern writer, and a number of these have been written by relative amateurs. Their analyses often read like autobiographies, the records of troubled souls wrestling with a personal angel or devil. At a more austere level we have the testimony of Claudel and Maritain, the two most jealous missionaries of the time, and their long effort to convert Gide. The conversion of a Maurice Sachs or a Jean Cocteau was spectacular enough. But Gide's conversion — the subjugation of an attitude rather than a pose — was the one which would have mattered.

In 1931 a few of the *Latinité* contributors could deny any influence at all, or could point hopefully to signs of indifference in the younger generation. Today the fact of an enormous influence on three generations is almost universally admitted. But the exact nature of this influence has never been analyzed, and names are rarely named. Henri Massis, whose whole career has been darkened by Gide's success, wrote a chapter called "L'Influence d'André Gide"; the chapter is merely another attack on Gide's ideas. So too did Gide's former secretary Yvonne Davet. But her chapter is limited to *Les Nourritures terrestres,* and devotes many pages to Gide's own attitude toward his book. Roger Martin du Gard offers one of the shrewdest analyses of Gide's persuasiveness, yet mentions no particular disciples. Are the exact contours of Gide's influence as difficult to trace as the contours of his thought, his psychology, his style? Or is the influence so general as to seem indefinable in particular terms? The subject, in any event, is one which will occupy future scholars and historians. The pages to follow offer no more than an outline, and a few skeptical warnings.

It is important to distinguish, at the outset, between *spiritual influence* (a general working on the mind and imagination of others) and that kind of specific *literary influence* which so preoccupies and bemuses scholars: the alleged direct transference from one writer to another of plot and attitude, of literary technique, even at times of phrasing. Such particularized transference need not detain us long. It is almost never recoverable with any accuracy and seldom has, when partially recovered, any serious interest. The important direct influences operate so deviously and so obscurely (often by reaction not imitation) that not the most minute and most imaginative scholarship can discover them. The real "source" for a chapter or even a whole novel may be a single sentence or page in a book opened by chance and at once put down.*

Direct literary influence is often most tangible where most minute, particular, and technical. And most interesting, perhaps, where we can observe the natural creative impulses of the disciple (or his natural deficiencies) assert themselves — after a few chapters of imitation — against the lesson of the master. We can hazard that *L'Immoraliste* exerted the same kind of influence on the opening chapters of Jacques Rivière's *Aimée* (1922) and Jacques Chardonne's *Eva* (1930). Both novels begin as compact retrospective "récits" of disturbed married lives, told in the first person. Both narrators are

---

* The dangerous consequences of source-hunting are legion. One of the least obvious but most serious is a natural inclination to interpret the meaning of a book in terms of its alleged source's meaning.

under the illusion that they are happily married. Just as the Ménalque of Gide intervenes to preach sincerity, rebellion, and pleasure (thus tipping Michel's scale toward anarchy), so Rivière's Georges Bourguignon intervenes in the life of François to preach exactly the same things.[3] And so too Chardonne's Etienne intervenes, to accuse the narrator of sacrificing integrity to a docile married life. At this point, however, the three books diverge. Rivière's novel becomes even more frankly a study of self-destructiveness than Gide's, while Chardonne's novel moves toward other Gidean themes and situations. It becomes an anecdotal story of sexual disgust and extreme self-delusion. As works of art the three books diverge even more sharply. Both disciples desert the admirable economy of their first chapters: Rivière to indulge his evil genius of abstract psychological analysis, Chardonne to indulge mere random recollection and meditative aside. Neither manages to maintain his intense concentration on the character of the narrator himself.

Rivière's *Aimée* repays further attention, if only because it illustrates some of the dangers latent in the study of literary influence. After its economical first chapters, *Aimée* recalls *La Porte étroite* even more than *L'Immoraliste*. Like Alissa, Aimée suffers a traumatic experience of sexual horror, and like Alissa she is hardened, isolated, and compelled to reject pleasure. We know less of François's childhood than of Jérôme's, little more than that he was reticent and given to idealization. But where Jérôme's adult passivity is unconscious, and deliberately shadowed by Gide, François's passivity is wholly conscious and is fully described (though not understood) by Rivière. François has a "perversity of a psychological order"; he does "not like happiness" and feels a "longing for misfortune." He is drawn to Aimée by their common love of rejection, "the perversity which brought us together." François at one point even formulates the plight he shared with Jérôme: "A man as unaggressive as I am . . ."[4] A lack of normal masculine aggressiveness caused the tragedy of *Aimée,* as it caused the tragedies of *La Porte étroite* and *Madame de Mauves.*

The student of influences, making these conjunctions, would certainly assume that Rivière saw this passivity in Gidean terms; that he could have written just such a contemptuous comment on François's flabbiness as Gide wrote on the flabbiness of Jérôme. The facts are very different. When he spoke of a "man as unaggressive as I am," Rivière was writing autobiography not fiction. In the letters to Alain-Fournier, Gide, and Claudel he not merely admitted his self-destructiveness but cherished it. His love of deprivation was self-pitying; the ego, by surviving its own flagellations, asserted its courage and strength. The impartial reader of *Aimée* might well arrive at just such an understanding of François. But the student of influence, noting the resemblances between the two novels, would probably credit *Aimée* with the mature psychological understanding of *La Porte étroite*.

The most solid ground we can stand on is that of technique: the transmission from one novelist to another of tactics and strategy. But here too the student of influence is tempted to prove too much. There is, for instance, the temptation to infer, from an apparent influence on technique, influences of a more general nature. Very probably the opening chapters of *Les Faux-Monnayeurs* affected the opening chapters of *Saint-Saturnin* (1931), an excellent novel by Gide's friend Jean Schlumberger. We have, after the first three pages, the same abrupt introduction of the characters; the same use of the present tense for immediacy and economy; the same unusual point of view of an unseen but vivacious narrator or "roving conductor," curious concerning the actors yet free to address the reader, a camera-eye approaching and withdrawing impudently. Schlumberger's narrator conducts the reader not the action (which is already *there*); he can only wish and protest, or speculate on the free life of an unfolding present. Like Gide, Schlumberger finds it impossible to sustain this difficult point of view throughout. He violates it much as does Gide: by moving directly into the characters' minds ("Méditation de Nicolas," "Méditation de Jenny Cheu"); by letters which take the place of summaries in the past tense, and even, as in the sixth chapter, by direct retrospection.

Confronted by such a marked resemblance in technique, we are tempted to look further. And now the follies and paranoid fantasies of old William may seem to be those of La Pérouse, and his impulse to destroy his own estate a reminiscence of Michel's. Both William and Michel take pleasure in the wanton felling of valuable trees. The narrator argues that William's savage outbreak in old age was caused by his lifetime of repression and orderly devotion to duty. What assumption could be more Gidean than this one? Our ground is very shaky now, but having progressed thus far there is no reason to stop. Only the deracinated adventurer Gilbert de Sinnis can save the family, as Claude-Edmonde Magny observes,[5] and the loyal Nicolas feels he has thrown his life away. Can we not then infer that Schlumberger shares all of Gide's feelings about close-knit families and in fact derived his attitudes from Gide? Perhaps. But it is much more plausible to recognize that William is even more Dostoevskian (or Faulknerian) than Gidean in his eccentricities, and that the stubborn self-denying Nicolas is a heroic figure. The problems raised by Gide may well have affected Schlumberger's choice of situations to dramatize, and so too Gide's reminder that novelists ignore the drama and pathos of senility. But it would be unwise to assert, more precisely than this, that the meaning of *Les Faux-Monnayeurs* had influenced *Saint-Saturnin's* meaning.

Literary historians will no doubt discover many such instances of limited but specific influence on particular novelists of the twentieth century, though the task of separating direct influence from indirect will become increasingly difficult. How directly, or through how many intermediaries and modulations, did the idea of the "acte gratuit" pass . . . from Gide's *Prométhée mal enchaîné* to Sartre's *Le Sursis?* How can we measure the share of *Les Faux-Monnayeurs* in the complex omnivorous structure of Sartre's novel, as against the share of *The Possessed,* of *Ulysses,* of *U.S.A.* or *Light in*

August? Rather than answer such questions precisely, scholars may find it more useful to assess, very generally, Gide's share in the literary changes of his time. Not Lafcadio but Dostoevsky's Kirilov may be the ultimate ancestor of Camus's Meursault, who shot an Arab without knowing why he did it. Who can tell? Perhaps not even Camus, who admires both Dostoevsky and Gide. But we can say that Gide deeply affected the French understanding of Dostoevsky. And we can say that he sharply increased our understanding of the "inexplicable act" as an act which can be explained only in terms of subrational needs and conflicts.

In the most general terms and the briefest: Gide helped perhaps more than any other writer to liquidate the symbolist heritage profitably, and to encourage both experiment and a new classicism. But how? It is already impossible to assign to each phase of Gide's activity its proper share: his personal help and encouragement (paying the publication costs of Jammes's first play, for instance, or "placing" unpublished authors, or advising such successful ones as Roger Martin du Gard and Julian Green); his editorial work for *L'Ermitage* and the *Nouvelle Revue française*; his lectures and critical essays, with their tendentious revaluations and insights; his systematic effort on behalf of disorderly foreign authors; his insistence that the new classicism be dissociated from the moral and political conservatism of Maurras and Brunetière. The least obvious role may have been the most important one: his share in the literary magazines. For it is in the pages of the "little" *Ermitage* and *Revue blanche*, as well as in those of the *Mercure de France* and the *Nouvelle Revue française*, that literary history occurs: those minute shiftings of current which may presently become floods.[6] We must weigh, against all this, the example of Gide's own creative example: his own withdrawal from symbolism, his own parallel movement toward surrealism and toward a new classicism.

This was not a solitary withdrawal or a solitary progress. It is therefore important to separate Gide's changing positions from the mannered *naturisme* of Saint-Georges de Bouhélier, from Jarry's purely destructive absurdity, and from Moréas's retreat to an imitative neoclassicism. No doubt Gide's first step was taken half-consciously. This was to charge symbolist forms with his own anxieties, and hence with a complex psychological content. The nebulous *André Walter* could elicit a very personal reaction from Jacques Rivière and *Le Voyage d'Urien* a very personal one from Francis Jammes.[7] These quasi-symbolist books, founded as they were on unresolved sexual conflicts, spoke intimately to attentive readers; Mallarmé was too easily reassured that the voyage of the "Orion" was not a real one. And *Le Traité du Narcisse*, in the very act of defining symbolism, maintained that the artist must represent and manifest everything — not merely (it soon appeared) some quintessential "soul," but all divagations of the mind and all the body's impulsions. Gide's exploratory "sincerity" is at the antipodes of Mallarmé's austere intellectualism, and it is fully implicit in the few pages of this treatise. The next step was *Paludes's* satire on a cloistered literary life, and the longest step was that of *Les Nourritures terrestres*. It asserted openly the claims of real life and unliterary sensuous experience, and offered itself as a guide to conduct.*

After *Paludes* and *Les Nourritures terrestres*, Gide's purely literary influence moves in the two directions: toward a destruction of the orderly realistic novel and toward a revitalized classicism. Historically, this is the secret of Gide's strength and importance; he refuses to choose finally between divergent paths, and leads the way along both. It is also the despair of the commentator, who must follow them separately. We may consider first the modernist tendency. The absurdity and inconsecutiveness of *Le Voyage d'Urien* in one sense seem closer to surrealism than do these elements in *Paludes*

* The reaction against symbolism was, as Yvonne Davet remarks, inevitable and "in the air." Marcel Schwob's *Livre de Monelle* (1894) also preached individualism, "disponibilité," and hedonism, but the impulsion was far more literary than Gide's. Zola announced the collapse of symbolism in 1896 and 1897, and hailed the new *naturistes*. The *Revue naturiste* was founded in March 1897, and contained a venomous attack on Mallarmé. The *Ballades françaises* of Paul Fort, published in 1897, became progressively less symbolist and more earthy during the years. But here too the revolt was more literary than Gide's. See Yvonne Davet, *Autour des Nourritures terrestres* (Paris, 1928), pp. 24–40.

and *Le Prométhée mal enchaîné:* they are at times truly gratuitous, dictated by mere whim and by less-than-conscious needs. But *Paludes* and *Le Prométhée mal enchaîné* are more surrealist in subject and over-all effect. As carefully calculated as *Tristram Shandy,* they yet come much closer than the *Voyage* to surrealist disrespect, humor, and illogic. They puzzled some young readers more than did Rimbaud and Laforgue, but *Paludes* inspired even the academic Rivière to imitation. And in the Preface to *Paludes,* a quarter of a century before surrealism and a half-century before the Wimsatt-Beardsley essay on "The Intentional Fallacy," Gide defined the role of the preconscious in creation, the tendency of the work of art to escape or transcend the artist's intentions.

The greatest influence on Dada and surrealism was, to be sure, that of the final "sotie," *Les Caves du Vatican.* It was scarcely surrealist itself, certainly not Dadaist. It neither professed to be a product of the liberated unconscious, nor attempted any assault on language. It even acknowledged the importance of ideas by playing with them so subtly. But it was a revolutionary book, a few years ahead of its time. It did arrive, by calculation, at the absurdity which the surrealists would try to achieve spontaneously. Ultimately the surrealists chose Lautréamont as their master — a less conscious artist than Gide, and certainly a more scabrous one. But only the final section of *Les Chants de Maldoror* can be called a novel or story. Lautréamont was unread at the turn of the century and little read in 1914.[8] It was Gide who prepared the way. Today a dramatized *Caves du Vatican* is fare for the youthful Thursday and Sunday matinee audiences at the Comédie Française. But it has not always been deemed so innocent.

Surrealism strictly defined produced no great fiction and could not have. The most obvious impact of *Les Caves du Vatican* has been on the fiction we call "post-surrealist." Claude-Edmonde Magny emphasizes the *Caves's* variety of tone, its varying degrees of stylization, the juggling of the planes of dream and reality; she finds reflections of these in various later novelists of fantasy.[9] Still more important, she observes, was its destructive bearing on the conventional real-

istic novel. For it anticipated by more than a decade some of
the most important innovations of *Les Faux-Monnayeurs*:
the suppression of description and slow transition, the tele-
scoping of psychological analysis, the point of view of a
sprightly narrator, the immediacy of the present tense and
the unpredictable plot, the fragmentation of structure.

The history of modern anti-realism has yet to be written.
But even Max Brod, the friend and biographer of Kafka,
recognized Gide's primary importance in freeing the novel
from its bondage to conventional psychology and mere brute
event.[10] The problem of priority is a particularly difficult one.
Raymond Roussel's *Impressions d'Afrique* (1910) is earlier
than *Les Caves du Vatican* but later than *Le Prométhée mal
enchaîné* and is certainly more surrealist than either. The
important thing, in historical terms, is that it had very few
readers. But what of the critical ideas and techniques and
impulses made famous by *Les Faux-Monnayeurs* and its attendant *Journal*? Many of these are latent in Gide's "soties"
and explicit in his lectures on Dostoevsky — especially the
demand for a vast complex of action and the preference for
shadowed characterization. Nevertheless, the first full critical
expression of the Gidean ideas is to be found in Jacques
Rivière's 1913 essay on "Le Roman d'aventure." Was Rivière
not Gide the innovator? Alain-Fournier referred to his un-
completed *Grand Meaulnes* as a "roman d'aventures" as early
as April 1910, but he did not formulate a detailed aesthetic.[11]
On the other hand Rivière was now in association with Gide;
the ideas for his essay may have been not merely "in the air,"
but pressing him very close. Certainly Rivière nowhere else
showed a capacity for original thought. Edmond Jaloux sums
up one view of the matter bluntly: "This essay obviously derived from the preoccupations of a small group of writers:
preoccupations which also led to *Les Caves du Vatican* and
Les Faux-Monnayeurs and to *Les Thibault* of Roger Martin
du Gard." [12]

The curious thing about Rivière's argument, originally
published in three issues of the *Nouvelle Revue française*, is
that it contradicts itself radically. Perhaps Rivière was con-

verted to Gidean principles while writing his essay. The first thirty pages, beginning with an attack on symbolist ambiguity and abstraction, seem to look backward rather than forward. Rivière demands careful and observable transitions, classical fullness and perfection of detail, clear distinctions, a freedom from ambiguity.[13] "Cards on the table; I want to see everything." [14] This is very far from *Les Faux-Monnayeurs*. But in the last seventeen pages we have a full reversal, and a detailed anticipation of Gide's and Edouard's theories.[15] Now the novelist (no longer striving for masterly structure or clear detail) is the astonished recorder of unpredictable adventure. He should not know where he is, what his characters signify, or how his story will end. He should be the helpless observer of life and not its lucid interpreter. The "aventure" will result, Rivière now argues, from an absence or abruptness of transition: one event should not seem to grow out of the preceding one. Anticipating Gide even more closely, Rivière argues that the new novel must be long and even contain *longueurs*; that it must be capable of assimilating everything; that it must be so multiple in structure as to admit even diaries and digressions; that it must depart completely from the "rectilinear" simplicity of the traditional French novel; that its plot must at last form a knot so difficult and so absurd that it cannot be untied. One particular passage suggests that Rivière's theorizing was based on a prepublication knowledge of *Les Caves du Vatican*. It describes fairly exactly the technique of Lafcadio's introduction. The general theory, in any event, is that which Gide would make famous more than a decade later, with *Les Faux-Monnayeurs* and the *Journal des Faux-Monnayeurs*. The natural assumption, difficult to verify, is that Gide had arrived at this theory by 1913. Charles du Bos believed that *Les Caves du Vatican* was a *Faux-Monnayeurs* "manqué"; that the earlier book was to have been Gide's abundant and multiple "first novel." [16] Claude-Edmonde Magny suggests, cautiously, that it is impossible to know how much of Gide's theory was his own, and how much he owed to conversations with Roger Martin du Gard, Rivière, or Jacques de Lacretelle.[17]

Whatever the just settlement of priority, and however startling the *Caves du Vatican's* innovations or Rivière's essay — *Les Faux-Monnayeurs* has left the largest impression. The measure must be taken not in immediate resemblances, such as those of *Point Counter Point* (a novel saturated with the old realism and psychologizing) but rather in terms of major tendencies in the novel: in such blendings of complexity and economy as we find in Malraux's *La Condition humaine*; or in the suppression of description and analysis by most of the best novelists since Gide; or, still more distantly, in the cross-sections of Sartre's trilogy and Camus's *La Peste*. Conceivably Camus did not think of *Les Faux-Monnayeurs* at all. Yet we observe that Camus's highly personalized narrator remains anonymous until the final pages. Is he not perhaps (having passed through many modulations) Gide's sprightly "roving conductor"? Questions as specific as this may well be unanswerable. But certainly (proceeding here along the same lines as the early E. M. Forster) Gide showed later novelists how to use the nineteenth-century omniscient author's freedom in a new and interesting way, and without loss of nominal objectivity. The narrator may confide in his reader as confidently as did Thackeray, or shuffle the cards as arbitrarily — and even admit, perhaps, that he is shuffling the cards. But he is no longer a man sitting at a desk.

Les Faux-Monnayeurs was, finally, a "roman critique": a manual on how to write novels. Much less radical as an experiment than *Ulysses*, it yet suggests more to the novelist trying to escape a bare realism. "If *Les Faux-Monnayeurs* and the *Journal* which accompanied it have exercised such an influence on theory, it is because they posed a certain number of critical problems. The history of the novel since Gide is a story of the efforts of novelists to escape — whether consciously or not — from the difficulties which he was the first to perceive." [18] Henry James thought about the art of the novel as intensely, though in very different terms, long before Gide. But it is safe to assume that James's essays were read in Europe even less than his novels. In France, before Gide, only Flaubert had worked as consciously toward a theory and art of fiction. At his most destructive and "modern," Gide was classically speculative and calculating.

A leader of the destroyers, Gide was also perhaps the strongest force behind the new "classicism" associated with the *Nouvelle Revue française* — a classicism which in turn strongly affected T. S. Eliot and *The Criterion*. The duality of Gide's role, as cautious radical and daring conservative, naturally offended the extreme partisans in either camp, whether André Breton or Julien Benda. So too did the seemingly contradictory impulses of the *Nouvelle Revue française*. Rivière's editorial in the first postwar issue (June 1919) summed up its position succinctly: a determination to correct and consolidate the findings of romanticism and symbolism through a vindication of the conscious mind; encouragement of experiment joined to a rigorous critical vigilance; a plea for "demobilization" of the intellect after the war years of propaganda; insistence on the autonomy of the work of art, and on the separateness of artistic and political convictions. In the August 1920 issue Rivière's "Reconnaissance à Dada" expressed the new classicism in more literary terms. Dada, by carrying to a dead end the subjectivity of romanticism, of Flaubert's pseudo-realism, of symbolism and of cubism, proved the need for a return to intelligence and to a more impersonal art.[19]

The Gidean "classicism," however, must be defined in much broader terms than these. It had begun to exert its influence long before the war, and in diverse ways. There was first of all the Goethean effort "to assume as much humanity as possible," and to universalize even the most intimate personal experience. We shall return to this impulse again, in trying to define Gide's spiritual influence. In formal terms it meant the enrichment of a literary genre, the generalizing spiritual autobiography. Amiel, absorbing all the intellectual currents of his time, marked some advance over the solitary introspections of a Maurice de Guérin. But Gide, progressing from diary to classical myth, could make his own special case and particular curve of experience seem general. The second aspect of Gidean classicism was its belief in art as an instrument of control: language and mastered form as protections against inner anarchy. Gide's personal example of patience and delayed publication was exceeded only by Valéry's — and Valéry's vain effort, after all, was to reduce all experience to the workings of the mind.

Gide's essays, almost from the beginning, proscribed "lyrisme" and preached restraint, a "mastered romanticism." His most original argument was that the artist is often more successful when he resists his natural creative impulses and energies. By resisting them, he puts them to work in a new and richer way. Once again it is impossible to fix the history of such an idea, which would have seemed absurd in 1900 but is accepted by many today. Alain-Fournier, who in 1910 was thinking of *La Porte étroite* as he planned the ending of *Le Grand Meaulnes*,[20] was long an extreme example of the "relaxed artist" who waits on inspiration and is determined to obey it slavishly. He was unwilling to weigh his own creative impulses, let alone combat them. Yet we find him (when at last he is working efficiently and about to complete his book) echo Gide familiarly: "I do well, I achieve what I do achieve only against myself — resisting my fondest tendencies, climbing back up my most cherished slope." [21]

In still another sense, art may be an instrument of control: by providing its own corrective. Gide's argument that each of his books contains a critique of a preceding one is relevant only if we consent to take a writer's work *en bloc*. The austere *Saül* does "correct" *Les Nourritures terrestres*, but *Saül* has had few readers and *Les Nourritures terrestres* many. Gide is on much stronger ground when he says that each book contains its own antidote. The "soties" turn irony inward and ridicule glib or theoretical rebellion. And in the "récits" Gide dramatizes, seriously, the possible dangers of his own ideas. Just so Camus — in *L'Etranger, Caligula,* and *Le Malentendu* — would dramatize the dangers of "indifference" and "absurd revolt," if carried to their logical conclusions. Gide's "classicism," and Camus's, is a classicism of irony and saving common sense.

The most obvious aspect of Gide's classical influence,

though the least apparent to many foreign readers, has been his influence on style. Even *Le Voyage d'Urien* shows that subtle interplay of inner mobility and unusual syntax which no translation can reflect. The early style was nevertheless luxuriant and full of mannerisms. The progressive chastening of this style in a few years, from *Le Voyage d'Urien* to *Le Retour de l'enfant prodigue,* offered a rare example of artistic control, rejection, discipline. Much later, with *Œdipe* and *Thésée,* the prose achieved an even barer surface. Gide's example of self-discipline and his own style have left their mark on French prose; on what Claude-Edmonde Magny calls, rather contemptuously, "le style *Nrf.*" It is to be found in members of the *Nrf* group (such as Schlumberger, Jacques de Lacretelle, Radiguet, and Alain-Fournier) but also in writers as far removed as Mauriac and Montherlant — a studied colloquialism, complexity underlying a spare surface, a gravity of tone. A typical *Latinité* contributor, Paul Reboux, anxious to discount a general influence on himself, yet admitted that Gide had taught him to write "in the barest possible way." [22] The greatest contemporary exponent of this classical style is certainly Albert Camus.

Finally, Gide revived and revitalized the traditional French "récit." His own "récits" belong to the remote line of *La Princesse de Clèves* and the more recent line of *Adolphe.* Claude-Edmonde Magny, who is committed to an ethic of extreme relativism and to an aesthetic of disordered immediacy, finds the moralism and quiet distinction of these twentieth-century "récits" tiresome: Rivière's *Aimée,* Chardonne's *Eva,* Jacques de Lacretelle's *Silbermann,* Radiguet's *Bal du Comte d'Orgel.* But Gide's achievement was to make the "récit" something more than a confession or problem novel, something more than a case study. Eschewing all explicit psychological analysis (as Rivière and the others did not), Gide gave his short novels a psychological content which Bourget and other immediate predecessors lacked. Once again his classicism looks forward to Camus, the Camus of *L'Etranger.* The influence of Hemingway on *L'Etranger* may seem more obvious than the influence of Gide. But long before Heming-

way, Gide saw that the task of correction and interpretation
must be left to the reader.

A lifetime of research could perhaps document and "prove"
Gide's influence on French prose style of the twentieth
century, or on the technique of the psychological "récit." It
would be far more difficult to fix with any exactness his place
in intellectual history; his part in the fluid development of
certain now familiar ideas. How many of these ideas were "in
the air," to which Gide merely gave a more forceful or more
courageous expression than others? The Gidean definition of
"sincerity," for instance — a conscientious listening to *all*
of one's inner voices, a determination to suppress no potentiality — has certainly widened the meaning of that word.
Jacques Rivière's 1911 essay on sincerity would seem to be
no more than a docile commentary on another man's thought;
the very close imitation of Gide's style suggests a mere echoing
of his ideas. Yet we find that Rivière had read the lesson of
this peculiar sincerity into Maurice Barrès' books before he
encountered Gide; he even claimed to have entertained just
such a conception since childhood. It is equally difficult, of
course, to determine when Gide acquired the ideas he would
refine upon and transmit. The concept of "sincerity" is implicit in the famous injunction of *Le Traité du Narcisse* to
manifest everything. This little treatise on symbolism, however subversive of symbolist detachment, owes something to
Gide's brief stay in the symbolist salons. But how much more
(or less) does the idea of sincere, complete representation
owe to his reading of Schopenhauer and Novalis?

The problem of priorities is confused, and hopelessly confused whenever we have to cope with more general movements of thought. Gide could say with justice that he had
been a Bergsonian before he read Bergson — in his relativism
and in his search for buried sources of energy, in his assaults
on the factitious personality. He could say just as truly that
he had been a Freudian before he read Freud — in his awareness of the unconscious life and of hidden sexual conflicts;
in his understanding of repression, sublimation, identification. Yet these matters too were "in the air." We can say

that Bergsonian ideas reached French intellectuals through Bergson and others more often than through Gide. But this is by no means so clear when we come to Freud. French intellectuals, including Gide himself, resisted Freud's books rather longer than did intellectuals in other countries. Gide had dramatized all his own psychological intuitions before Freud found, outside of academic circles, any wide acceptance in France. And what is the relative share of Bergson, Freud, and Gide (not to mention more obvious "ancestors") in the structure of French non-Christian existentialism? At best we can point to very small segments of that structure. *Paludes*, for instance, dramatized man's tendency to become a function, and his imprisonment by his illusory conception of a coherent and single self (which he feels obliged to imitate), more brilliantly than the existentialists of the 1940's ever would.

Gide may not have been a very original thinker. We can say that his attack on traditional ethics and his theory of self-transcendance are Nietzschean, or that his concepts of eternal life and of affirmation through renunciation are Dostoevskian; or that his "disponibilité" is merely a graver version of Oscar Wilde's. Even should we reject Gide's insistence that he arrived at these positions independently, we would still have to admit that he refined upon and qualified them, often by playing them against each other, and that he was largely responsible for their dissemination in France and Germany. But Gide's true originality may consist rather in his willingness to express ideas which others refused to "verbalize," and to dramatize situations which others glanced at, then turned away. He was "ahead of his time" most of all in this. As a scientific treatise, *Corydon* may be neither original nor convincing. But it did, like the Kinsey report, break through a discreet silence. It posed frankly a problem which, when it leapt embarrassingly to consciousness, was usually pushed down.

The most difficult task of all is to measure the degree to which ideas move and grow beneath the level of full consciousness. For the voyage of any idea is in part an underground adventure; we may resist the idea yet nourish it all the same. The half-century history of *L'Immoraliste's* reception poses this problem strikingly. A few early readers detected the homosexuality of Michel. And to a modern reader *L'Immoraliste* may seem one of the most flawless of Freudian novels. Yet the large majority of critics to this day have not seen, or have not admitted seeing, the homosexual element. They have observed instead an intellectual conflict between Nietzschean and Christian principles. This being so, can we still say that *L'Immoraliste* (through its brilliant dramatization of repression and sublimation) contributed to the advance of Freudian conceptions? Can we say that it enlightened those who, unconsciously, "refused to understand" it? The most significant evidence is that so many of these readers were yet profoundly moved by the novel; found it "terrible" and "frightening." Resisting its meaning, they nevertheless absorbed some of that meaning against their will. The novel pushed a real and harrowing human situation closer to full consciousness; it prepared readers for the more abstract definitions of Freud. In this sense, *L'Immoraliste* perhaps belongs to the history of Freudian understanding.

At this level, however, intellectual history becomes very speculative and perilous. There remains a great deal of more modest groundwork to be done. The danger is that many diverse positions will come to seem, after another half-century or so, one rather crude position. The danger is that our multiple age will seem as coherent as the "Romantic Period" seemed not very long ago. So far as Gide and his period are concerned, much close discrimination will be necessary. Most obviously Gide's mobility and restlessness must be separated from the tired skeptical relativism of Renan and Anatole France. His hedonism must be separated from Marcel Schwob's, his pursuit of simplicity from Francis Jammes's. It is not impossible that Maurice Barrès and Gide, those bitter antagonists, will one day be subsumed under the convenient heading "le culte du moi" in manuals of literary history. One way to avoid such confusion is to observe the successive impact of the two egoisms on such a docile mind as Rivière's, or to compare their influence on more masculine minds. To compare, for instance, the amplitude and complexity of Albert Camus with the infinitely narrower "toughness" of Henry de Montherlant, who is Barrès' most famous disciple. But this kind of question takes us already into the area of "spiritual influence," of an influence operating in very personal terms. Why, apart from conveyed literary forms and transmitted ideas, did Gide have such a strong influence? How did his books and his personality *work*?

And first of all, there has been the personality of the living man: a presence wholly different from the somber and troubled self conveyed by the *Journal* and the spiritual autobiographies. Personality and temperament, a particular way of looking at things, the intimate appeal of a speaking voice — these have their share in our liking for Hardy's and Conrad's books. But the visitor at Max Gate would find a shy and commonplace cottager, and the visitor at Bishopsbourne a reserved man who now and then broke out into rages. Gide's personal magnetism, on the other hand, often approximated the magnetism of his books. He could be charming, gracious, fun-loving, and eternally youthful; yet seemed to demand the gravest self-inquiries and the most intimate confessions from his friends and even from strangers. There are many intangibles here, which ideally we should want to consider and perhaps discount: the appeal of the respected and justified homosexual for the troubled fellow homosexual such as Maurice Sachs, or the fatherly appeal of any great writer for the unknown beginning his career. (Sachs knelt daily, for a time, before the portrait of Cocteau.) We must not be deluded by the public indifference to Gide's books before *La Porte étroite* or even before 1925. He had, from the days of Mallarmé, a real prestige among fellow writers.

There is also to be discounted the legendary Gide, the Byronic figure of literary gossip and chameleon attraction — the legendary Gide, not the exemplary or representative.

There was first of all the image of the saintly ascetic in a black cape, who theorized on desire and liberty: "Frizeau claims the immoralism and Nietzscheism of Gide are very superficial, a kind of mask; his morals are very chaste." [23] But there was also the legend of the dark adventurer: the discoverer of North Africa who brought Athman to the 1900 Exposition in Paris, the man who was always leaving or arriving, the repository of underground rumors and unspeakable vices, the moralist whose mission was to corrupt. There was the great sinner who confessed his sins; and who was careful to remind his admirers that he had not given up these sins. There was also the "enfant terrible" of the "beau geste" — who disposed of some of his friends' manuscripts and autographed books at public auction. And there was, finally, the political Gide, attacking atrocities in the Congo and in Berlin — important enough to plead with Goebbels for Dimitrov, and who appeared on lecture platforms.

These are some of Gide's "public personalities." We are concerned, rather, with the Gide who strongly influenced so many personal friends, and who was sought out by so many strangers asking consolation or advice. Roger Martin du Gard writes of this Gide eloquently:

Here, I must make an effort to forget my personal experience and how useful and quickening his affection has been for me. Let it suffice to speak of others. I have had many and many an occasion to verify the salutary influence of André Gide — not merely on his close friends, which would already be conclusive, but on so many unknown friends who have assailed him with letters and visits, who have confessed to him their inward debates, who have demanded help and advice; on all these anxious beings of such different nationality, age, religious background, taste and outlook, who have almost never sought his moral support in vain. [24]

Roger Martin du Gard wrote that he might some day "tell what a conversation with André Gide is like." But he has not yet done so. The personal figure of Gide may well become more and more austere with posterity. Most of the books about Gide, preoccupied with graver matters, say nothing of his great personal charm. Even Charles du Bos, in the midst of his careful assault on Gide's work, regretted that "our descendants" would know nothing of a charm which could be "irresistible." Yet this intangible of personality played an important part in the *viva voce* influence. The inward figure of lassitude, longing, and discontent was doubled by one of outward energy and fun. Julian Green speaks of the extraordinary "youthfulness of expression and of voice." He could never get over the impression that he was speaking to a man of his own age, a "camarade"; in 1936 Gide seemed to him younger than ever. The sober young Rivière, invited to Cuverville, was astonished by Gide's talent for humorous mimicry. What so many friends have referred to but none has conveyed is an infectious warmth: "Ah how Gide excels at helping each maintain his fever," Roger Martin du Gard wrote. "And how he knows how, suddenly, to send one's temperature up!"

But also (and here the living personality corresponds to the personality of the writer) there was the seduction of an evasiveness and even coyness: the attraction, in Armand Pierhal's words, of the "homme fuyant." [25] With Paul Claudel, Gide played an intricate cat-and-mouse game: first in offering and withdrawing the possibility of their meeting, then in offering and withdrawing the possibility of his own conversion. Rivière and Maurice Sachs both described Gide as a man who says "no," yet smiles as he says it; Rivière complained that he could never discover exactly what Gide thought of him. Even as a young man, Francis Jammes — so grateful for Gide's "warmth" — complained of his flarings of severity. The embittered Jammes of 1932 emphasizes the capricious "homme fuyant" in his novel about Gide's influence: *L'Antigyde, ou Elie de Nacre.*

The terrible biblical epigraphs promise a somber attack on pederasty, but Elie de Nacre is an older Lafcadio. He courts disciples, then ridicules them. He invites friends to his wedding feast, but sends a telegram to the restaurant announcing the birth of a baby. The guests must pay the bill. He duplicates, with Norbert, Michel's experiment on Moktir, allowing himself to be robbed. Within a few hours he detects a more serious theft, has Norbert arrested, rescues him from the police, and admonishes him in a moralizing letter. He courts election to the French Academy, then attacks all his fellow-academicians in his inaugural address. The simple, noble, and forgotten poet Rustique (Jammes himself) spends an evening with Elie in Bayonne. He is appalled by the swift alternation of Elie's "two personalities, that of the monk and that of the clown." An insult is followed by an exotic gift, and flattery by another insult. Does Jammes's caricature correspond to a certain reality — an incorrigible love of caprice and coquetry, a refusal to grow up? Despite the deep bitterness of Jammes's portrait, a certain charm shines through. The ending of *L'Antigyde* is embarrassing wish-fulfillment. The famous Elie seeks out Rustique (shamefully neglected by a corrupted younger generation), asks for the affection of the old days, and takes him on a trip to Spain. There the regenerate Elie is converted and dies.*

Many of the friendships nevertheless took on (and certainly the early friendship of Jammes and Gide) a gravity almost at once. The commonest impulse — provoked by what intangibles in Gide's voice and manner? — was an impulse to confess and confide. "Are you not," wrote the Jammes of 1897 to the Gides, "one of those evangelizing families who give alms on the outskirts of cities? Then receive my moral misery as you would receive a suffering man." [26] Of his first solitary meeting with Gide, Rivière wrote thus to Alain-Fournier: "To sum it up, I told him everything . . . I never before had this experience of feeling that my own thoughts were coming to life, as I talked, in someone so close to me. I think he understands me, terrifyingly and with his whole being." [27] "You have become for me," Charles du Bos wrote, "that one friend to whom it is natural to reveal all the depths I hide from others — the friend who always understands, who always 'sees through' and anticipates." [28]

Claudel overpowered interlocutors by his missionary

* For Gide's comment on this paragraph, see his letter of December 18, 1950, at the end of this book.

faith and Valéry by his missionary skepticism; and both
overpowered others by their brilliant flood of words. The
conversations became monologues. But Gide's effect appears
to have been entirely different. His voice might have an
"almost august gravity"; or the visitor might feel a frightening "lucidity, a great self-possession and self-knowledge." [29]
Yet the achievement was that, again and again, of a sympathetic "directeur de conscience." The visitor was impelled
to a frank confession, then led back — even Maurice Sachs admits this — to his own best qualities. This influence through
personality and conversation is perhaps best summed up by
Roger Martin du Gard:

> The fact is that he brings to each a new strength. One of the
> strongest elements of the influence he exerts is the persuasive
> and intoxicating encouragement he gives us to persevere, reso-
> lutely and happily, each in his own being; and to demand of
> ourselves the most particular, the most authentic, the best . . .
> He has the gift of sharpening each man's critical sense and of
> increasing his insight, without *diminishing his fervor*. He does
> more: he exalts in others — not pride, certainly, and I don't know
> quite how to put it: an upright vision of self; a confidence, a
> modest confidence in oneself. [30]

We are concerned with Gide the writer, not with Gide the
man. These testimonies to a maieutic personal influence
are nevertheless worth noting because they correspond so
closely to other testimonies on the influence of the books.
Du Bos said he had to escape the persuasiveness of Gide's
voice before he could take a detached view of his writings.
Yet something of this voice gets into the written style: the
interplay of gravity and youthful gaiety, a tone of clair-
voyant sympathy, a labyrinthine texture which invites probing, and even the undulant coyness. The style as well as the
matter (and here we must certainly include the large amount
of "primary " sexual imagery in the early works) suggest to
the most diverse readers a wide area of shared experience and
shared prohibitive longing. By 1941, according to the Talvart and Place bibliography, some thirty books had been
written on Gide, over 150 other books dealt with his work

at length, and to these may be added over five hundred articles or reviews. But the real clue to the range of Gide's influence lies in the fact that many of these books and articles, hostile or sympathetic, are extremely personal as well as polemical. Over and over one detects a reaction of identification and recognition, followed by a shocked determination to define one's own separateness. "You may ask yourself why I insist on afflicting you with such confessions," Rivière wrote to Gide. "But at times I feel myself so close to you, to such a degree share the same attitude toward things, that — to reassure myself — I have to let you know how I think we differ." [31]

Some of these autobiographical *critiques* express an equal enthusiasm for each of Gide's diverse messages. The critic, having identified himself completely with his subject, offers mere summary and lyric paraphrase. But others betray their subjective bias by the fact that their interpretations are so partial or limited. Thus Jacques Rivière (who had a mania for discipleship) emphasizes, in *L'Immoraliste*, the enrichment of the ego through identification with others. Another autobiographical critic may, like Van Meter Ames, operate almost exclusively in intellectual terms, and show himself equally selective. Ames's *André Gide* (1947) offers vast personal speculations on the nature of freedom, progress, love, beauty, God, et cetera. His analysis of Gide is a dialogue, but usually an inward dialogue. Gide, we may surmise, here provided his critic with just that provocation which education is supposed to provide — and it may be ungrateful to complain because Ames turned his subject into a Columbia Teachers College enthusiast, devoted to science and to "sharing."

The longest and best-known of these autobiographical critiques is Charles du Bos's *Le Dialogue avec André Gide*, a collection of circular musings dictated over many years and accompanied by footnotes of retraction and emendation. For 139 pages the study is not merely friendly but naïvely sympathetic; the contemplative and solitary Du Bos is attracted, perhaps, by Gide's adventurous hedonism. There-

after — having become a practicing Catholic, and having protested in vain against *Si le grain ne meurt's* publication in
Gide's lifetime — Du Bos struggles to identify and cast out
Gide as one might struggle with a slippery Devil. We observe first (and this may account for many of the books on
Gide) the extreme rationalist's need to understand the complex, order the contradictory, classify the intangible. But the
dialogue (which was obviously an inward dialogue and not a
seventeen-year dialogue with Gide) soon becomes much
more personal. As in Van Meter Ames's book, so here the
critic's own speculations far outnumber Gide's. How dramatic this struggle became, how obsessive the need to define
one's own separateness, we see in Du Bos's *Journal* (Volume
III) as well as in the *Dialogue* itself.

The diary is a minute record of Du Bos's effort to trap
Gide in logical absurdities and verbal contradictions; to
prove, through a skillful confrontation of titles and texts,
that Gide's writing was getting worse and worse. What obsessive desire to demolish, or what complex of personal inhibitions, could lead such a puritan as Du Bos to defend the
amoral "grand viveurs" (Byron, Wilde) as against the moral-
istic Gide? No doubt there was some of Jammes's envy of a
more successful contemporary. But more probably Du Bos
felt much of Gide in himself, which he had to extirpate,
while he felt in himself none of Byron's or Wilde's supposed
casualness and ease. The alliance was indeed so intimate
that Du Bos could not understand why Gide, reading such
an ill-willed critique, should see in it an end of their friendship.[32]

We have the impression, in reading Du Bos, that Gide
must have awakened a congeries of suppressed impulses and
dangerous thoughts, which had to be wrestled with, not
merely denied. A significant number of critics (including
Du Bos himself) testify to Gide's great general influence, yet
disclaim any influence on themselves. Surely they protest
too much. Jacques Rivière shrewdly surmised that such half-
identification accounts for the obsessive and repeated attacks
of Henri Massis: "Gide has affected you profoundly, far more

than has Maurras or Barrès or Péguy. But you have known how to react to him only defensively: by accumulating aggressions, to serve as barricades." [33] In essay after essay, Massis harried Gide as passionately as Babbitt harried Rousseau. We think of Massis as the incubus. But was the incubus not rather Gide? The prolonged attention to Gide's soul of Maritain, Du Bos, Jammes, and Claudel is usually attributed to the particular zeal of the convert, who has himself traveled through skepticism. But this does not account for the equal persistence of Mauriac, who was always a practicing Catholic. No doubt these men hoped, in converting Gide, to convert his disciples too. But perhaps they also saw in Gide, still stubbornly open and verbalized, too much of their own inward anarchies. These are highly speculative matters, to be sure. The demonic in Mauriac, for instance, is unmistakably stronger than the demonic in Charles du Bos.

The curious epistolary friendships with Jammes and Claudel may illustrate, rather, Gide's appeal to persons very different from himself. Or they may suggest the multiple nature of Gide's personality, which could offer something to every taste. Certainly no two men would seem more different, at a glance, than the transparent Jammes and the complex, mobile, and self-critical Gide. Jammes was a simple and sentimental poet, deeply rooted in his isolated Orthez; conceited and demanding, a painfully dedicated spirit. The friendship began when Gide agreed to represent Jammes with Paris editors. Jammes was duly grateful, but it was Gide who began the "tutoiement" in their letters. Jammes referred to himself as "the faun" and to Gide as "the shepherd of the riverbanks." His letters were lyric and nebulous in the manner of *André Walter*, and Gide replied in kind. Reading the letters of 1897, we seem to observe Gide in a role he had already outgrown. It would be easy to say that here too, as in some of his fiction, he was turning a human relationship into a complicated game. Yet he was, in the long run, the more patient sufferer of the two. He could not, out of friendship for anyone, suppress the vagabond pages of *Les Nourritures terrestres* or the sexual meanings of *Le Voyage d'Urien* and *L'Immoraliste*. But he was willing to offer Jammes, as long as possible, the kind of cloudy companionship his correspondent needed. And he was not merely acting; he genuinely responded to Jammes's simplicity.

Gide's friendship with Claudel, like his friendship with Jammes, flourished in correspondence and was strained by personal meetings. No doubt Gide can be accused of a certain coyness in pretending on various occasions to be nearer conversion than he was. He emphasized the piety of *La Porte étroite* but did not emphasize its final skepticism; and he apparently sent Claudel a copy of *Numquid et tu . . . ?* without explaining that he no longer felt its religious impulses.[34] Yet he seems to have been the more patient of the two. He admired Claudel's poetry, looked out for its interests in Paris, and hoped to develop a "literary" friendship; he enlisted Claudel in the *Nouvelle Revue française*, long after the attempts at conversion had begun. But Claudel gave him no peace. Five days after their first meeting in 1905 Claudel asked him coldly why he had not been converted; by 1912 he could write Gide that he believed him under the influence of the Devil, who was furious to see conversion approach. The fury of bafflement was in the end Claudel's, not the Devil's. In 1947, he cast out Gide more ferociously than did Jammes in *Elie de Nacre*: "I will not admit that he has any talent . . . He has given a horrible example of cowardice and weakness . . . He is a poisoner, I say it advisedly. How many letters haven't I received from young sinners. You will always find Gide at the beginning of their progress toward evil." [35]

The Gide-Claudel correspondence is of major interest, not merely because it offers certain new information on Gide and his work, [36] but because it helps define the attitude of his Catholic critics. "I don't know one Catholic," Claudel wrote in 1926, "who isn't concerned with you, who doesn't think about you and almost all the time — and in a manner, whatever you may say, strangely combining affection and a wholly legitimate horror." [37] Claudel's own horror began in 1914, when he understood the homosexual implications of a page of *Les Caves du Vatican*. "If you are a pederast, miserable one, cure yourself and don't parade these abominations." [38] Only a week later Claudel was to insist on the position which Maritain, Du Bos, and others would take before the publication of *Si le grain ne meurt*. To be a pederast was serious enough, but to admit it even worse. These vices are "neither permitted, nor excusable, *nor may they be confessed*." [39] The Catholic opposition was to a fundamentally Protestant attitude, which took too literally the injunctions of sincerity and of individual salvation. Beyond this, the Claudel correspondence shows how early and how seriously Gide was taken as a spiritual influence: "Your course is not yet finished," Claudel wrote in 1926. "You are one of those whose life has the value of a parabola; who achieve completely a curve of which others merely sketch the beginning — and that is in fact one of the reasons for the interest I take in you, an interest in which anxiety has as large a share as hope." [40] But already in 1910 he had called Gide one "of the guides of present-day youth." [41]

One of the young men of 1910 who looked to Gide as a guide was Jacques Rivière, the brother-in-law of Alain-Fournier and editor of the *Nouvelle Revue française* from 1919 until his death in 1925. It may be profitable to look into at least this one instance of Gidean influence and spiritual "action" in more detail — and not merely because Rivière's discipleship is more frequently cited than anyone else's. The fullness of his correspondence with Alain-Fournier helps us to see Gide as young men of 1905–1910 saw him: before criticism and Gide's own *Journal* had sorted the major from the minor works and assigned each of the books to a category, before a clear chronological pattern had set in. (In 1905, for instance, Rivière begins with the *Philoctète* volume, perhaps because it was the one available, and not with *Les Nourritures terrestres* or *L'Immoraliste*.) Rivière is also interesting as a "representative" figure, responding to many of the moral anxieties and nearly all of the literary suasions of his time. Lacking Gide's originality and strength, he is in one sense more representative than Gide of the twentieth-century intellectual. For he took few of his many steps independently. He echoed Barrès, Claudel, Gide, Freud, and Proust as glibly as a later generation would echo Toynbee and Sartre.

Rivière is also interesting on his own grounds — not as a minor writer or as a very gifted editor, but as an interesting person: a man who meditated at length on his own self-destructive impulses, who applied a rage for academic classification to his own mind and life, and who experienced a "desire to be influenced" by great men to an obsessional degree. Rivière was the narcissistic Amiel of his time, the fine sieve through which twenty years of literary history passed. And this, of course, suggests his ultimate interest for us. We have an enormous amount of data on the influences Rivière underwent, yet we cannot define any of these influences confidently. Rivière proves that the study of "source and influence," like any other aspect of literary history, cannot pretend to scientific accuracy. For every fact discovered, ten more important ones may escape detection.

Rivière is nevertheless the delight of the literary historian, inviting even a François Mauriac to textbook summary: "Thanks to the leaven of Claudel, and to that of Gide, extreme and incompatible feelings ferment in him . . . henceforth to come under his control. Gide helps him to free himself from Claudel and Péguy; Claudel and Péguy to free himself from Gide; Proust and Freud lead him far from the other three — and already, to judge by certain signs, I discerned that he was beginning to detach himself from Proust." [42] Rivière once intended to call his *Etudes* (a book of critical essays) "L'Imitation des maîtres" — with what justice a few excerpts from the letters to Alain-Fournier will show:

Barrès revealed to me, when I left Maeterlinck's placidity, Desire . . . These days I think only in and through Barrès . . . To tell the truth, it is my intellectual sensibility or my felt thought that Barrès taught me to cultivate . . . Basically, it's for the cult of Desire (under diverse forms) that I moved to-

ward Barrès, Claudel, Gide; Maeterlinck's impassiveness turned
me away from him . . . Gide always prepares one for Claudel
. . . Who will deliver me from Claudel, and from God . . . ?
Having experienced Claudel, and since I reject him, who shall I
now experience? [43]

The letters are full of such references to the influence of
masters. Even at nineteen and twenty Rivière could refer to
their combat as "the novel of my inner life," and could accept
the humble role of an Amiel initiating nothing. Alain-Fournier protested frequently against this impulse to record and
classify one's "sources." On July 5, 1907, Rivière defended
himself eloquently, but his diagnosis was probably incomplete:

You smile a little to see me undergo influences almost as on
my life and my flesh. You — you quickly extract from those you
most admire what is essential to you, the novelty they bring
you, because you have your own writing, and you are too busy
to see anything in the world but material for it. But I, I who
have no other task than to understand, I who offer myself and
my vacancy to every invasion — I must submit myself to him I
welcome, I must become his body and soul . . . in order to understand, in order to possess him. And then I must rid myself
of him in order to welcome another. And the more perfect has
been my understanding, the more laborious and cruel the separation. There is a tearing of filaments.
But, most of all, to keep oneself free and nude.[44]

This curious sexual imagery of the intellectual life is significant — and even Rivière himself, in 1924, regretted the "voluptuous" phrasing of *Etudes*. Gide's own comment of 1922
was much more succinct: "Jacques Rivière constantly seeks to
caress himself in others. His extraordinary pursuit of affinities
and his predilection for what resembles him. His admirations
always have an element of flattery and self-indulgence."[45]

A full study of Rivière invites the student of personality
rather than the literary critic. But even a brief survey of his
career describes a circular movement of personal and literary
change. The Rivière of nineteen and twenty already possessed

a precocious culture and fully developed academic style, and possessed also the love of orderly classification, the addiction to introspection and broad psychologizing, the *"volupté* of destructive analysis."* He was highly emotional. But — and here he differed radically from Alain-Fournier — his sensibility fed on ideas and abstracted feelings rather than particular memories and things. At this age too his need to define himself to others was fully developed. "These reflections, in spite of their infuriating form, tell you a great deal about me," he wrote to Alain-Fournier. "Therefore I pass them on . . . That had become the chief object of my introspection; I studied myself largely so that I could talk about myself to you." [46] So he would address himself later to Gide ("There are times when I want you to know every detail of my life, which of my aunts I liked best, etc.") [47] and particularly to Claudel — to whom he gave a detailed account of his feelings. And so it appears he would later favor his wife, as did the François of his novel *Aimée.* Describing to her his feelings, tendencies, and the "habits" of his heart, Rivière's "happiness would turn to exaltation." [48] He said his Gidean essay "De la foi" was written, for one reason, to make himself better known to Gide, who was by then a close friend.[49]

Accompanying the adolescent narcissism (or adolescent loneliness) were a sexual timidity and idealization, and a paralyzing reticence (*pudeur*) which he tried to overcome.[50] Rivière's sympathetic essay on Amiel, whose adolescent shame was said to have determined his vice of passive revery, may offer an important clue to his own troubles.[51] Be that as it may, the young Rivière of nineteen seemed ready for the pallid lesson of Proust. In 1905 he had to satisfy himself with the early Maurice Barrès, not the Barrès of sensual energy but the Barrès of refined introspection and complex inward conflict. His next great enthusiasm was for Claudel, into whom he read much Barrès and no little Gide: an ethic of sincerity and self-realization, relativism, the primacy of life over virtue. He had written a large part of his essay on Claudel before he discovered that Claudel was a Catholic and even a proselytizing Catholic. So be it: Claudel was a greater writer than Dante. But four months later, while on military service and maneuvers, Rivière discovered *Les Nourritures terrestres*. After three weeks only (August 28, 1906) this pure intellectual not merely wrote in Gide's style but preached the harshest Nietzschean doctrine. By November he was offering Alain-Fournier a shameless rehash of Gide's attacks on timidity, education, authority.

However disturbing this may be to the historian, Rivière's Gide and Claudel "periods" were roughly contemporary. If the letters give higher praise to Claudel, the published essays of 1911 and 1912 show rather the influence of Gide — not only the essay on Gide himself, but also the essays on sincerity and faith. "De la sincérité envers soi-même" points to the dangers of mere self-indulgence, yet affirms man's obligations to each facet of his own nature. "De la foi" is a most eloquent and reasonable apology for faith. But the final section, in pure Gidean palinode, expresses a radical, incorrigible refusal to submit. Harried (as he wanted to be) by Claudel's letters, Rivière did briefly submit and did kneel before the Abbé Fontaine; as a prisoner in Germany he developed an intense solitary zeal. Both believers and skeptics claim the Rivière of 1919–1925, who remained discreetly silent about religious matters.

In purely literary terms, Gide and others led Rivière very far from Barrès and from Proustian introspection. We have seen that his "Le Roman d'aventure" of 1913 demolishes the old symbolist ideals and offers a purely Gidean theory of the novel. "Reconnaissance à Dada" (1919) goes further in attacking all the subjective, analytic, psychologizing movements of the last hundred years: "It [Dada] develops relentlessly everything in the subjective tendency. How forcefully it shows that to try to gather up one's entire self means giving no importance at all to any particular state of feeling." [52] But Rivière was to discover, before he died, one more master.

His Monaco lecture on Proust, "the most important author of our time," shows a complete return to the ideals of 1905: to the novel as a way of psychological knowledge, to introspection and the narcissistic recreation of the inner life, to

a love for minute detail, to the rational ordering of experience. The analysis of Proust marks a complete rejection of
the 1913 and 1919 essays. Temporarily misled into "real life"
by Gide, Rivière at last recovers his own nature of passive
contemplation and pure spirit. In the final hours of his life,
unresigned, Rivière fought death with all his analytic powers:
he begged the friends at his bedside to proceed methodically.
The memorial issue of the *Nouvelle Revue française* separated, with a singular appropriateness, the first two install-
ments of *Les Faux-Monnayeurs*. However truant to Gide in
his admiration for Proust, Rivière tried to live the ethic of
Edouard and Bernard. Beyond good and evil, he worked out
an individualist ideal of precarious harmony; sought a delicate equilibrium based on the juxtaposition not the suppression of antagonistic impulses.*

With Rivière as with Gide, we must be careful to separate
the public figure from the introspective and isolated personality of the letters, the essays, and *Aimée*. Like many others
who see no need for concepts of good and evil, Rivière was
a man of docile, loyal, and kindly temperament: an innocent
who could scarcely conceive of evil impulses, according to
his wife; for Mauriac, "Anima Naturaliter Christiana." Several of the contributors to the *Hommage* testify to his generosity, kindliness, and energy as editor and as friend to beginning writers. We are concerned, however, with the "novel"
of his "inner life." Significantly, Rivière continued to write
confessional letters to Gide even after they were closely associated on the magazine, and were meeting frequently. The
active editor still harbored another self which asked for
spiritual guidance.

The peculiarities of this other self must be taken into
acount in any serious study of Rivière's discipleships. The
data are too slight, perhaps, to permit easy diagnosis: "latent
homosexuality," or "search for a substitute father," or "self-

---

* He anticipated, incidentally, the most succinct definition of Bernard's
ideal, the famous image of the taut wire: "il veut répondre au coup qui le
frappe, par un cri pur, juste et surpris" (Cited by Jean Schlumberger,
Hommage à Jacques Rivière, p. 482).

punishment for childhood guilt," or "compulsive reënactment" — the courting of catastrophe to prove that one can
survive catastrophe. Rivière's relationships with his various
masters were, nevertheless, unmistakably neurotic. "This
disgust with myself; this desire to destroy myself in you as in
a dear love, to think only through you — I am angry with
myself for feeling these things. Are they not the worst injuries
one can do you?" [53] So the Rivière of 1906 wrote with reference to Barrès, whom he had never met. "And yet I have a
desperate need to confess," he wrote to Gide in 1911, "a need
that tears me apart." He compared his "malady of sincerity"
to that of characters in *The Idiot*.[54]

The self-destructiveness, expressed repeatedly in the letters
to Alain-Fournier, emerges most clearly in the correspondence
with Claudel. Rivière was afraid of Claudel before he met
him, even before he wrote his first astonishing letter: "I want
you to brutalize me, to throw me to the ground, to injure
me." [55] His humiliating and chaotic letter of April 5, 1907,
is as appalling as anything in Dostoevsky's fiction; or, perhaps,
in Dostoevsky's confessional visit to Turgenev. Rivière's impulse was in part the normal one of the young unknown who
wants to be recognized — have his mere existence recognized
— by the admired great man. But it was much more than this.
He both paraded his self-destructiveness and asked Claudel
to cure it:

I chose my painful hunger and anguish. There is my malady,
of which I must nevertheless cure myself . . . Since childhood I
have always refused myself joy, rejected happiness, saying to myself secretly: "I will always have *myself, me* . . ." My love has
finally clarified for me my need to perish . . . I can fulfill myself
only by destroying myself ceaselessly . . . I must lose self-possession; otherwise I despair, and become evil. [56]

Rivière's self-destructiveness must be reckoned with, whatever its origins, when we come to measure Gide's influence
on him, or the influence of anyone else. Most of all, however,
we must discount the various Gidean ideas and attitudes
which Rivière harbored before he read Gide. He had already

found in Barrès that double impulsion to isolate or protect
the ego and to submerge it which we have seen as the fundamental contradiction of Gide's inner experience. And as early
as January 1906 he had urged "that our life is founded on the
oscillation, within our deepest self, of contrary tendencies."
Like Gide, he based his own "lucidity" on his awareness "of
the totality of possibilities" which exist at a given moment.
When he defined his "sincerity" to Claudel, he admitted its
resemblance with Gide's. "But books corrupt only those who
are by nature ready to receive their poison." Even in childhood he had been afraid to limit his love, "to forget the rest,
the innumerable immensity of the rest." [57]

The recorded impact of Gide on Rivière, as Rivière himself saw it, is available to any reader of the correspondence
with Alain-Fournier and of his own essay on Gide. In November 1905, reading the *Philoctète* volume, Rivière liked particularly "La Tentative Amoureuse": its "indefinable deli-
cacy," a "subtle irony," an "incomparable charm." He is
aware of obscurities in *Le Traité du Narcisse* and *El Hadj*,
but clearly lacks the enthusiasm for further study. The great
revelation came in 1906, with *Les Nourritures terrestres*. Gide
now is an "adorable being, who will not pass without influ-
encing me." At this first reading Rivière emphasized neither
the doctrine of sincerity (which he already knew), nor the
exhortation to rebel against family, habit, and one's past self,
nor the impulse to volatilize the ego. He saw, instead, the
sanctification of sensuous desire, indiscriminate and unreflec-
tice: "Hungers and thirsts for everything." Three weeks later,
and though referring more directly to Nietzsche, he gives
Alain-Fournier a sermon on "force": "The important thing
is to transcend myself." But still he emphasizes Gide's lesson
of hedonistic pleasure and desire. Two months more, however
— two months during which the book has "worked" in his
mind — and the full impact of *Les Nourritures terrestres* is
felt:

Our education is wretched. It consists in frustrating and dam-
aging all the child's desires. Why do we punish a child? For his
curiosity, his brutality, his violence? What do we teach him? Not

to get his shoes or clothes dirty, to speak respectfully to strangers, to eat less, to become less. Timidity: that's what education produces in us; that is what I am dying of, strangling in spite of all my efforts . . . I want to shake up all that. I want to see myself naked and free, without respectful prejudices, without unreasoned venerations. I want to put aside once and for all my reserves and timidities; I want the sight of things to awaken in me only an immediate desire to possess them, only the act of rushing upon them. Like Ménalque, I want — having buried my knowledge and my false riches in the darkness of my room — to leave: walk ahead with empty hands . . . Ethics should teach us to find our true desires beneath our prejudices and the timidities we have been taught. What an odious machination — all society's against our instincts! [58]

Such was Rivière's reaction in November 1906. By 1911, in the *Etudes* essay on Gide, he could look on the book with some of his original equanimity; could, for instance, devote much attention to form and style.

Rivière's changing reactions to *Les Nourritures terrestres* — more exactly, his "delayed reaction" to this book — tells us a good deal about the way Gide's books penetrate. First Rivière experienced an area of feeling very foreign to his own placid temperament, then he discovered a revolutionary message, and finally he enjoyed the stylist. Most readers of *L'Immoraliste* and *La Porte étroite*, I suspect, identify themselves at once with Michel's lawless aspirations and Alissa's aspirations toward sanctity. Later they may perceive Gide's interpretation of these aspirations, and his message on the dangers of suppression; still later the minute artistry of the "case exposed." Rivière shows the same delayed reaction toward *Paludes*, but in a slightly different form. At a first reading he finds his own masochism: "What is splendid in it is the hatred of happiness." This in February 1907. But by May 1908 he has reached a much more impersonal judgment, and is even inspired to write a Gidean novel on the relativism and gratuity of ideas. In August this novel — which if written would surely have been as abstract as Valéry's — had a title, "Bel Eté." And we can see that Rivière has already begun to meditate on the surrealist technique of *Paludes*; has already begun to move toward the revolutionary aesthetic of "Le Roman d'aventure." His reaction to *Paludes*, at first highly personal, became moral and finally literary. The characters of his own novel

must be as unreal as Ydier, Alain or Nathanael. And at the same time as precise, as individual and as living as Coeuvre or Isidore de Besme. The plot must be as banal as possible, so that the ideality of the relationships will always show through. And at the same time the plot must be as complex, as confused, as infinite as life itself . . . And what is even more disturbing — these are not problems to be solved in advance coldly. The book must, once written, find that it satisfies all these contradictory demands . . . One must realize that it will be perhaps the first book which will try to justify everything, refuse nothing; force the reader to accept — as though it were equivalent with himself — everything that is contrary to himself. [59]

On September 14, 1908, Rivière made one of his rare efforts to assert his independence. Saying that he could summarize "in three sentences" what distinguishes his own thought from Nietzsche's, Gide's, and Claudel's, he feels that he has now achieved an attitude of his own. His conception of happiness is different from the self-conscious joy of Ménalque: "We can never apprehend our happiness, because to do so would be to destroy it. How could Ménalque fail to see that the mere awareness of desire would suffice to exhaust it, and that the kind of exploitation he prescribes would make it as cold and unfeeling as a meaningless exercise." [60] Happiness (significantly defined as "peace" and "rest") is unattainable, but we should not give up the illusion that we can attain it. Rivière, temporarily seduced by Gide's sensuous delight in *things*, has recovered his old fleshless idealism. In the same letter he similarly deprives the idea of "sincerity" of its sensuous content. Sincerity is not the living realization of contrary or buried impulses, but a "progressive description of the truth. . . The series of perhaps contradictory confessions of a whole life." Desire is an impalpable aspiration toward the unattainable; sincerity an exercise in intellectual honesty.

This is all we know of the purely bookish spiritual influence of Gide on Rivière: the way *Les Nourritures terrestres* and *Paludes* "worked" and developed in his mind. For in December 1908, Rivière met Gide himself at André Lhote's house, and in January had his first intimate conversation with him. Thereafter the letters to Alain-Fournier cease to have any real value as evidence. We can no longer distinguish the effect of reading Gide from the effect of listening to him talk. We see Gide's personal encouragements, we see him sharpen Rivière's interest in Dostoevsky, we see him accept Rivère as a junior associate in the *Nouvelle Revue française*. But we have no way of measuring Gide's influence on Rivière's own writings; no way of separating, from the mass of Gidean arguments, the particles of thought which were Rivière's own. The 1909–1913 letters to Gide propose at times to define their differences, but reflect rather Rivière's confessional need and longing for a closer friendship. At the end of the final letter Rivière claims to have achieved in it the last depth of human friendship, "a kind of renunciation of self, and a devouring preference for others." But the letter itself offers a minute description of his own feelings. A complete narcissism gave Rivière the exultant feeling that he had achieved a complete friendship with Gide.

It is thus difficult, perhaps impossible, to draw up a neat balance sheet. Benjamin Crémieux argues against the idea of a slavish discipleship. Rivière, he says, rejected the "moral torment" and demonic side of Gide, who inculcated only a "complete accessibility [*disponibilité*] to all feelings which may offer themselves, and even to misfortune itself." Valéry Larbaud admits that Gide influenced Rivière, as he influenced "most of the best minds of his generation and especially of the generation that followed," but he says that Rivière freed himself of this influence long before his death. "What he sought so avidly in the thought of others," according to Jules Romains, "was the nurture which he needed at the particular season his mind had then reached." [61] Chaix's ambitious study of Gide's corrupting influence (*De Renan à Jacques Rivière*) is vitiated by a marked Catholic bias and by an obtuse failure to understand Gide's ethic of self-correcting tension. But even Chaix finds it hard to separate Gide's perversity from the perversities of Renan and Barrès. He accuses Gide of delivering Rivière from his last scruples and of placing him "beyond good and evil." [62] But the most fundamental differences between Rivière and Gide were surely here: that Rivière thought he could accept the Church without refashioning his moral life, and that he insisted on separating (as Gide would not) literature and morality.[63] "Yes, I need a moral liberty which disgusts you. It is not in order to use it. I wouldn't know how. It's in order to be free of that kind of preoccupation. I cannot admit the primacy of moral sanctions, whether positive or negative." These words, coming at the end of their published correspondence, are Rivière's, not Gide's.

Gide's own analysis of the problem must be read with an important fact in mind: it was written for the memorial number of the *Nouvelle Revue française.* He points out the areas of moral and religious difference, and notes Rivière's much greater belief in abstract psychological analysis — not only as one of the means but as an end of art. Beyond this he loyally attributes to Rivière a real independence of thought and masculine resistance to influence. "He was not a man to be imposed upon; on the contrary I think he most appreciated, in his relations with me, the clearer awareness which he could find — and which I unceasingly provided him — of the force of our divergence. . . We were resolved and resigned to remain, with all the strength of our friendship, adversaries." [64] Gide perhaps wrote more accurately when he recorded his wearied reading of the circular *Aimée*, and when he said that Rivière "constantly seeks to caress himself in others."

The balance sheet, or this heavily documented instance of one man's influence on another? The Rivière of nineteen was narcissistic, rational, analytic, reserved, consciously self-destructive, and a precocious amateur psychologist. He found in Gide his own (or Barrès'?) ideas concerning sincerity, "disponibilité," desire, the value of inward contradiction. For a brief period he may have been led, under Gide's guidance, to give those ideas a fleshly rather than intellectual significance. Verbally, his self-destructive impulses may also seem to resemble Gide's. But Rivière seldom analyzed those feelings accurately, or combated them with a real will. Gide may have postponed Rivière's movement toward the Church, and may have influenced his silence on religious matters in the last years of his life. Gide's "récits" may have affected the structure of *Aimée*; his conversation and example may have suggested the "Roman d'aventure" and "Reconnaissance à Dada" essays; his style seems to have left its mark on the essays on sincerity and faith. The verbal echoes and resemblances are perhaps striking. But did Rivière ever reach more than a verbal understanding of Gide? In the last years of his life — justified, it may be, by Proust's unquestionable greatness — he returned to reason and analysis with relief, to abstract psychology, to a timid and passive observation of inward experience, to a narcissistic subjectivity. Should we say that Rivière was almost saved by Gide but not quite saved? Or that, for a few years, he gave a specious impression of being saved? The important thing to observe is that nearly every sentence in this concluding paragraph has been tentative.*

Once we have thus admitted the impossibility of defining spiritual influence with exactness, we can begin to talk profitably about such influence: about the very real life that books live in the minds of their readers; about the exemplary, corrective, or consoling image that a writer's total achievement leaves. These are, of course, two different things. And any full study of Gide's influence will have to distinguish its two phases: the effect of particular books and particular ideas, and the effect of the whole life and career. A single book may save or corrupt us by its single message or particular energies. Only a series of books is likely to provide the contours of an attitude and a full image of our age.

* And how dubious even the best first-hand evidence may be one sentence of Jean Schlumberger on Rivière may suggest! "Ses articles et ses notes avaient apporté dans nos pages quelque chose d'intuitif, qui trahissait une formation moins rationaliste que la nôtre" (*Eveils* [Paris, 1950], p. 220).

It could perhaps be proved that *Les Caves du Vatican* had a more tangible influence than any of Gide's other books. Lafcadio was for many, Du Bos says, the Julien Sorel of "our time" — and especially of the years 1917–1923.[65] But Lafcadio's example was for the most part theoretical and "literary." *Si le grain ne meurt*, again, may have caused the greatest initial shock and for a few careful readers the most lasting disquiet. But the reactions to such a confession were often simple and predictable. *Les Nourritures terrestres* offers the clearest instance of a book's *diversely* liberating or disturbing effect on widely diverse readers, and on several generations. It sold only 500 copies in the first eleven years, only 1007 in the next eight, yet is today the most widely read of Gide's early books and one of the two or three books most commonly associated with his name.[66] Success finally came with Roger Martin du Gard's reference to it in *Les Thibault*, in 1923. Yet the book had an underground existence during the quarter-century of neglect. And even the scattering of 1897 and 1898 readers took very different forms of comfort from it, according to their personal needs. A few early critics found a narrow egoism; Léon Blum discovered a romantic and concrete yet unsystematic pantheism; still others attended only to form and style. But the strongest reactions were very intimate ones. Francis Jammes took the luxurious nomadism as a personal affront, yet on another occasion discovered much of himself: "torrents of chastity, of asceticism and moral frugality." Georges Rency found a "religious austerity" in Gide's frank celebration of "sensual joys." Jammes said the one voluptuous desire it awoke in him was a desire to drink water, thought by some to be dangerous. But Charles Guérin said the *Nourritures* filled him with desires. Albert Samain wrote of "fervor" and "love"; Raymond Bonheur of the "intoxication of the open air." Edmond Jaloux, speaking of the Ménalque fragment, testified to a real change in his own life. His letter of 1897 has the very tone which many later readers would adopt:

The first time I read it, I did not understand its real message — for my way of looking at things was still too distant from yours.

I reread this fragment many times, and then understood your full message. It impregnated me slowly; it did not leave me again — and, thanks to it, I have known how to resist ennui and to interest myself in things as they are. All the vital revolt against my stagnation, accumulated within me, awoke. You have led me toward life, toward nature and toward love. Certain words of Ménalque's have become my constant rules of life. [67]

Gide himself has preferred to emphasize the "apologie du dénuement" — the disvestment of inherited ideas, feelings, and vanities. Many readers, indifferent to the sensuous appeal, have found in the *Nourritures* a plea to think independently. But Jaloux's experience of personal revelation and conversion has been the commonest response of all. It was the experience of Daniel in the famous page of *Les Thibault*. Opening the *Nourritures* by chance, he

had never known a similar fever, such a glorious exaltation . . . He knew that this was a solemn hour, that a "working" — a mysterious burgeoning — was taking place in the most secret part of his consciousness. When at dawn he had once again finished the last page, he realized that he looked on life with new eyes . . . The feelings which he had hitherto entertained only against his will suddenly freed themselves, and took the first place. That night, and in a few hours, the scale of values was overthrown, which since childhood he had thought immutable.[68]

Much depends, to be sure, on the needs of this or another Daniel. The peculiar effect of *Les Nourritures terrestres*, Maurice Sachs observes, is that it responds to the needs of each reader, and whatever his particular state of mind may be. "Those who are born to order learn from it a salutary disorder. Those who are born to disorder, as I was, learn order from it." [69] As with Jacques Rivière, or Charles du Bos, or Francis Jammes, it could elicit a series of changing reactions in the same reader.

Les Nourritures terrestres lends itself as much as any book of Gide's to academic abstraction: to comparisons with Whitman or Nietzsche, to lectures on restraint and unrestraint, to generalizations on the perdurance of romantic naturalism.

But the most eloquent testimonies have been those of non-professional readers who wrote directly to Gide. A young seminarist thanked him for a liberation from puritanism and from "ideological balderdash"; the book prepared him to accept his vocation wholeheartedly. One R.S. wrote thus from Greece: "To the sinister imbeciles who reproach you with having corrupted youth I should like to offer my own case: a human being who underwent no influences in his youth, who attended school and college only five years, who learned to read and write decently through his sole efforts at twenty — and to whom *Les Nourritures terrestres* revealed morality and the human conscience." [70]

Most of all, *Les Nourritures terrestres* has conveyed a desire to live more fully to these nonprofessional readers — and, in some instances, the very courage to live. Yvonne Davet quotes letters from two persons dying in hospitals, in 1934 and 1935:

I take this occasion to let you know how much good I derive, at the present time, from the *Nourritures terrestres* — which has greatly helped me to "interest myself in life," and in part at least to resist the flood of pessimism and despair . . . as a result of the ravages of sickness and the waiting for a problematic cure . . . I have been sick five years, I am twenty years old and I first read one of your books — it was *La Porte étroite* — only six months ago. Since then I've read others, and little by little you have taught me the beauty of life, giving me thus at first the will to get well, and then to react against this horrible state of mind in which, between myself and all my desires, all my aspirations and the faith that was left me, the sinister question intervened: "What's the use?" (G.B.)

Because I'm perhaps going to die soon, I am writing to you at last.

You have been the guide and support of my life in the worst hours of suffering. The *Nourritures terrestres* not merely helped me to live; it saved me from death. At seventeen I copied the gist of the little book in a notebook which has never left me; I have found in it the will to live and if I am still alive it is thanks to you because through you I understood that the smallest instant of life is stronger than death and denies it.

And I have liked Michel and Lafcadio, Bernard and Olivier.
They have been my companions. I am twenty-two and I am going to die, although with all my
strength I will to live. A general tuberculosis has wasted me for
the last five years. I've lived on my back for two years and I've
known the worst depths of pain, but I've always passionately
loved life (or, no, rather since I was seventeen and read your
books) . . . (M.L.)[71]

There has been, finally, the "exemplary" or "representative" career and character: the image of a single mind har-
boring so many intense contradictions and personalizing so
much moral conflict. The friendly *Hommage à André Gide*
and the hostile *Latinité* survey alike testified to Gide's position as "le contemporain capital." The Union pour la Vérité
debate, called to analyze Gide's communist leanings in his
presence, eventually took up most of the issues which have
divided twentieth-century man. His opponents and his admirers alike have found his presence symbolic. For Gonzague
Truc, Gide was one of those writers who, from century to
century, "seem to incarnate the spirit of disorder and dissolution." For Heinrich Mann, Carl Sternheim, and others,
he was a representative "honnête homme" of his period. Even
François Mauriac could say that he "has helped all of us to
know ourselves. One has the impression that his work has
been for our generation a kind of landmark, which has permitted each of us to locate himself." [72] Mauriac's statement
for the program of the Comédie Française production of
Caves du Vatican is, coming from such a source, one of the
most eloquent tributes Gide's influence has received.*

* Mauriac's full statement is as follows: "Il ne faut pas attendre de
moi un jugement sur André Gide; j'apporte ici un témoignage. J'étais très
jeune quand j'ai commencé de lire, à Bordeaux, *les Nourritures terrestres* et
l'Immoraliste. Un adolescent qui se croit prisonnier de sa province, de sa
famille, de ses 'principes,' cherche de livre en livre la clef du cachot imaginaire
où il étouffe. Barrès, d'abord, le Barrès du *Culte du Moi*, l'avait secouru. Mais
entre eux, les idéologies barrésiennes (la terre et les morts, le nationalisme)
déjà faisaient écran. Gide, lui, s'était dépêtré de toute doctrine: il avait rompu
la dernière amarre qui le rattachait au calvinisme, il ne cherchait plus de
défense contre lui-même. Avec le Jammes de *l'Angélus de l'Aube* et des *Elégies*,
avec le Claudel de *Tête d'Or*, il nous rendait conscients de cette merveille: être

This representativeness will perhaps be, for future historians, the darkest of many Gidean mysteries. How could such a special and difficult writer, generally unknown before the First World War, and with a very special personal history, become "le contemporain capital" by the middle or late 1920's — the exemplary figure of his time? The answers are complex and several, and there is at least one answer which would puzzle most American readers: Gide's position as the greatest prose stylist of the period. We may be willing to single out our best prose stylists — say Glenway Wescott, Katherine Anne Porter, Janet Lewis, Caroline Gordon, Josephine Johnson, as well as the early Hemingway and the Faulkner of parts of *The Bear* — but we do not for that reason listen to them more attentively. Of the seven, only Hemingway and Faulkner (and a more tempestuous Faulkner) are generally considered major writers, and only Hemingway has a large public.

The first historical paradox is that Gide was an "exemplary" figure for fellow-writers even before any of his messages had penetrated fully: before *L'Immoraliste* was understood, before *Les Caves du Vatican* provided a popular image of youthful revolt, before *Les Nourritures terrestres* was

---

un jeune vivant. De sa rigueur huguenote, l'oeuvre d'art seule gardait le bénéfice.

"Mais la rigueur de l'artiste exige la pratique de certaines vertus: honnêteté intellectuelle, sincérité envers soi-même; nous les admirions dans Gide. Qu'au long de sa vie, il n'y ait jamais contrevenu, et en particulier dans le débat religieux, on en pourrait discuter et c'est là une autre histoire. Il reste que nous avons appris de lui à ne pas nous payer de mots: notre génération lui doit d'avoir été lucide.

"Le dialogue qu'il a longtemps mené avec les chrétiens, avec Claudel, avec Du Bos, se poursuivait au dedans de nous. Je lui sais gré, quant à moi, de m'avoir montré, dans la pure lumière de ses livres, le choix qui, dès le départ, s'impose à un jeune être: jouissance de soi-même ou dépassement de soi-même. A-t-il pesé sur ce choix? C'est le secret de chacun de nous et de Dieu. Ce Lafcadio redoutable dont l'acte gratuit va être joué devant vous, ce soir, lorsqu'il fit son apparition en 1914, préfigurait le jeune surréaliste qui n'existait pas encore. Mais peut-être aussi l'a-t-il suscité.

"Qu'on ne voie, dans cette note, nulle complaisance: je suis de ceux qui ont vécu "à contre-courant" d'André Gide. Mais le courant que nous remontons dans une tension de tout l'être nous est plus salutaire que le courant qui nous porte."

fully rediscovered. For young writers of 1905–1910 Gide was a leader in the drift away from symbolism and an exceptional example of artistic integrity. But the art not the mind was exemplary. By 1911 however (with Rivière's essay, for instance) some of the Gidean contradictions had become apparent. How could the same writer have produced *L'Immoraliste* and *La Porte étroite?* Gide had anticipated much with *Paludes* and *Le Prométhée mal enchaîné.* But his ability to meet a younger generation's needs was most apparent with *Les Caves du Vatican.* The success of the *Nouvelle Revue française,* as we have already observed, made a special and *avant-garde* attitude seem general. The change in Gide's fortunes, over the war years, was very similar to the change in Sartre's between 1940 and 1945.

The full transition from exemplary self-contradictory artist to representative and contradictory moralist occurred in the 1920's. This is a moment in literary history which it may some day be worth while to document in detail. The first important episode may have been the *Morceaux Choisis* of 1921 — a selection intended for young readers, and carefully planned to underline rather than minimize the contradictions. No doubt the repeated attacks of Henri Massis, emphasizing Gide's assault on a whole conception of human nature, helped to establish his representative interest. Finally there was the swift succession, within a very few years, of five disturbing books: the public issue of *Corydon* (1924), the religious diary *Numquid et tu . . . ?* (1926), the full public version of *Si le grain ne meurt* (1926), *Les Faux-Monnayeurs* (1926), and the *Voyage au Congo* (1927). All the major impulses and astonishing contradictions of Gide's mind descended on the general public virtually at once. How could one mind show so much perversity and so much piety, so much somber honesty and so much amusing vivacity, and finally such a social conscience?

Looking back from our present dark vantage, over the six decades of Gide's career and of our modern unrest, the representativeness takes on a different and less voluntary character. We see Gide then as typical of the twentieth-century intellectual, oscillating between isolation and commitment; tempted to identification with some group at each moment of spiritual crisis. Like so many others he understood the comforts of inertia and submission. But he presently withdrew, after each partial commitment, to his own difficult individualism. This is the representative career described in my first chapter. But it would be wrong to suppose that Gide elected it, that he *chose* to be tempted by the Dreyfusists or the Action Française or communism. The total experience was partly chosen for him by his age. We can say, on the other hand, that the contradictions of the 1920's were deliberate; that Gide fashioned with some care his multiple and inconsecutive image. And this was perhaps the most disturbing, and most "exemplary," fact of all: that he insisted on an inconsecutiveness which other men deny or try to conceal. Most men strive to prove their fidelity: fidelity to a past self which has moved in a single direction, fidelity to an ideal image of the future self. Gide's argument, which he made a living argument, was that each new moment should elicit a new self. Could a man really be so accessible to an unknown future, and so contemptuous of his own "figure"? Mauriac would have been happier, perhaps, had Gide committed himself finally to communism or to Dada. And Breton would have been much happier had he submitted at last to the Church. For radical and conservative alike such a restless image of freedom was intolerable.

And yet, Gide was not contemptuous of his own figure. His consciousness of an exemplary role — the endless retracings of his own curve in so many changing autobiographies — helped convince others that he did indeed offer an example. *Si le grain ne meurt* and particularly *Thésée* are the autobiographies of a man who has accepted greatness, who knows himself to be a living classic. But even *Le Retour de l'enfant prodigue* makes a personal crisis representative. Almost from the start Gide tried to universalize his most private experience; and, conversely, to interpret public dilemmas in the most personal terms. It is easy but I think misleading to say that he moved from a Dostoevskian ideal of disquiet to a

Goethean ideal of harmony. Like Thomas Mann, Gide had long been attracted by the image of Goethe's comprehensiveness and equilibrium — "the finest example, at once smiling and grave, of what man himself, unaided by grace, can achieve." [73] Goethe's one great weakness according to Gide was his hatred of darkness. Gide's own example, also both smiling and grave, is of what man himself can achieve, unaided by grace or dogma, and though handicapped by a serious neurosis. It is also an example of darkness frankly faced and made to serve.

Gide's representative idea, for the 1920's especially, was that the free man — freed from family, church, and indeed all external sanction — could still have an ethic; could still lead a humane, decent, and reasonably disciplined life. Deliberate conscious exercise, and not merely Babbitt's Freudian "inner check," could take the place of traditional punishments and fears. This was a comforting message. So too was his more general optimism: an optimism that survived a full awareness of the cosmic *néant* and the inward nightmare. So too was his personal example of anomaly transcended and guilt appeased. Who could not, feeling himself "different from the others," look to Gide's triumph with comfort? We may nevertheless doubt that Gide's final mission was to bring comfort. The mission was rather to disturb.

A certain amount of disturbance may have been whimsical or diabolic: undertaken, that is, for its own sake and amusement. But this pleasure in making the respectable squirm must be conceded to any great writer, however placid his century. Gide's serious attempt, as "demoralizer," was to bring as much conflict, longing and self-delusion as possible to the level of consciousness; to get individuals and groups to explore their instinctive premises. The Pontigny conferences corresponded, on a public level, to the private self-inquiries which the novels, autobiographies, and essays instituted. Gide's prolonged effort was to make men look into themselves, and recognize the motives for their acts and beliefs. The effort was psychiatric, maieutic. Or, to put things more simply, Gide was ahead of both his readers and his time.

A study of Gide naturally ends with a personal statement. I first tried to assess Gide's role as a "demoralizer" in 1947. Much of what I wrote then seems to me true. As demoralizer, Gide encourages tolerance, a reasonable sympathy, suspended judgment, moral independence — all very real virtues of the critical spirit. He wants us to question our most cherished institutions, as well as our preconceptions. The only valuable demoralizer is the one who, like Gide, has much respect for the tradition he hopes to purify, and who has a strong natural impulse to order. The destructive intellect, to be of value, must be a controlled intellect. In this connection America, with its lingering puritanisms and its tendency to slogan-thinking, particularly needs *coherent* demoralizers, not Menckens and Philip Wylies. It would hardly be possible to overestimate the benefits an American André Gide would confer.

In more general, philosophical terms, Gide's position, if taken very literally, has serious and obvious limitations. Were it not for his natural inclination to logic and belief, he would have fallen into the purest phenomenology. The danger of Gide's attitude is that it removes, theoretically, the possibility of choice. It could give comfort to those who, between the two wars, tried to argue value out of existence. This objection, which has been made by many others, could be developed at length. But Gide has been a moralist, not a metaphysician. What particularly struck me in 1947, a year of uneasy peace, was that the value of the demoralizer varies greatly with time and place. I saw a Gidean demoralizer as more necessary to a confident America than to a discouraged France. Further, the mind which dissolves slogans and questions all assumptions seemed to me essential in times of peace but actively dangerous in time of war; such a mind discourages rapid choice and makes easy obedience difficult.

Now in 1951 this statement seems to me too bare, too abstract, too unqualified. Since 1947 the pressure of events has more and more forced upon us — upon education as well as government — the expedient decision and convenient fiction, the virtuous rationalization of impulses to power or survival, the collective hypnotic illusion. We have become pragmatists on a monstrous scale, and are much closer than most people think to the world of Orwell's *1984*, where what ought to be is "honestly" mistaken for what is. The pragmatist's truth (which Gide hated more than anything else) has gradually come to seem more true than fact. The mechanisms of propaganda grow constantly more powerful, and with them our capacities for self-flattery and self-delusion. It is hard to see how, in the years that face us, young people will learn to think truthfully, rather than to think usefully or patriotically. In such a world, we can be sure, there will be few demoralizers to combat the radio, the newspaper, the communiqué, the leaflet. These few may seem merely decadent, and Gide himself the product of a dead culture and leisure class. Yet perhaps only these few demoralizers shall save us.

APPENDIX (1969)

THE POSTHUMOUS REVELATIONS

"I must, I absolutely *must* disperse the cloud of lies which has
sheltered me since my youth, since my childhood in fact . . .
I'm stifling behind it!" [1] Thus Gide insisted in March 1922, regarding publication of *Si le grain ne meurt* and *Corydon*. And to
the very end he was concerned with the image he would present to
posterity. A writer so elusive, capable of such complex evasions
and tantalizing confessions (and who felt such a need to alienate
respectable admirers) could well be counted on to deliver a few
posthumous shocks. There was good reason to hope for further
light on the marriage, that "essential" and "secret" drama of his
life. The commentaries of friends after 1951 were less bound
than before by reasons of discretion. Many questions remained
that inevitably had to be asked — not for the sake of scabrous or
redeeming anecdote, but in order to define more exactly the pressures under which Gide wrote and lived. Had they intended a
normal marriage with children? How close was the real honeymoon to the tormented honeymoon of *L'Immoraliste?* How
much, at any given moment, did the sheltered Madeleine-Em-
manuèle know — about Gide's homosexual activities or about
his writings? About the major attachments to Marc Allégret and
Elisabeth Van Rysselberghe? About his casual pederast adventures? About his daughter, "la petite Catherine"? And did Gide
believe (who was so aware of the tragic impact of Michel's rebellion in *L'Immoraliste*, and aware too of *Jérôme's* crippling
passivity in *La Porte étroite*) that he had deeply hurt, perhaps
irreparably damaged, the person he loved most of all? *Si le grain
ne meurt*, ending with the engagement, cried out for a sequel —
though Gide had declared to Claude Mauriac that one would be
impossible. "Ce serait trop compliqué, trop délicat." [2] He said
Roger Martin du Gard would in due time give an account of
the marriage.

Et nunc manet in te (1951, private edition 1947), published
in English as *Madeleine* (1952), undertook to answer at least
some of these questions. It is one of the most beautiful,
most compressed, and most contrite of Gide's writings: an

act of penance coming from inward necessity no doubt,
but also one bound to lend ammunition to his narrower detrac-
tors. From beyond the grave Gide's sincere utterance seemed to
prove them right: he had been guilty of criminal dissimulation,
disregard, neglect! We surmise from Gide's narrative that no
sexual relationship ever occurred; may even surmise none was
ever attempted. (The well-informed Jean Delay, in *The Youth of
André Gide*, argues instead a humiliating failure. He says the
hedonistic fragment "Ménalque" in *Les Nourritures terrestres*,
was the compensatory dream of an impotent husband.) Gide tells
of being advised by a doctor, consulted before the marriage,
that he would return spontaneously to the "natural instinct." *
He did not. But it is evident the young Gide assumed his wife
could accept without qualms or distress a sexless marriage and
a continuation of their childhood spiritual companionship. He
modified this view only much later: "I am amazed today at that
aberration which led me to think that the more ethereal my love
was, the more worthy it was for her — for I was so naïve as never
to wonder whether or not she would be satisfied with an utterly
discarnate love." ³ He had "doubtless" told himself — "and with
what remorse! — that she might have liked to be a mother"; but
had reasoned that they would have disagreed about the education of children, and that there would have been other sorrows
and disappointments. In long retrospect these reasonings seemed
to him inadequate: "I have the remorse of having warped her
destiny." The most poignant note of all is that over the forty-two
years of marriage no explanation was achieved: only a wall of
silence on the question of their sexual relations, as on the question of his sexual relations with others. "Never a complaint
from her; nothing but mute resignation and an unconfessed
rebuff."

What I fear she was incapable of understanding is that it so happened that the spiritual force of my love inhibited all carnal desire.
For I was elsewhere able to prove that I was not incapable of the impulse (I am speaking of the procreative impulse), but only providing that
there was no admixture of the intellectual or the sentimental. But how
could I have got her to admit that? And probably she modestly attributed that deficiency of my desires to her insufficient charms. Skillful
and ever ready to disparage herself, she probably said to herself: "Oh,

* He also made enquiries, elsewhere, as to the dangers to children of con-
sanguinity.

if only I were more beautiful and knew better how to charm him!"
Just to think such a thing is painful to me; but how could it have been
otherwise, at least so long as she remained uncertain of the direction
of my instincts? How could I have convinced her that of no feminine
face, of no look in the eyes, of no smile, of no gesture, of no inflection
of the voice, of no grace so much as hers could I have become en-
amored? [4]

How long did Madeleine remain uncertain of the direction of
his instincts? In 1939 (she died in 1938) Gide believed her ignorance had lasted a much shorter time than he had earlier supposed.
Looking back forty-two years, Gide describes three humiliating
episodes of the honeymoon. She had been surprised by his
"animation" when, descending into Italy, their carriage was
"escorted by the *ragazzi* of the villages we were going through."
And she had been aware of the male models he took to the apartment they had rented in the Piazza Barberini in Rome, in order
to photograph them. Madeleine, he now believed, understood
the photographs were only pretexts. Most terrible of all is the
recollection of a train ride from Biskra, when three schoolboys
occupied the compartment next to theirs:

At each of the frequent but brief stops the train made, by leaning
out of the little side window I had lowered, my hand just reached the
arm of one of the boys who amused himself by leaning toward me from
the next window, laughingly entering into the spirit of the game; and
I tasted excruciating delights in touching the downy amber flesh he
offered to my caress. My hand, slipping up along his arm, rounded the
shoulder. . . . At the next station, one of the two others would have
taken his place and the same game would begin again. Then the train
would start again. I would sit down, breathless and panting, and pretend to be absorbed by my reading. Madeleine, seated opposite me, said
nothing, pretended not to see me, not to know me. . . .
On our arrival in Algiers, the two of us alone in the omnibus that
was taking us to the hotel, she finally said to me in a tone in which I
felt even more sorrow than censure: "You looked like either a criminal
or a madman." [5]

The second half of *Et nunc manet in te* is a portrait, already
adumbrated in the *Journal*, of the bruised, self-mutilating, self-
abnegating Madeleine, prematurely aged, withdrawing into
housework and deepening moral conservativism. No clear chronological distinctions are made, though in fact 1918 brought a
sharp break in their lives. Thus a grayness is cast over the whole

marriage, and over Madeleine's piety, resignation and silence. "It was entirely up to me to keep her from forsaking life." Moreover, "the zone of silence extended ever farther between us." The memoir nevertheless concludes with a beautiful evocation of the "deep feeling of harmony" he had so often felt in Madeleine's presence. A particular harmony emerged too, in the late years, out of "the very wreckage of our love": "I never loved Madeleine more than aged, stooped, suffering from varicose veins in her legs, which she would let me bandage, almost disabled, at last surrendering to my attentions, sweetly and tenderly grateful." [6]

Et nunc manet in te is so free of contingencies, of names and places and dates, as to have an almost Racinian purity and compression; by the same token, it is something other than autobiography. It is followed, in *Madeleine*, by the *Intimate Journal*: passages of the *Journal* relating to Madeleine that do not appear in the standard editions. Here (though again with little circumstantial detail) we see reflected one of the most dramatic moments of the marriage: Gide's discovery, after having gone to England with Marc Allégret, that Madeleine had destroyed all his letters to her. (We must turn to Jean Schlumberger, quoting Roger Martin du Gard, for an account of the confrontation prior to that journey, when Madeleine for once revealed that she knew of a clandestine relationship; and that she dreaded, moreover, her husband's corrupting influence on a family friend.) [7] The loss of the letters seemed to Gide an immeasurable calamity. He felt they contained the best of himself and of his work, and would alone have assured his literary survival. On certain sexual and moral matters there was silence. But on other subjects, we may infer, Gide and his wife achieved a rare degree of communication; each was truly part of the other. Gide says he wept for a week, and not only out of literary vanity:

> . . . I suddenly became conscious of the anguish in which my personal happiness kept her, whom, in spite of all, I loved more than myself; but also, more surreptitiously, I suffered at knowing that she had reduced to nothing all of me that seemed to me to most deserve survival. That correspondence, kept up since our childhood, probably belonged to both of us at once; it seemed to me born of her as well as of me; it was the fruit of my love for her . . . and for a week I wept without stopping, unable to exhaust the bitterness of *our* loss." [8]

In a moment of terrible if unconscious irony Gide writes: "I am suffering as if she had killed our child."

Such is Gide's moving and quiet utterance of an almost unrelieved guilt and remorse, tempered only by rare moments of
reasserted individualist faith. And such is his picture of a marriage that had failed, because of his own delinquencies and because of radical incompatibilities of temperament and attitude,
as well as because of sexual deprivation. Gide would seem more
than ever to have wanted to present the truest (even the worst)
face to posterity; and to be loved or hated for what he was. But
two authoritative books of 1956, written by knowledgeable
friends, cast a very different light on these events, and on the
darkness of Gide's behavior. Jean Schlumberger (*Madeleine et
André Gide*) was not only one of the closest and oldest of family
friends but a writer of great psychological discernment. He raises
the even more complex question of why Gide wanted so to
blacken his name. He suggests that he who accuses himself thus
is in reality seeking to excuse himself. But is there not also a
sharp need for self-abasement? Madeleine herself spoke of Gide's
"thirst for martyrdom." [9] Did Gide have to put himself to still
another test, this one posthumous? Would his good name survive
even *Et nunc manet in te?* Be this as it may, Schlumberger asserts bluntly that the marriage was not a failure. On the contrary,
there was a perfect harmony for the first twenty years. It was only
after the marriage that the solemn Madeleine became capable of
gaiety. And the Cuverville estate was known as a happy place for
visitors. Pierre de Lanux, who lived with the Gides from 1907 to
1912, speaks of a vivacious household where husband and wife
gave the impression of brother and sister living together by choice
and out of a "profonde affinité mutuelle." [10] The abstinence from
a sexual relationship occurred quite naturally, Schlumberger sur-
mises, probably to the relief of both.[11] In her 1891 Journal,
Madeleine notes that neither she nor Gide feels passionate desire:
"Amour implique, me semble-t-il, désir — quelque chose de brû-
lant, de passioné qui n'existe pas (ni en lui ni en moi)." [12] Shortly
before the marriage she wrote to Gide of herself as his sister:
"*Soeur* paraîtrait peut-être bien ridicule à d'autres — a mes yeux
il répond très bien aussi à ce que je suis, ce que je sens." [13] The
crisis for Madeleine came not in 1895 but more than twenty
years later. Moreover, the Madeleine of even 1935 was not,
Schlumberger says, an exhausted invalid, surrendering at last to
her husband's tender attentions, but a smiling talkative woman
full of curiosity about people and books.

In 1928, ten years after the incident of the burned letters, and the sharp spiritual separation, Madeleine wrote that the marriage had not been a mistake. But even in 1918, shortly after revealing that she knew of his intention to go to England with Marc, she wrote a beautiful letter that radically attenuates the severity of Gide's self-portrait. Yet even at Schlumberger's urging Gide refused to include it in his self-incriminating account:

André cher,

Tu te méprends. Je n'ai pas de doutes sur ton affection. Et lors même que j'en aurais, je n'aurais pas a me plaindre. Ma partie a été tres belle. J'ai eu le meilleur de ton âme, la tendresse de ton enfance et de ta jeunesse. Et je sais que, vivante ou morte, j'aurai l'âme de ta viellesse.

J'ai toujours compris aussi tes besoins de déplacement et de liberté. Que de fois dans tes moments de souffrances nerveuses, j'ai eu sur les lèvres de te dir: "Mais pars, va, tu es libre, il n'y a point de porte à la cage où tu n'es pas retenu." (Je ne le disais pas, de peur de t'affliger en acquiesçant si vite à ton absence.)

Ce qui m'angoisse — et tu le sais sans te l'avouer — c'est la voie où tu t'es engagé, et qui ménera à la perdition toi et les autres. Ne crois pas, là encore, que je te dise cela avec un sentiment de condamnation. Je te plains autant que je t'aime. C'est une terrible tentation qui s'est dressée devant toi et armée de toutes les séductions. Résister. Adieu, au revoir.

Ta Madeleine.[14]

The picture of a tormented honeymoon was also, Schlumberger claims, utterly distorted; and he notes significantly that Madeleine always spoke nostalgically of her own four trips to North Africa. A crucial document of Roger Martin du Gard,[15] summarizing a conversation with Gide, puts the terrible incident of the schoolboys on the train several years after the honeymoon. Moreover, a letter to Valéry of 1898 would seem to indicate that it was then, rather than during the honeymoon, that Gide rented the Piazza Barberini apartment. More generally, Schlumberger argues a separation between the world of the Alis and Athmans, a world of animal joy, and the world of Madeleine: Gide did not consider them rivals. Yet the Roger Martin du Gard document does add a third confession of major interest, though the incident itself would seem to have occurred perhaps twenty years after the marriage. It evokes, many years after that novel was written, the nerve-wracking constraint of Michel at La Morinière. The interpreter of *L'Immoraliste* who sees, in Michel's interest in Charles and Alcide, only an attraction to youthful vitality or youthful rebellion, should at least acknowledge Gide's own conflicts and suppressions:

Le troisième souvenir est situé en Normandie. Vous n'imaginez pas ce que sont parfois pour moi ces semaines en réclusion à la campagne: certains jours, le désir me fait errer comme un insensé à travers la maison, et sortir, et courir dans les champs, comme un possédé, vers les petits bergers, vers les enfants qui jouent dans les ruisseaux. Oh, il ne se passe rien, c'est impossible. Mais j'ai besoin de *voir* des enfants, de les faire causer, de les imaginer nus, de les avoir autour de moi. Il faut aussi vous dire que, autrefois, lorsque ma femme était encore une toute jeune fille, un scandale domestique avait détruit le ménage de ses parents. Ma femme avait eu la révélation fortuite de l'inconduite de sa mère, et cette découverte lui avait causé alors un tel ébranlement, ce secret avait été si lourd à porter pendant sa jeunesse, que sa sensibilité, malgré le temps passé, en conservait encore l'empreinte. Donc, une année que je m'étais pris d'intérêt pour un fils du jardinier, que j'attirais le bambin dans la maison, que je cherchais à le faire travailler, ma femme m'a dit, un soir, en me regardant avec une expression de supplication anxieuse: "Il ne faut pas que, dans notre maison, nous ayons encore à rougir." [16]

Jean Schlumberger's account thus modifies considerably Gide's picture of mutilation through neglect. On the other hand, it reports Gide's confession of cruel rebellious response, in 1918: a letter he describes himself as a "geste de criminel".* Above all, it emphasizes the appalling drama of suppression, dissimulation, and silence extending over many years. We wonder again how much Madeleine knew of Gide's wanderings or understood (or even read) of his writings. Schlumberger believes her suspicions were first aroused in the summer of 1917. In 1893 and 1895, Schlumberger remarks, people did not talk openly of homosexuality; the general public saw in it only a bizarre aberration of the ancient Greeks. (Jean Delay's view of public consciousness is quite different.) In any event, we are led to understand that Gide never spoke to Madeleine of his daughter Catherine, and was not sure, while his wife was alive, how much she knew of an event fairly well known in literary Paris. Madeleine disapproved of the toler-

---

* "Je lui écrivais que je ne pouvais plus séjourner en Normandie, auprès d'elle; *que j'y pourrissais,* — je me souviens de ce mot affreux; que toutes mes forces vitales s'y liquéfiaient, que j'y mourais, et que je voulais, que je devais vivre, c'est-à-dire m'évader de là, voyager, faire des rencontres, aimer des êtres, créer!" (Schlumberger, *Madeleine et André Gide,* p. 190).

ance with which Elisabeth Van Rysselberghe's having an illegitimate child was accepted, and for this reason did not want to
occupy the Rue Vaneau apartment adjoining that of the Van
Rysselberghes. Then, at least, she may not have known that the
father of the disapproved illegitimate child was her husband. Why
not, Elisabeth's mother eventually asked, tell Madeleine at last?
— to which Gide responded, "Mais, chère, cela est impossible. Il y a
des mots que je ne puis plus prononcer devant elle." [17] Schlumberger accepts Gide's version: that his silences were intended
to protect Madeleine, and were not motivated by cowardice. Yet
the need to dissimulate — the intense pressures of concealment
as well as constraint, the unending vigilance demanded in the
presence of one loved so sincerely — was conceivably more harrowing than any particular suppression of desire. It was, Schlumberger
says, "une dissimulation particulièrement pénible dans une union
fondée sur de si hautes exigences morales." [18]

The appalling drama centers finally, then, not on the lawless
or adventurous behavior but on this inability to communicate
and confess. Gide said on a number of occasions that his books
before *Les Faux-Monnayeurs* were written to "convince" his wife;
to convert her, as it were, to the individualist ethic. Should this
not be amended to say that they were at least in part written in
order to confess to her, but most obliquely and gently, what he
could not bring himself to say aloud? Wouldn't she finally guess
the awful truth? Of the Biskra section of *Si le grain ne meurt* he
said to Roger Martin du Gard: "You realise, don't you, my dear
Roger, that all that is for my wife? It was with her ever-present
in my mind that I wrote it." We may never know whether
Madeleine read *Si le grain ne meurt*. To Claude Mauriac, Gide
said that *Les Faux-Monnayeurs* was the first of his books not
written in order to convince his wife: to explain himself, to give
her the means for judging him fairly.

Was *L'Immoraliste*, too, a hard-wrought oblique confession?
Or can we say that the domestic drama of half-concealment is
responsible for its energizing reticence and subtlety, the saving
absence of overt explanation, that gives *L'Immoraliste* so much
of its fictional strength? The ultimate irony, if we are to believe
Jean Schlumberger, is that Madeleine herself would have read
L'Immoraliste in terms of literary conventions, would have been
reassured by the absence of any indecency of phrasing, and so
would have found nothing in the novel to trouble her. She would

not, that is, have recognized the novel's tragedy as her own. Jean Delay, on the contrary, believes Madeleine would have understood even the much earlier Ménalque fragment of *Les Nourritures terrestres*; and would therefore, understandably, have taken alarm.

II

The other major work published in 1956 was Jean Delay's *La Jeunesse d'André Gide* (*The Youth of André Gide*, Chicago, 1963), perhaps the most valuable of all the many books on Gide. It supplies, among much else, a number of important corrections to *Si le grain ne meurt*'s account of the North African journeys of 1893 and 1895. Gide's major attempt to achieve absolute sincerity of confession is not in the least brought into question. However, his memory for dates was defective, and his fiction-writer's incorrigible need to recompose experience at times had its way. Working from the unpublished notes to *Si le grain ne meurt*, and from a very rich collection of unpublished letters, Delay takes us a little closer than before to the drama as it was actually lived. He also brings evidence (to go back to an earlier time) that the dependence on the mother was even more sinister than had commonly been supposed. From his father's death until he was twenty-three, Gide was not away from his mother for a single day. Incidentally, Delay reminds us (as does Schlumberger) of Gide's failure to mention one of the most extenuating of circumstances, as we look at the conflicts and truancies of those years — that Madeleine had repeatedly refused his offers of marriage. It was, Schlumberger sums up, "un débat qui dure cinq ans."

The story of Gide's spiritual crisis of 1893–95 is rather more complex than *Si le grain ne meurt* would suggest, and distinctly more complex than Michel's story in *L'Immoraliste*. Books and intellectual influence play a larger part; indeed, a full novelistic treatment of those years might seem to invite the labyrinthine talents of a Thomas Mann or Marcel Proust, rather than Gide's classical spareness. Delay's ample record clearly discriminates between Oscar Wilde's generalized influence on Gide in 1891 and his critical psychosexual intervention in 1895. *Si le grain ne meurt* notably minimizes the meetings with Wilde in December 1891, perhaps because Gide had already written about them in his 1901 article "In Memoriam" (published 1905). Gide had not yet read Wilde's books in 1891; moreover, he claimed to have been unaware of Wilde's homosexuality at that time. The impact in 1891 seems to have been comparable to that of Ménalque: the seductive charm of a flamboyant personality and living legend, preaching heady doctrine. Gide's unpublished notes speak of Wilde "always trying to instil into you *a sanction for evil.*" He was fascinated by Wilde's paradoxes on life and art, by his disparagement of sincerity, and by his attack on the Christian virtues generally — the spirit of renunciation, the condemnation of instinct and mortification of the flesh, the concern for the "weak" not the "strong." The December 1891 meetings, Delay concludes, "represent an important stage in Gide's de-Christianization and demoralization." [20]

Another great de-Christianizing force was neglected by *Si le grain ne meurt*: Goethe. The battle between the influence of Christianity and the influence of Goethe was, Delay claims, the "great and perhaps most important battle in Gide's life." [21] The claim is surely excessive. Had no Goethe existed, Gide would have found some other mentor to help in his struggle against inherited inhibitions, or would have done without a mentor. In March 1892 Gide went to Munich and there began four years "of almost uninterrupted reading of Goethe's works." [22] (But how "uninterrupted," since he read and did so much else in those years?) On the brink of the first North African journey Gide hoped to learn from Goethe the art of giving in to temptation; the *Roman Elegies* had awakened dormant wishes and a faith in the primacy of beauty, a faith, too, in the joy of living in plenitude. Later, Gide would emulate Goethe's more classical concern for harmonious self-fulfillment. In 1893, too, Gide read and responded to Ibsen's dramas of revolt and emancipation, and to his pleas for individualist joy combating Christian renunciation.

Paradoxically, Gide's selective unbookish record in *Si le grain ne meurt* (and the even barer *L'Immoraliste*) may come closer to the essential psychological truth than Jean Delay's scrupulous summary of books read and issues debated. Delay suggests Gide hoped to improve his story by attributing to "fruits of the earth" what were in fact owing to "fruits of literature." But can we not assume the essential struggle was really inward and unintellectual, and that Gide would have won his way to "immoralism" (and to the full discovery of his homosexuality) without benefit of Wilde or Goethe or Ibsen? The essential combatants were not ideas but inward voices — an insubordinate voice of his own and the mother's internalized harsh one. Michel moved toward self-discovery without recourse to books; one suspects he would have done so without Ménalque. Nevertheless, Delay argues with some persuasiveness that Gide's "inward revolution" had begun before the first trip to North Africa in October 1893. Gide himself said he and Laurens set out in pursuit of an "ideal of equilibrium, plenitude and health," and that his decision not to take his Bible with him was of the highest importance. But an unpublished letter to the mother, written only days before leaving on the great adventure, asks her to send the Bible, and two other books: *La Logique de Port-Royal* (that "masterpiece of Jansenist rigor") and the *Elective Affinities*, with its discarnate mysticism. Now on the brink of a first liberation, as two years later after the definitive breakthrough in Algiers, Gide felt compelled to throw in counterweights of order and control. (In Biskra in 1892–93, it is fascinating to learn, Gide read Rousseau's *Confessions* for the first time.) [23]

Jean Delay's record of the divers sexual episodes confirms what we already know, and underlines the very close connection between Gide's homosexual conflicts and those of Michel in *L'Immoraliste*. Like Michel, the convalescent Gide was attracted by the youth, health, and vitality of the Arab children. "I feel better when I sense the presence around me of some beautiful child who breathes." Unlike Michel, he was aware of his pederast interest in them, and he still struggled against it. (It is amusing to learn that in Biskra Madame Gide was pleased to see her son go off with Arab children; at least then he was not in bad company.) These children were even more numerous than in *Si le grain ne meurt* or *L'Immoraliste*.* Significantly Gide records his attraction to one Hamma, who had the reputation of being a thief, and above all to Mohammed, Mériem's brother. He would seem to be the prototype both of that brother preferred

---

* Gide's obsessive onanism and its attendant narcissism is partly responsible, Delay argues, both for Gide's paedophilia, itself a sign of arrested development, and for the fact that mutual masturbation was his chosen mode of homosexual activity — the commonest among inverts, according to Freud. The imagery of *fellatio* in *Le Voyage d'Urien* (with its vampires as sinister as those of *Les Chants de Maldoror*) may represent an unconscious repudiation rather than wish-fulfillment. We may note the horror expressed in *Si le grain ne meurt* of Daniel's assault on Mohammed: "he was like a huge vampire feasting on a corpse."

in the last line of *L'Immoraliste* and of the insubordinate and evil Moktir:

Mohammed-Fantasio-Heinrich Heine — The tassel of his *chechia* was attached to his hair — a sneering head — or a serious death-head — vice or madness in his eyes — his burnoose constantly hiding the side of his face one could have seen in profile — a torn burnoose, an enormous flap of it always thrown over his arm — constant gestures with his hands. A highway prowler, he shot birds with stones which he threw admirably. You meet him at night in the Oulad quarter, always prowling, always in the shadows. He goes into the long and narrow café and chats — sitting in a circle with other children. Brushing against women, training for vice. . . . I had been out looking for him every day; so as to vary the opportunities, I would go down the road at different hours . . . and I dared not talk about him to anyone.[24]

The second trip to North Africa, as we read Jean Delay's full report, involves an even more intense and more intricate struggle than Gide's own narrative described. In *Si le grain ne meurt* Gide speaks of regretting Biskra, and of his "nostalgic longing for that great featureless land and its people in their white burnooses"; and he notes that he was "mad enough," before leaving France in 1895, to invite Madeleine and his mother to join him. Delay believes Gide knew returning to North Africa would mean, eventually, an acceptance of homosexuality. The invitation to mother and cousin, days before sailing, was a last desperate attempt to stop himself: "his one chance for salvation." But it remains true that only with the open acknowledgement to Wilde of his desire did his commitment and self-recognition become definitive. He then said aloud what had so long been repressed, toyed with, or consciously suppressed.

The familiar rhythms of Gide's spirit (and Michel's) — that compulsion to correct every swing toward anarchy by some reestablished order, and every impulse toward order by a compensating freedom — were in play immediately after the extraordinary night of sexual fulfillment with the little musician in Algiers. Gide soon returned to Biskra, not to emulate the debaucheries of Lord Alfred Douglas there, but to throw himself into work. The struggle against his mother's constraining influence continued, however. Hitherto unpublished letters concerned with the project of bringing Athman to France show Gide more openly and violently in revolt against her than the *Journal* or *Si le grain ne meurt* would ever suggest. Back in Algiers, unable

to return to France, immobilized in North Africa and fascinated
by a "quite Biblical corruption," Gide may have affirmed through
random revolt and sexual adventure his continuing protest
against the mother's puritanism. His voice, in an unpublished
letter of April 3, 1895, is very close to that of the directionless
Michel:

It seems to me that I have not yet seen enough, savored enough . . .
the desire, no, the *will* to push everything right to the very end and the
horrible realization that one is never at the end of anything . . . ;
the *will to dare* to do everything, understanding that our whole life is
compromised by each one of our acts. I'm staking everything I have in
this tragic game.[25]

Having achieved sexual release, Gide felt a need to go further,
achieve some other frontier. It was no absolute of anarchic or
lawless behavior he sought, one suspects, but rather freedom:
freedom from the tyrannizing voice, the outward maternal voice,
that was also, obviously, still lingeringly internalized.

The mother, in any event, seems to loom in the darkest background of that shadowy struggle, and the prowling of the Algiers
and Blidah alleys. Her severe harrowing puritanism and aura
of saintly sexlessness had without doubt crippled any impulses
toward normal sexuality long since. In 1895 the acceptance of
homosexuality and, beyond it, the need to "push everything to
the very end" (and the need at least to hint at some form of liberation, in his letters to her, the need to confess it obliquely)
were also modes of protest against the mother's domination.
There had been the surprising letters to her speaking of Douglas
and Wilde. Delay fascinatingly suggests that the private drama
was perhaps illumined, suddenly, by the public drama of Wilde's
disgrace:

Between Wilde's conviction on May 25 and the attack that paralyzed
André Gide's mother at the end of May, the chronological coincidence
is indeed disturbing. Did he himself never think of it? As a child, and like
many other religious and scrupulous children, he was inclined to make his
"sin" responsible for any unfortunate events that may have occurred in
his immediate surroundings: in *Les Faux-Monnayeurs* he described his
alter ego, little Boris, as terrified by the idea that his vice had made
him responsible for the death of his father, and I have already pointed
out the chronological link between Paul Gide's death and his son's fits
of anguish. Fifteen years later, upon the death of his mother, at the
point when moral suffering causes childish terror in even the most

reasonable of adults, did he not feed his guilt feeling on that kind of remorse? This hypothesis would more clearly explain the state of panic brought about by his bereavement, and the immediate and absolute need he had for "clinging" to his love for Madeleine, a pure Beatrix floating over the hells, the ideal image of a *vita nuova*.[26]

We will return briefly to the critical days following sexual liberation in re-examining the problem of *L'Immoraliste*. But for the moment we may anticipate the marriage itself, and concur in Jean Delay's definitive summation. Gide and Madeleine were more like brother and sister than cousins in their childhood years. But the marriage could be doubly incestuous:

> The note he wrote three months after his marriage: "How often, with Madeleine in the next room, have I mistaken her for my mother," confirms these hypotheses. It was impossible for Gide to desire a woman he mistook for his mother, not only because the prohibitions of incest were involved, but because no image was more apt to inhibit his virility than that of the puritanical Mme. Paul Gide. As a general rule neurotics — and Gide was sexually a neurotic — tend to repeat throughout their lives the complex-ridden situations of their childhoods in relation to substitutes for the parental images, thus perpetuating the early basic conflict. Gide's struggle against his wife, which began as soon as they were married, was simply the unconscious repetition of his struggle against his mother.
>
> When the couple finally settled down in La Roque, after the nine-month journey through Switzerland, Italy and North Africa, it became less and less probable that the inhibition could ever be removed. In the family environment, which had been created by Mme. Paul Gide, all the habits and memories helped to accentuate the unconscious identification between the two images of mother and wife.[27]

III

The unpublished letters and journals, and the unpublished notes for *Si le grain ne meurt*, make clearer than ever the autobiographical basis of *L'Immoraliste* and the centrality of its psychosexual theme. Yet a number of books published since 1951 either minimize the story of homosexual repression and discovery or ignore it altogether. Gide himself, though complaining that I had overpraised the novel, acknowledged its "freudisme latent et précurseur." [28] Neither Wallace Fowlie (*André Gide: His Life and Art*, 1965) nor G. W. Ireland (*Gide*, 1963) refers to these matters. The new version of George Painter's *André Gide: A Critical Biography* (1968) seems to have learned nothing from Jean

Delay or even from Gide's *Madeleine*. The well-informed Justin O'Brien (*Portrait of André Gide*, 1953) recognized the theme of unconscious pederast leanings, but was reluctant to stress it; so too J. C. Davies in *L'Immoraliste* et *La Porte étroite* (1968). Davies consulted the manuscript first draft of *L'Immoraliste* in the "Fonds Gide" of the Bibliothèque Doucet, and he refers to an illuminating (subsequently suppressed) passage that shows the violence of Michel's desire for his wife, "which immediately disappears as soon as he comes into her presence." [29] Stephen Ullmann, *The Image in the Modern French Novel: Gide, Alain-Fournier, Proust, Camus* (1960), manages to discuss the imagery of *Le Voyage d'Urien* and *L'Immoraliste* without discerning homosexual or even sensual elements in either. It is a relief to turn from such naïve academicism to Jean Delay's expert discussion of the sexual imagery in *Le Voyage d'Urien*.[30] And one recent critic, Ralph Freedman (*The Lyrical Novel: Studies in Herman Hesse, André Gide and Virginia Woolf*, 1963), does offer some illuminating commentary on *L'Immoraliste*.*

What shall we say of this appalling blindness to a subject any bright undergraduate would be likely to discern? It is true that the theme of latent homosexuality is no longer as startling as it was twenty and thirty years ago. Moreover, it is entirely legitimate to generalize Michel's conflict, and to think also in terms of other forms of conformity and rebellion. This Gide himself has asked us to do. But to ignore a novel's original and manifest content entirely — the very *données* of the narrative — would seem an instance of singular obtuseness or bad faith or both. Every academic discipline has its anxieties and shibboleths, and no resistance is more durable than that of the run-of-the-mill literary historian

---

* Freedman stresses Michel's passive role as observer, a role already evident in the scene of Moktir's theft of the scissors. "In a revealing scene, Charles superbly imposes his will on a wild colt while Michel and Marceline *look on*" (p. 151). Freedman comments on Michel's taking Moktir's mistress in his presence: "The importance of this scene lies not only in the further displacement of obvious homosexuality but in the way in which Gide chose to cast his transparent veil. Michel sinks passively into the mistress' arms while Moktir plays impulsively with a white rabbit whose anxiety he tames. Echoing Michel's observation of Charles' taming the horse, it reverses the perceivers while it retains the theme of taming as an act of the strong or liberated self. The inversion of the percipient's roles is similarly important — Moktir's indifferent presence makes possible Michel's release — because it reenacts his view of Moktir's theft with opposite roles and so completes the novel's cycle" (pp. 152-53).

to any suggestions of psychosexual content and to any "psychologizing" interpretations. Has it become a sign of soundness among professors of French to read *L'Immoraliste* in very general nonsexual terms? To see only an intellectual debate between rebellion and conformity, or to talk only in terms of the rights of the individual, is to oversimplify a great and dramatic book. Gide saw sexual conflict (and sexual nonconformity) as the cornerstone of his personality; they are the cornerstone of Michel's too. Gide wrote to Marcel Drouin in 1894: "The psychological truth of (such) thoughts *with relation to the person* who expresses them interested me more than their *absolute truth* . . ." [31] Again and again he speculated on the secret or buried psychological motivation of ideological commitments. The great beauty of the novel lies here: in its understanding of the relationship between the person and the idea, repression and anxiety, suppression and ideology; and in its dramatic rendering of the fitful struggle toward recognition. The formal beauty of the novel in part derives, moreover, from the fact that the pederast preference is not mentioned until the book's very last sentence. But to fail to detect its vibrating presence throughout the narrative, on a second reading at least, is to be unresponsive to language; to what can be said through nuances of diction, imagery, rhythm. And to see in Michel's interest in Arab children only a convalescent man's attraction to vitality and health is to pose too radical a separation of creator and creation. The great difference is that Gide soon recognized the pederast impulse, whereas Michel did not until the very end of his narrative. (The intensity of that impulse, in later years at least, had better be frankly acknowledged. His close friend Roger Martin du Gard acknowledges it; so too, of course, does Jean Delay: "When Gide was possessed by his 'demon', when he was prey to his pedophilic obsessions, he would lose all control and any feeling of decorum, respect for others, or even the most elementary caution. His features and his eyes would change; he would become someone else." [32]

What precisely is the relationship between Michel's repression, his ideological revolt, and his self-destructive frenzy? In Gide's own words though in a different context, "Il est bien difficile de préciser ces choses." [33] Jean Delay, it should be noted, finds it "simplifying to an extreme" to see a link of cause and effect between Gide's "immorality" and his "immoralism." Yet the data he has summoned so carefully seem to establish that link very strongly. Delay does not agree with Gide that homosexuality is the cornerstone of his personality; he is, in fact, surprisingly hostile both to the "immorality" and to the "immoralism." And of course it does distort a complex book to see repression as the *only* source of Michel's violent outbreaks and taste for clandestinity, or unrecognized pederast longing as the sole force behind his search for a "new self" or behind the new philosophy of barbarism and non-culture. Delay does, as it happens, record the virtually overnight consequences of Gide's crucial adventure in Algiers and the extraordinary sexual expenditure and release of that night. For the very next day Gide writes his mother that he is *"counting on a radiant springtime"* and that he is writing "all sorts of notes for my *Nourritures terrestres*. That frightful title is exactly right — and now I shan't change it any more." [34] Three days later he writes again, still in high spirits, but still conscious of an "unconscious" not yet fully discovered:

> I now feel that my youth is over. In this book I'm planning to write, I should like to bury it altogether. I feel myself maturing and ready for more serious and stronger works. — You might find it indecent that I talk so much about myself — but it's because I'm unable to write a line or a sentence so long as I'm not in *complete possession* (that is, WITH FULL KNOWLEDGE) of myself. I should like very submissively to follow nature — the unconscious, which is within myself and must be *true*.[35]

The fact is that Gide was ready, immediately after liberation, to reimpose bonds. Yet this was also the moment when he conceived "Gidean Christianity" with its freedom from restriction and rule. The *Journal* of 1895 already embodies its essential heresies.

All this is but to say that self-recognition and sexual liberation could not solve all problems, nor operate in one direction only. The random debaucheries, or at least wanderings, while Gide lingered in Algiers, were themselves a form of rebellion against the mother. And in letters of March 15 and 17 he sums up some of the great themes of the later individualist ethic.[36] At this point, at least, the doctrines of liberation were not simply compensatory. But there remained the fact that the mother did not know everything; full confession might have been needed, for full relief of the spirit. And on April 3 (to quote again a crucial comment), and still drawn by that "quite Biblical corruption," Gide seems to partake of Michel's directionless rebellion. A vital restlessness remained:

> It seems to me that I have not yet seen enough, savored enough . . . the desire, no, the *will* to push everything right to the very end and the horrible realization that one is never at the end of anything . . . ; the *will to dare* to do everything, understanding that our whole life is compromised by each one of our acts. I'm staking everything I have in this tragic game.[37]

It was a game that Michel lost; that Gide, more or less, won.

A Note on the Manuscript of *L'Immoraliste*

The distance between turbulent personal experience and classically ordered art is long. The working, or "first draft," manuscript of *L'Immoraliste*, in the Bibliothèque Jacques Doucet, exists at a fascinating intermediate stage between the two, and illumines both life and art.* We may surmise from internal evidence, for instance, that the still chaotic pages on Ménalque were apparently written before the rest; in them Michel is regularly called "Bernard." The last pages of the published novel are entirely missing, on the other hand, and the manuscript ends with the words "dix ans." The most fascinating internal evidence indicates that certain passages were written in a state of high creative excitement, either rapidly or with an intense groping concern for the right word. The landscapes so rich in sexual overtone involve (as on sheet 78) many insertions and corrections. Elsewhere, when concerned with the children Bachir and Lachimi, for instance, Gide appears to have written rapidly, not pausing for precise nuance or even always to indicate dialogue (22, 49 verso, 50). The handwriting leaves its normal even keel

---

* A manuscript (B-V-25) of 225 sheets, some of them incorrectly numbered or out of order, and on paper of different sizes and quality. Sheets 85–94 inclusive are missing. A few sheets include penciled marginalia and plans. Sheet 38 is written on the stationery of the Hotel and Kurhaus Arco. The manuscript was read in June 1969 with the permission of Madame Catherine Gide and other members of the "Fonds Gide" committee. Permission to quote could not be obtained in time for the present note. A later and more detailed report on the manuscript will, it is hoped, include ample quotation.

at certain moments of excitement, and curves more and more sharply toward the right-hand bottom of the page. Thus with the conversation that follows Michel's capture of the poaching Alcide (181). The theft of the scissors by Moktir, psychologically one of the novel's most enigmatic scenes, involves many corrections, and at last a handwriting so exceedingly small as to suggest either that Gide had no more paper at hand or, as plausibly, that he felt a strong compulsion to encompass the dark material on a single page, to box it in as it were (58).

To move from working draft to printed text is to observe, again and again, Gide's concern for compression, economy, definition. A certain amount of North African local color disappears, and a full realistic evocation of the twenty-year old Sadek is removed, presumably because an Arab of that age would have little appeal for the anxious pederast. An intense dramatic component (the progressive demoralization and increasing rudeness of the servants at La Morinière, as Michel's authority is undermined) is also minimized, as we move from first draft to last; it might have diverted attention from the novel's internal conflict (173). The movement toward published text involves, as is normal with great writers, a purified discovery of theme. Art triumphs over original intention.

The first draft is no more explicit than the last in defining or talking about the homosexual *données*, but in a number of scenes it treats those *données* more intimately. Gide's desire to generalize his personal conflict may be seen in a change from "ma chair" to "mes sens." The sound of a youthful singing voice at La Morinière is desperately compelling, in the first draft, and significantly recalls voices in Naples, voices of Arabs, and the voices of Granada gypsies (170). The little Sicilian coachman embraced in Taormina is described erotically as not much much "prettier" (joli) than many others and there is a reference to his dark flesh (216); in the final version he is, "beau comme un vers de Théocrite . . ."

The crucial evocation of sexual collapse noted by Davies appears also in the nearly final manuscript consulted for the Pléiad edition of the novels, though in slightly different form (*Romans, récits et soties*, p. 1527). Desire for Marceline, experienced intensely when Michel is alone, vanishes in her physical presence. There are two versions in the Doucet manuscript (82-83): the first uses the language of physical erection, and this appears also in the manuscript cited in the Pléiad edition notes: "gonflait et raidissait ma chair." It speaks, too, of an impulse whose strength had been unsuspected, though the "impulse" itself was not unknown. The second version speaks more generally of a reflux of life and joy. Later, two important commentaries are juxtaposed, though perhaps not intentionally; neither appears in the published text. In the first, Michel speaks of his guilty neglect, and of Marceline's affectionate patience (112–113). In the second, Michel refers to Marceline's constraining moral influence in terms very similar to those Gide would use for Madeleine (114–115).

A single sentence in the eighth chapter of Part One takes on, as we examine the Doucet manuscript, an intense and harrowing significance: "Ce fut cette nuit-là que je possédai Marceline." This is the first and, so far as we know, the only sexual relationship to occur between husband and wife; and a rough calendar at the top of sheet 149 duly measures the eight and a half months from conception in Sorrento to the "accident." Yet this crucial sentence — "Ce fut cette nuit-là que je possédai Marceline" — does not appear in the Doucet manuscript at all. Instead, at precisely this point, the manuscript breaks off (after sheet 103) and a different quality of paper is used. Sheet 104 moves ahead to events at La Morinière, and to reflections on Athalaric, and only at 130 do we find the old paper again and further references to the night at Sorrento. And only at this point do we have the next paragraph in the published text, beginning "Avez-vous bien compris." The movement of the manuscript is considerably more complex than this summary suggests, and perhaps indicates a need for evasion and concealment as radical as that of Stavrogin's confession. Suffice it to say that memory of the one night of sexual love hovers over the first draft far more than over the final text. Much later (194), when Michel proposes that they go to Switzerland, he says that they will live as they had lived at Sorrento; and, again, that he will love her as he had loved her there.

All this is but to emphasize that the first draft of *L'Immoraliste* is even more autobiographical than the last, even more deeply rooted in the personal drama described in *Et nunc manet in te*. The pathos of sexual failure and neglect is less muted than in the published text of the novel, while the sensual appeal of young boys, both in North Africa and in Normandy, is more confused and at times more intense. Gide did not begin his novel in order and generalized understanding, though he ended there triumphantly enough. The beginning was instead, as is often true with the highest classical art, in suffering and confusion, in moral and visceral uncertainty. Gide did, as he commented in the crucial letter to Scheffer, live through this book as through a disease. At the far end of the struggle was an almost perfectly modulated fiction.

A BRIEF CHRONOLOGY OF ANDRE GIDE'S LIFE AND WORKS

The following list does not include all the works issued as separate volumes or Gide's translations from Rilke, Tagore, Conrad, Whitman, Goethe, Shakespeare, Pushkin, and Blake. The English titles, unless otherwise indicated, are those of the earliest American editions. The dates of the works are those of regular publication. In some instances a small edition "hors commerce" was published before the regular edition. Several of the dates found in the books themselves are misleading; *Les Faux-Monnayeurs*, for example, is dated 1925 but was published February 27, 1926.

1869	November 22. Born in Paris.
1880	Death of his father.
1891	Attends salons of Mallarmé, Hérédia.
	Les Cahiers d'André Walter.
1892	*Le Traité du Narcisse.* An edition of twelve copies was published in 1891.
	Les Poésies d'André Walter.
	Two parts of *Le Voyage d'Urien* published in *La Wallonie*, May–June.
1893	First trip to Algeria, with Paul-Albert Laurens. Tuberculosis and convalescence. First homosexual experience at Sousse.
	Le Voyage d'Urien (Urien's Voyage, to be published).
	La Tentative amoureuse.
1895	January. Second. trip to Algeria. Meets Oscar Wilde, acknowledges homosexuality.
	Summer. Death of his mother.
	October 8. Marries Madeleine [Emmanuèle] Rondeaux.
	Paludes.
1897	Contributes to *L'Ermitage.*
	Les Nourritures terrestres (Fruits of the Earth, New York, 1949).
1898	Supports Captain Dreyfus.
1899	*Philoctète.*
	Le Prométhée mal enchaîné (Prometheus Illbound, London, 1919).
	El Hadj.
1900	*Lettres à Angèle.*
1901–07	Period of apathy and disquiet.
1901	*Le Roi Candaule.*
1902	*L'Immoraliste (The Immoralist*, New York, 1930).
1903	*Prétextes.*
	Saül.

1906   *Amyntas.*
1907   *Le Retour de l'enfant prodigue.*
1909   One of the founders of the *Nouvelle Revue française.*
        La Porte étroite (Strait Is the Gate, New York, 1924).
1911   *Isabelle* (in *Two Symphonies,* New York, 1931).
        Nouveaux Prétextes.
1912   On jury of the Rouen Cour d'Assises.
1914–16 Works at the Foyer Franco-Belge (for Belgian refugees).
1914   *Souvenirs de la Cour d'Assises (Recollections of the Assize
        Court,* London, 1941).
        Les Caves du Vatican (Lafcadio's Adventures, New York, 1928).
1916   Religious crisis; writes most of *Numquid et tu . . . ?*
1919   Begins crucial second part of *Si le grain ne meurt.*
        La Symphonie pastorale (in *Two Symphonies*).
1921   *Morceaux choisis.*
1923   Birth of Catherine Gide, daughter of Gide and Elisabeth van
        Rysselberghe.
        Dostoïevsky (Dostoevsky), New York, 1926).
1924   *Corydon (Corydon,* New York, 1950). First published anony-
        mously in 1911, as *C.R.D.N.*
        Incidences.
1925–26 Trip to Congo and Tchad.
1926   *Les Faux-Monnayeurs (The Counterfeiters,* New York, 1927).
        *Journal des Faux-Monnayeurs (The Counterfeiters with "Jour-
        nal of The Counterfeiters,"* New York, 1951).
        Numquid et tu . . . ? Published anonymously in 1922, but the
        edition was not for sale.
        Si le grain ne meurt. . . The title-page is dated 1924, but the
        book was not published until 1926. Twelve copies of the first
        part were printed in 1920; thirteen copies of the second part
        were printed in 1921. These editions were not for sale.
1927   *Voyage au Congo (Travels in the Congo,* New York, 1929).
1928   *Le Retour du Tchad* (in *Travels in the Congo*).
1929   *L'Ecole des femmes (The School for Wives,* new edition, New
        York, 1950).
        Robert (in *The School for Wives*).
        Essai sur Montaigne (Montaigne, New York, 1929).
        Un Esprit non prévenu.
1930   *L'Affaire Redureau.*
        La Séquestrée de Poitiers.
1931   *Œdipe* (in *Two Legends: Œdipus and Theseus,* New York,
        1950).
1932–39 *Œuvres complètes,* 15 volumes.
1933–36 Anti-fascist speeches and articles: presides at various leftist
        meetings; goes with Malraux to Berlin, to demand release of
        Dimitrov (1934).

A Brief Chronology 261

1934	*Perséphone.*
1935	*Les Nouvelles Nourritures* (in *Fruits of the Earth*).
1936	Summer. Disillusioning trip to Soviet Russia.
	Geneviève (in *The School for Wives*).
	Retour de l'U.R.S.S. (*Return from the U.S.S.R.*, New York, 1937).
1937	*Retouches à mon Retour de l'U.R.S.S.* (*Afterthoughts on the U.S.S.R.*, New York, 1938).
1938	Death of his wife.
1939	*Journal, 1889–1939* (*The Journals of André Gide*, Volumes I–III, New York, 1947–1949).
1942–45	In Tunisia and Algeria.
1942	*Interviews imaginaires* (*Imaginary Interviews*, New York, 1944).
1943	*Attendu que . . .*
1944	*Pages de Journal, 1939–1942* (*The Journals of André Gide*, Volume IV, New York, 1951).
1946	*Thésée* (in *Two Legends*).
1947	Receives Nobel Prize for Literature.
1948	*Francis Jammes et André Gide, Correspondance, 1893–1938.*
	Notes sur Chopin (*Notes on Chopin*, New York, 1949).
1949	*Anthologie de la poésie française.*
	Paul Claudel et André Gide, Correspondance, 1899–1926.
	Feuillets d'automne (*Autumn Leaves*, New York, 1950).
1950	December 13. Première of *Les Caves du Vatican* at the Comédie-Française.
	Journal, 1942–1949 (*The Journals of André Gide*, Volume IV).
	Littérature engagée.
1951	February 19. Dies in Paris.
	February 22. Buried at Cuverville.

TWO LETTERS FROM ANDRE GIDE

The first of the letters to follow was written after Gide had read an earlier version of Chapters 1–4; the second after he had read a slightly different version of Chapter 5. The page numbers referred to in the first letter are those of my original manuscript: the allusions to Renan and to Nietzsche's life at Sorrento have been suppressed. The analysis of Armand is now a little less complicated than in my first version, but says essentially the same things. The letters are printed in full.

Cher Albert Guérard,

Paris, le 16 Mai 47

J'ai pris l'intérêt le plus vif à votre étude dont je viens d'achever la lecture, sans en sauter une seule ligne, un seul mot. Elle éveille ma curiosité très vive pour ce que vous aurez pu dire dans les deux études précédentes sur Hardy et sur Conrad. Je ne connais le premier que par ses livres, mais vous savez la profonde amitié qui me liait au second. Ces deux études précédentes sont-elles aussi poussées que celle que voici? Aurez-vous su et pu y apporter un regard aussi perçant, aussi indiscret? J'applaudis d'avance. . .

Pour ce qui est de mon oeuvre, je reste émerveillé de la connaissance que vous avez su prendre, non seulement de mes récits, mais de tout le reste. Eussé-je pu lire cette étude de mes livres (absurde supposition!) avant d'avoir écrit ceux-ci, quel profit n'en eussé-je pas tiré! Mais à présent que la partie est jouée-gagnée ou perdue-, déjà tout retiré du jeu, je m'en détache et ne sais plus trop qu'en penser. A chaque éloge ou blâme, je me dis: le critique a peut-être raison. Seules de manifestes erreurs ou des interprétations malignement tendancieuses parviennent à me faire encore sursauter. Je n'ai sursauté qu'une fois en vous lisant: c'est à propos de l'extraordinaire cas que vous faites de mon *Immoraliste,* livre auquel vous accordez votre majeure louange. Se peut-il vraiment que vous ayez raison? Perhaps, perhaps. Pourtant je m'étonne. Je sais que certains lecteurs, mais de très rares, partagent votre opinion: Louis Martin-Chauffier, par exemple, qui me disait récemment à quel point ce livre l'avait bouleversé. Mais combien plus de lecteurs — et parmi les plus importants — furent également ou davantage encore, bouleversés par ma *Porte Etroite* (même Claudel!). Et s'il ne s'agissait que de réussite artistique, je ne suis pas assuré que la majorité des suffrages n'aille pas à la *Symphonie Pastorale* et à *Isabelle* (je ne parle ici que de mes courts récits). Il n'est pas jusqu'à mon *Ecole des Femmes* qui n'ait su me valoir des sympathies enthousiastes jusqu'alors refusées à mes autres livres. Je vous dis ceci, non certes en protestation de ce que vous en pensez, mais parce que *ce cas litraire* [*sic*] me parait assez exceptionnel, d'un auteur dont tour à tour tel ou tel livre peut-être jugé le meilleur ou le plus important. Nombre de mes plus avisés lecteurs ont une prédilection marquée pour *Paludes*. Quant à moi-même, je ne parviens à considérer mon *Immoraliste* comme supérieur aux autres sous aucun rapport, littéraire, moral, psychologique, . . . Toute fois ce que vous dites de son freudisme latent et précurseur me paraît forte juste et mériter d'être pris en considération.

Vos remarques et observations me paraissent toutes extrêment judicieuses. Je ne crois pourtant pas qu'il y ait à tirer grand argument du temps plus ou moins long occupé par la composition d'un livre, car intervient ici la question déplacements et dérangements divers, interruptions dans le travail; mais, ainsi que vous le dites, mon *Ecole des Femmes*, ou du moins la troisième partie (*Geneviève*), est de tous mes livres le plus péniblement écrit (et de beaucoup). C'est tout ce qui reste d'un grand naufrage: le nombre des pages écrites, puis déchirées, eût formé un volume épais, qui sans doute eût été détestable. J'étais alors empoisonné par la question sociale. N'en parlons plus.

Je viens de regarder à neuf, y prêtant une attention particulière, les passages indiqués dans votre lettre et marqués en marge par des points d'interrogation au crayon. Il n'en est qu'un seul que je vous invite à supprimer, car il est nettement inexact: p. 79, l'allusion à la "Cité Engloutie" de Renan . . . Je ne sais même pas de quoi il s'agit ici.

P. 149: je ne sais pas trop non plus à quoi vous faites allusion lorsque vous parlez des "crucial hours at Sorrento."

P. 195: au sujet des *Possédés*, je ne sais trop que dire; il se peut que vous ayez raison.

De même pour les autres points d'interrogation, je dis: perhaps.

Mais j'avoue que le long passage (p. 206) à propos du double personnage d'Armand ne me paraît pas très juste; je crois qu'il est et reste le même à travers ses apparentes contradictions.

Oui certes, votre étude m'a paru tout au long de ma lecture des plus remarquables. Mais l'intérêt, dans les dernières pages, fléchit, et la sorte de conclusion que vous apportez à un aussi important travail, déçoit. L'action que peuvent avoir mes livres, l'influence qu'ils semblent exercer aujourd'hui, n'est évidemment pas due à certaine qualité de romancier que je comprends fort bien que vous me déniiez, surtout si vous me comparez à Thomas Hardy ou à Conrad, et je ne proteste nullement. Mais l'ébranlement profond de l'esprit ou de l'âme est donc provoqué par autre chose, et c'est là ce qu'il eût été intéressant de montrer; ce que l'on n'entrevoit qu'à peine à travers et tout au long de votre écrit.

Je suis trop fatigué pour vous écrire aussi explicitement et pertinemment que je le voudrais et que le mérite votre étude; mais ne veux pas vous faire attendre davantage l'expression de ma sympathie et de ma reconnaissance.

J'aurais voulu vous parler encore de bien des choses: de Proust, entre autres, si important sans doute, mais qui n'a jamais quitté les données fournies par la réalité; n'a pas, que je sache, inventé, créé, un seul personnage; à mon avis, mémorialiste, à la manière de Saint-Simon, et non pas précisément romancier.

J'aurais voulu vous parler aussi de Simenon, à mon avis, notre plus grand romancier aujourd'hui, *vrai* romancier.

Le temps et les forces me manquent. Je vous serre la main bien cordialement.

André Gide

23 Mai

P. Scr. Cette lettre est depuis 8 jours sur ma table. Je voulais ne la faire partir qu'après qu'Armand Pierhal en aurait pris connaissance; mais celui-ci est souffrant et n'a pu venir au rendez-vous. J'envoie donc la lettre pour ne point vous la faire attendre davantage; et ma secrétaire va porter ce matin votre dactylographie chez l'éditeur Laffont, qui vous la fera parvenir. Tout attentivement votre

A. Gi.

Le 18 décembre 1950

Cher Monsieur,

Je vous récris tout aussitôt; d'abord pour m'excuser de vous avoir si mal reçu l'autre soir: j'étais, vous avez pu le voir et le comprendre, extrêment fatigué et à peu près incapable de vous prêter une attention suffisante; mais le soir même, ayant commencé à lire votre dactylographie, j'y ai pris un intérêt si vif que je n'ai pu la quitter avant de l'avoir lue presque tout entière.

Je n'ai pas précisément de critiques à y apporter: il me semble que tout ce que vous y dites est exact et d'une perspicacité très plaisante. Vous me permettrez pourtant de vous dire que je crois que vous attachez une importance excessive à ce pénible livre de Francis Jammes, "Elie de Nacre": absurdité sans conséquence, où il fait preuve d'une grande sottise et qu'il regretta, je crois, par la suite, d'avoir écrit.

Toute votre étude révèle une extraordinaire connaissance de notre littérature et me fait vivement regretter de n'avoir pas su, ou pu, causer davantage avec vous l'autre soir. Oserai-je ajouter qu'elle m'invite à emporter dans ma valise votre roman, en réserve, pour le premier temps de liberté spirituelle. J'en dirai autant de vos deux publications sur Conrad et sur Thomas Hardy.

Veuillez croire, cher Monsieur, à mes sentiments de bien cordiale attention.

André Gide.

P.S. — Par courrier différent (recommandé), vous recevrez les pages dactylographiées que vous m'aviez confiées.

NOTES

Since several editions of Gide's *Journal* exist, references only to the date of entry are given. The initials AJG following a reference indicate that the translation from Gide is the author's. Otherwise, the standard English translations are used; where the passages are of sufficient importance, page references to both the original and the quoted translation are given. The author is responsible for all translations from untranslated books or articles by writers other than Gide.

CHAPTER 1. THE CRISIS OF INDIVIDUALISM

1. André Gide, "A propos des Déracinés," *Œuvres complètes,* ed. Louis Martin-Chauffier (15 vols.; Paris, 1932–1939), II, 437 (tr. AJG). This edition is referred to hereafter as *OC.*
2. Georges Lemaitre, *Four French Novelists* (New York, 1938), pp. 116–117.
3. *Si le grain ne meurt* (48th ed.; Paris, 1928), pp. 128–129 (tr. AJG).
4. *Ibid.,* p. 247.
5. Compare *Journal* entries for July 14, 1914, and August 5, 1922.
6. *Si le grain ne meurt,* p. 369 (tr. AJG).
7. *Journal,* July 1, 1931.
8. *Journal,* June 9, 1928; June 16, 1931.
9. *Journal,* June 19, 1924.
10. *Journal,* June 3, 1893.
11. "Lettres à Angèle," *OC,* III, 177–179.
12. "Feuillets," *OC,* XIII, 445 (tr. AJG).
13. Mario Praz included Gide in his chamber of horrors. See *The Romantic Agony* (London, 1939), pp. 365–369.
14. "Notices," *OC,* V, ix. (The "Notices" referred to here and later were presumably written by Louis Martin-Chauffier, and not by Gide.)
15. *Journal,* Dec. 3, 1924. Massis's first important attack, "L'Influence de M. André Gide," dates from 1921. "La Confession d'André Gide" (1923) is perhaps the best of his critiques. Both essays are included in the second volume of *Jugements* (Paris, 1924).
16. Gide's greatest editorial mistake, later corrected, was to refuse the first volume of *A la recherche du temps perdu.*
17. For a fuller list, see Alphonse V. Roche, *Les Idées traditionalistes en France de Rivarol à Charles Maurras* (Urbana, Ill., 1937), p. 28.
18. Gide's earlier attitude is perhaps best expressed in "Lettres à Angèle," *OC,* III, 198. For an account of a worker's university, see Jean Schlumberger, *Eveils* (Paris, 1950), pp. 125–133.
19. See for instance "En Marge du 'Fénelon' de Jules Lemaître," *OC,* VI, 299–306.

20. "Avant-Propos de l'édition de 1926 de Numquid et tu . . . ?" *OC*, VIII, 344. Published in present editions of the *Journal* following *Numquid et tu* . . . ?
21. "Souvenir de la Cour d'Assises," *OC*, VII, 3, 27–29, 62–78.
22. "Réponse à une enquête," *OC*, VII, 93–99.
23. "Feuillets," *OC*, VI, 387, 391.
24. *Journal*, March 3, 1918; "Appendice," *OC*, IX, 466.
25. "Billets à Angèle," *OC*, XI, 52–53.
26. A translation of "Dindiki" appears in *Autumn Leaves* (New York, 1950), pp. 56–69.
27. "Voyage au Congo," *OC*, XIII, 190 (tr. AJG).
28. "La Détresse de notre Afrique équatoriale," *OC*, XIV, 281.
29. *André Gide et notre temps* (Paris, 1935), pp. 62–63, 15.
30. *Journal*, May 30, 1940 (tr. AJG).
31. *Journal*, October 14, 1940 (tr. AJG).
32. The translation is Malcolm Cowley's, *Imaginary Interviews* (New York, 1944), pp. 153–154. The French text appears in *Attendu que* . . . (Algiers, 1943), pp. 13–19.
33. "Oscar Wilde," *OC*, III, 487.
34. " 'L'Amateur' de M. Rémy de Gourmont," *OC*, VI, 296.
35. Letter to Montgomery Belgion, *OC*, XV, 551–553.

CHAPTER 2. THE SPIRITUAL AUTOBIOGRAPHIES

1. Henri Massis, *Jugements* (2 vols., rev. ed.; Paris, 1924), II, 8–9, and *passim*.
2. *Journal*, September 6, 1924.
3. *Journal: Numquid et tu* . . . ? (March 4, 1916).
4. "Préface aux 'Fleurs du Mal,' " (1917), *OC*, VII, 503–504 (tr. AJG).
5. "Feuillets: pages retrouvées," following the *Journal* for 1923. A slightly different version appeared in the 1918 *Journal* as published in *OC*, IX, 452–454.
6. "Feuillets: du déterminisme et de la contrainte," following *Journal* for 1896.
7. "Et chacun de mes sens a eu ses désirs. Quand j'ai voulu rentrer en moi, j'ai trouvé mes serviteurs et mes servantes à ma table; je n'ai plus eu la plus petite place où m'asseoir. La place d'honneur était occupée par la soif; d'autres soifs lui disputaient la belle place. Toute la table était querelleuse, mais ils s'entendaient contre moi" ("Les Nourritures terrestres." *OC*, II, 138). The ghost of Samuel gives Saul a very similar warning: "Crois-tu que Dieu, pour t'en punir, n'ait pas déjà connu de loin les derniers chancellements de ton âme? — Il a posé tes ennemis devant ta porte; ils tiennent ton châtiment dans leurs mains. Derrière ta porte mal close, ils attendent; mais ils sont depuis longtemps conviés" ("Saül," Act III, scene 7, *OC*, II, 339). See also Gide's letter to the Reverend Ferrari, March 15, 1928, *OC*, XV, 532.

8. *Journal,* January, 1912 (tr. AJG).
9. "Essai sur Montaigne," *OC,* XV, 9–10.
10. *Les Nouvelles Nourritures* (Paris, 1935), p. 115; *The Fruits of the Earth* (New York, 1949), p. 259.
11. See letter to A. R., October 31, 1897, *OC,* II, 482.
12. *Journal,* February 1902.
13. "Dostoïevsky," *OC,* XI, 289–290. Maritain objected above all to the assumption that eternal life could begin here and now.
14. "Le Traité du Narcisse," *OC,* I, 215 (tr. AJG).
15. *Si le grain ne meurt,* p. 275.
16. "Pages inédites," *OC,* XI, 26 (tr. AJG).
17. "Pages du Journal de Lafcadio," *OC,* XIII, 79 (tr. AJG).
18. "Journal des Faux-Monnayeurs," November 15, 1923, *OC,* XIII, 49.
19. "Feuillets," following *Numquid et tu . . . ?* and *Journal* for 1916.
20. *Journal,* May 1906 (tr. AJG).
21. "Les Cahiers d'André Walter," *OC,* I, 151.
22. "Mopsus," *OC,* III, 7 (tr. AJG); *The Immoralist,* translated by Dorothy Bussy (New York, 1930), pp. 69–70; *Si le grain ne meurt,* p. 321 (tr. AJG).
23. *Les Nouvelles Nourritures,* p. 33; *Fruits of the Earth,* p. 203.
24. "Le Renoncement au voyage," *OC,* IV, 339 (tr. AJG).
25. *Fruits of the Earth,* p. 165.
26. *Journal,* November 30, 1917 (tr. AJG).
27. In *Les Nouvelles Nourritures* (p. 98), contradicting his other general statements, Gide gives still a third answer: "Il n'y eut là délibération ni méthode . . . le désir travaillait sourdement vers une confusion charmante, et me précipitait hors de moi."
28. *Fruits of the Earth,* p. 171.
29. "Les Cahiers d'André Walter," *OC,* I, 66–67 (tr. AJG).
30. *Fruits of the Earth,* p. 59.
31. See Paul Iseler, *Les Débuts d'André Gide vus par Pierre Loüys* (Paris, 1937). Loüys encouraged Gide in his formlessness (pp. 88–89). See also *Si le grain ne meurt,* pp. 216–224, 248.
32. Loüys seemed unduly concerned with supposed resemblances with Huysmans' *A Rebours.* See Iseler, p. 89.
33. *Si le grain ne meurt,* p. 247 (tr. AJG).
34. "Les Cahiers d'André Walter," *OC,* I, 130 (tr. AJG).
35. *Ibid.,* pp. 157; 170 (tr. AJG).
36. *Si le grain ne meurt,* p. 346 (tr. AJG).
37. I am indebted to Martha Winburn England's discussion of this problem in my Harvard seminar on the modern novel, in the spring of 1950.
38. Robert O'Clair, in the same seminar.
39. *Si le grain ne meurt,* p. 322.
40. "Tandis que d'autres publient ou travaillent, j'ai passé trois années de voyage à oublier au contraire tout ce que j'avais appris par la tête. Cette désinstruction fut lente et difficile; elle me fut plus utile que

toutes les instructions imposées par les hommes, et vraiment le commencement d'une éducation" ("Les Nourritures terrestres," *OC*, II, 61).

41. "Préface de l'édition de 1927," *OC*, II, 229, 228.
42. *Fruits of the Earth*, pp. 65–66.
43. *Ibid.*, p. 169, with very slight changes in the translation.
44. *OC*, II, 437–444.
45. See *Philoctète*, Act IV, scene 2, *OC*, III, 57–58.
46. *Le Prométhée mal enchaîné*, *OC*, III, 119 (tr. AJG).
47. *Ibid.*, pp. 158–159 (tr. AJG).
48. *Journal*, June 1905.
49. *Journal*, November 1904.
50. *Ibid.*
51. "Le Renoncement au voyage," *OC*, IV, 328, 273, 290, 307, 266, 340.
52. *Journal*, February 6, May 1, 1907.
53. *Journal*, June 22, 1907.
54. See for instance *Journal*, March 4, 1918.
55. *Journal*, October 15, 1916.
56. Letter to Sir Edmund Gosse, January 16, 1927, *OC*, XIV, 400.
57. *Ibid.*
58. *Si le grain ne meurt*, p. 13.
59. First part, Chapters IX and X.
60. *Si le grain ne meurt*, p. 368.
61. *Journal*, June 9, 1928.
62. Mathurin Régnier, "Epitaphe de Régnier."
63. *Œdipe* (9th ed.; Paris, 1931), Act II, p. 52. *Notre Inquiétude* is the title of a book by Daniel-Rops (1927), who subsequently became a conservative Catholic writer.
64. *Ibid.*, Act III, pp. 118–119 (tr. AJG).
65. ". . . Je pense que quelque tare originelle atteint ensemble toute l'humanité, de sorte que même les meilleurs sont tarés, voués au mal, à la perdition, et que l'homme ne saurait s'en tirer sans je ne sais quel divin secours qui le lave de cette souillure et l'amnistie" (*Thésée* [New York, 1946], p. 121).
66. Perhaps as early as 1912. "C'est en nous que sont les écuries d'Augias, les hydres, les marais à nettoyer. C'est en nous que doit œuvrer Hercule. Le christianisme — l'opération intérieure . . . Thésée s'aventurant, se risquant *parmi* le labyrinthe, assuré par le fil secret d'une fidélité intérieure" (*Journal*, February 28, 1912). On January 18, 1931, Gide imagines a decisive encounter between Oedipus and Theseus, "en manière d'épilogue," in which the two heroes throw light on each other's lives. On July 24, 1931, Gide considers telling Theseus' life through a diary. "Mais voici vingt ans que j'aurais dû l'écrire." The three page fragment on Theseus' search for his arms must have been written about 1924. Theseus develops his muscles while lifting rocks to look for his hidden weapons; when at last Pythias offers him the arms, Theseus replies that

The Early Novels   269

they are no longer worthy of him. This parable is shortened and much simplified in the final version, and Theseus' language has become far more colloquial ("Feuillet," *OC*, XIII, 405–407; *Thésée*, pp. 13–14). The dialogue between Oedipus and Theseus did in fact provide the concluding pages of the finished monologue.
67. *Thésée*, p. 123 (tr. AJG).

CHAPTER 3. THE EARLY NOVELS

1. Jean Hytier, *André Gide* (Paris, 1945); Claude-Edmonde Magny, *Histoire du roman français depuis 1918*, Tome I (Paris, 1950).
2. "Feuillets: Projet de préface pour Isabelle," *OC*, VI, 361.
3. The remainder of the list is fairly conventional. Gide admitted that he had not yet read the tenth book on his list! See *Imaginary Interviews* (New York, 1944), pp. 165–166.
4. "Préface à 'Armance,'" *OC*, XI, 81.
5. See for instance *Journal*, July 31, 1905, and December 8, 1907.
6. Gide wondered why Conrad disliked Dostoevsky's work. *Journal*, March 10, 1928.
7. *Journal*, April 22, 1922.
8. *Journal*, February 23, 1930.
9. *Journal*, March 28, 1916.
10. "Billets à Angèle," *OC*, XI, 49.
11. Letter to Charles du Bos (1920), *OC*, X, 548 (tr. AJG).
12. *Ibid.*, p. 550 (tr. AJG).
13. "The New American Novelists," *Imaginary Interviews*, pp. 140–146.
14. "Conférences sur Dostoïevsky," *OC*, XI, 280.
15. "L'Évolution du théâtre," *OC*, IV, 213; "Quelques Livres," *OC*, III, 449.
16. "Journal des Faux-Monnayeurs," July 26, 1919, *OC*, XIII, 14.
17. "Lettres à Angèle," *OC*, III, 181.
18. "Billets à Angèle," *OC*, XI, 57 (tr. AJG).
19. Undated letter to F.J., *OC*, III, 562.
20. Undated letter to Scheffer, *OC*, IV, 616–617.
21. Letter to Jammes of July 1897, Francis Jammes et André Gide, *Correspondance, 1893–1938* (Paris, 1948), pp. 117, 330.
22. "Jeunesse," *OC*, XV, 83.
23. See Jean Schlumberger, *Eveils*, p. 144; Jammes et Gide, *Correspondance*, pp. 109–110, 144, 158.
24. Jammes et Gide, *Correspondance*, pp. 109–110.
25. Gide was aware of this negative influence as early as 1898: "Nous mêmes, plus personnellement, nous risquions de laisser s'encombrer toute notre oeuvre par d'informes mouvements de pensées — de pensées qui maintenant sont dites" ("Lettres à Angèle," *OC*, III, 236). "Mon *Immoraliste* était à moitié écrit déjà et tout composé dans ma tête lorsque j'ai rencontré Nietzsche. Je puis dire que d'abord il m'a beaucoup gêné; mais

grâce à lui j'ai pu expurger mon livre de toute sortes d'idées adventices qui me tourmentaient confusément, qui n'avait plus besoin d'être dites, puisque je les trouvais exprimées par lui bien mieux que je n'aurais su faire" ("Feuillets," *OC*, XIII, 441). On another occasion Gide felt, wrongly no doubt, that his book had been impoverished because of his unwillingness to restate these ideas (*Journal*, August 4, 1922). In 1927 he recalled again that discovering Nietzsche had proved a handicap at first, but had served to free the book from a theorizing "qui n'eût pas manqué de l'alourdir" (*Journal*, November 4, 1927).

The Nietzsche in whom Gide found his own ideas is perhaps best represented by *The Birth of Tragedy*, with its attack on inertia and its insistence on the value of inner contradictions and antagonisms: ". . . tous ses futurs écrits sont là en germe" ("Lettres à Angèle," *OC*, III, 232). *The Birth of Tragedy* is one of the most striking nineteenth-century analyses of the impulses toward concentration and dissolution of self. Henri Drain's *Nietzsche et Gide* (Paris, 1932) is an interesting but unreliable study, depending too exclusively on a one-volume selection from Gide's work and on *Also Sprach Zarathustra* — which, as we know, Gide tried on several occasions to read and could not. Drain does make a valuable distinction between Nietzsche's desire to absorb the cosmos and Gide's to be absorbed by it (p. 94). We must recall, in any consideration of this problem, that the influence of Nietzsche generally preceded a real knowledge of his books, and that Nietzsche was admired especially for the openness of his attack on Christianity. In the light of these facts, Renée Lang's attempt to prove that Gide read Nietzsche earlier than he said he did, and to prove a particularized influence on *L'Immoraliste*, seems irrelevant (see *André Gide et la pensée allemande* [Paris, 1949], pp. 81–120, 177–185). Even a few catch-phrases from an author who is "in the air" may influence us. By 1901 Gide had not fully assimilated Nietzsche, whom he had read at least in part, but he had thoroughly assimilated Freud, whom he had not read!

26. In an article, not yet published, on forty-seven years of criticism on *L'Immoraliste*. D. L. Thomas' *André Gide: The Ethic of the Artist* (London, 1950), the most recent book on Gide, offers a long and sympathetic account of *L'Immoraliste* which makes no mention of homosexuality. It similarly ignores the conscious sexual background of *La Porte étroite* and, of course, the unconscious or half-conscious sexual background of *Le Voyage d'Urien*. The reader will be forewarned by Thomas' prefatory praise of Charles du Bos. Several of Thomas' dates are wrong; he even suggests that *La Symphonie pastorale* (1919) was written before *Philoctète* (1899). His book is nevertheless one of the best written yet published on Gide; it has a Victorian innocence and grace.

27. Du Bos, *Le Dialogue avec André Gide* (Paris, 1947), p. 218.
28. *Journal*, November 26, 1915.
29. *Ibid.*

30. See my introduction to the Signet Book edition of *Heart of Darkness and The Secret Sharer* (New York, 1950).

31. Gide's Preface to *L'Immoraliste*.

32. Charles Neider's excellent essay on *Death in Venice* detects five men "with odd features in common," and calls the second and the third (the sailor with the goatee, the ancient dandy) "secondary symbols." See *Short Novels of the Masters*, ed. Neider (New York, 1948), p. 49.

33. "Feuillets," March 3, 1929, *OC*, XV, 518.

34. "Réponse à la lettre de Jules Renard," *OC*, VI, 135; "Feuillets: Projet de préface pour la Porte étroite," *OC*, VI, 359–361; *Journal*, February 7, 1912.

35. Letter to M. Deherme, May 19, 1911, *OC*, VI, 470; "Journal sans dates," *OC*, VI, 40; "Feuillets," *OC*, XIII, 439.

36. "Lettre de Jules Renard," *OC*, VI, 134; "Feuillets: Projet de préface pour la Porte étroite," *OC*, VI, 359.

37. Paul Claudel et André Gide, *Correspondance, 1899–1926*, ed. Robert Mallet (Paris, 1949), pp. 90, 104.

38. See *Si le grain ne meurt*, pp. 128–129, 226, 247; *Journal*, February 7, 1912.

39. Of loving Emmanuèle while playing more with the other children (*Si le grain ne meurt*, p. 125); of his aunt Lucile's infidelity (p. 128); of initialing for Emmanuèle the passages he wanted her to read (p. 210); of Emmanuèle's insistence that she could not marry before her sisters (p. 329).

40. See *Journal*, June 1905; October 18, 1908; July 31, 1905. The "Geneviève" of this last entry is presumably Alissa.

41. Letter to A.R., 1909, *OC*, V, 419.

42. "Journal sans dates," *OC*, VI, 40.

43. "Mais qu'il me tarde d'écrire autre chose! J'en ai pour dix ans avant d'oser employer de nouveau les mots: amour, cœur, âme, etc. . . ." (*Journal*, November 7, 1909). See also *Journal*, March 1913.

44. *Journal*, July 31, 1905.

45. "Notices," *OC*, VI, x–xi. See also Robert Mallet's introduction to Jammes et Gide, *Correspondance*, p. 20.

46. Letter to Jean-Marc Bernard, September 21, 1911, *OC*, VI, 470.

47. "Isabelle," *Two Symphonies*, translated by Dorothy Bussy (New York, 1949), p. 71.

48. Letter to Bernard, *OC*, VI, 470–471.

49. *Journal*, November 14, 1910.

50. Letter to Bernard, *OC*, VI, 471.

51. *Journal*, November 14, 1910.

52. Dust-jacket description, Knopf's Alblabook edition (New York, 1943).

53. *Journal*, July 12, 1914. The *Journal* entry for January 5, 1902, suggests an area of speculation which would lead to the conception of Lafcadio's crime.

54. *Journal*, April or May 1905, *OC*, IV, 510. Pléiade edition, p. 153, will locate this indefinitely dated entry.
55. *Journal*, March 28, 1906; October 15, 1906.
56. *Journal*, December 3, 1909.
57. *Journal*, April 24, 1910: ". . . d'un style tout gaillard, très différent."
58. *Journal*, May 7, 1912.
59. See Claude-Edmonde Magny, *Histoire*, pp. 238–239.
60. "Lettres à Angèle," *OC*, III, 226–227.
61. See for instance *Journal*, November 4, 1929.
62. "Petits Poèmes en prose," IX (tr. AJG).
63. "Journal des Faux-Monnayeurs," May 27, 1924, *OC*, XIII, 55.
64. *Journal*, May 1, 1927.

CHAPTER 4. THE LATER NOVELS

1. *Si le grain ne meurt*, p. 291.
2. "Billets à Angèle," *OC*, XI, 55 (tr. AJG).
3. "Feuillets," *OC*, XIII, 444; letter to R. P. Victor Poucel, November 27, 1927, *OC*, XIV, 406.
4. *Journal*, June 24, 1924.
5. *Journal*, July 16, 1914.
6. "Journal des Faux-Monnayeurs," June 17, 1919, *OC*, XIII, 6.
7. *Journal*, October 20, 1928.
8. Dedication to *Robert*.
9. *Journal*, March 31, 1930.
10. *Journal*, May 25, 1931; March 9, 1930; "Journal des Faux-Monnayeurs," June 17, 1919, *OC*, XIII, 6.
11. *Geneviève, ou la confidence inachevée* (Paris, 1936), p. 127 (tr. AJG).
12. *Ibid.*, p. 166 (tr. AJG).
13. "Feuillets: Projet de préface pour Isabelle," *OC*, IV, 361 (tr. AJG).
14. "Journal des Faux-Monnayeurs," *OC*, XIII, 14.
15. *Ibid.*, pp. 5, 18.
16. *Journal*, December 18, 1921; April 17, 1928.
17. "Journal des Faux-Monnayeurs," January 3, 1924, *OC*, XIII, 50.
18. *Journal,* November 12(?), 1922. The question mark appears in the *Journal*.
19. "Journal des Faux-Monnayeurs," June 17, 1919, *OC*, XIII, 5.
20. *Ibid.*, June 17, 1919, and June 16, 1921, pp. 6, 25. The plight of the woman may be reflected to a certain extent in the unhappy marriages of Pauline and Mme Profitendieu.
21. *Ibid.*, June 17, 1919, p. 6.
22. *Ibid.*, p. 7.
23. *Ibid.*, July 30, 1919, p. 15.
24. *Ibid.*, August 1921, p. 32; January 3, 1925, pp. 58–59.
25. Duchamp's Mona Lisa served as a cover for Picabia's magazine *391*, which appeared in 1920 and 1921. It is reproduced in Albert Schinz, *Dadaïsme, poignée de documents (1916–1921)*, Smith College Studies in

Modern Languages (Northampton, Mass., 1923), p. 52. See also Maurice Nadeau, *Histoire du surréalisme* (Paris, 1945), pp. 49–50, 356.

26. "Journal des Faux-Monnayeurs," January 1, 1921, *OC*, XIII, 19, 21.

27. *Ibid.*, February 23, 1923, pp. 44–45. See also "Appendice: Identification du démon," pp. 79–82.

28. *Ibid.*, July 16, 1919, pp. 12–13. Cp. *The Counterfeiters*, translated by Dorothy Bussy (Modern Library ed.), p. 132. Gide has compressed into a few lines the material for half-a-dozen chapters.

29. "Journal des Faux-Monnayeurs," June 17, 1919, and July 6, 1919, *OC*, XIII, 5, 10. See also "Appendice: Pages du Journal de Lafcadio," *OC*, XIII, 75–79.

30. The transition seems to be occurring in May 1921. See "Journal des Faux-Monnayeurs," May 3, 1921, *OC*, XIII, 22.

31. *Ibid.*, February 23, 1923, p. 44.

32. *Ibid.*, January 3, 1925, pp. 58–59 (tr. AJG).

33. *Ibid.*, August 20, 1922, p. 39.

34. *Ibid.*, March 29, 1925, p. 61.

35. *Ibid.*, April 10, 1924, p. 53.

36. *Journal*, June 17, 1923; October 3, 1924.

37. Hytier, *André Gide*, pp. 253–271.

38. Crémieux, "André Gide et l'art du roman," *Hommage à André Gide* (Paris, 1928), p. 95. I have rigidly curtailed Crémieux's summary.

39. "Journal des Faux-Monnayeurs; Appendices," *OC*, XIII, 65–68.

40. *Ibid.*, March 31, 1924, p. 52; *Journal*, October 3, 1924.

41. "Journal des Faux-Monnayeurs," November 3, 1923, p. 50.

42. *Journal*, February 8, 1902.

43. "Anna Shackleton! . . . Raconterai-je un jour votre modeste vie? Je voudrais que, dans mon récit, cette humilité resplendisse, comme elle resplendira devant Dieu le jour où seront abaissés les puissants, où seront magnifiés les humbles. Je ne me suis jamais senti grand goût pour portraire les triomphants et les glorieux de ce monde, mais bien ceux dont la plus vraie gloire est cachée" (*Si le grain ne meurt*, p. 29). For a suggestion of Rachel, see *Si le grain ne meurt*, p. 178.

44. "Journal des Faux-Monnayeurs," *OC*, XIII, 71; *Si le grain ne meurt*, pp. 178–185.

45. The original for Pastor Vedel. See *Si le grain ne meurt*, pp. 179–180.

46. *The Counterfeiters*, pp. 208–211 ("The Author Reviews his Characters"). Cp. "Journal des Faux-Monnayeurs," *OC*, XIII, 16.

47. At one of the *Mercure* dinners. See Eugène Montfort, *Vingt-Cinq Ans de littérature française*, I, 196, for a reference to this incident. Gide gives an account of it in his essay on Christian Beck, translated in *Autumn Leaves* (New York, 1950), pp. 131–135.

48. "Journal des Faux-Monnayeurs," May 27, 1924, *OC*, XIII, 54.

49. *Ibid.*, November 15, 1923, p. 49 (tr. AJG).

50. See *Journal*, October 29, 1929.

51. *The Counterfeiters*, p. 65.
52. "But my vocation was to write *The Nocturnal Vase*" (*ibid.*, p. 352).
53. "Journal des Faux-Monnayeurs," December 27, 1923, *OC*, XIII, 49–50.
54. *The Counterfeiters*, p. 81.
55. *Ibid.*, p. 68.
56. "Journal des Faux-Monnayeurs," January 2, 1921, *OC*, XIII, 19.
57. Claude-Edmonde Magny, *Histoire*, pp. 230–278.
58. *Ibid.*, p. 241.
59. *The Counterfeiters*, p. 44.
60. *Ibid.*, p. 176.

CHAPTER 5. THE CORRUPTOR OF YOUTH

1. "Enquéte sur André Gide," *Latinité*, January 1931, p. 46.
2. *Ibid.*, p. 201.
3. Armand Pierhal, Rivière's private secretary in the last months of his life, says that *Aimée* is commonly supposed to be a "roman-à-clef," with Gaston Gallimard as Bourguignon and Rivière as François (conversation with author, December 1950).
4. Jacques Rivière, *Aimée* (Paris, 1922), pp. 20, 22, 89.
5. Claude-Edmonde Magny, *Histoire*, pp. 103–104.
6. Speaking of Gide's influence as exerted through the *Nrf*, René Boysleve writes that "on ne louera jamais assez le rôle de bienfaiteur de la littérature et de pensée nettement indépendantes" ("Hommage à Jacques Rivière," *La Nouvelle Revue française*, No. 139, April 1, 1925, p. 544).
7. Jacques Rivière et Alain-Fournier, *Correspondance, 1905–1914* (2 vols.; Paris, 1948), II, 95 (referred to hereafter as Rivière-Fournier). Jammes objected to Angaire's disgust with normal sexual relations, in a letter of December 1894 (Jammes et Gide, *Correspondance*, p. 38).
8. Gide read the sixth Chant for the first time in November 1905 (*Journal*, November 23, 1905).
9. She asks whether, without the *Caves*, such books as Cassou's *Légion*, Queneau's *Enfants du Limon*, Ribémont-Dessaignes's *Adolescence*, or Guilloux's *Le Sang noir* would have been possible. "I don't mean to claim that these novelists were directly or consciously inspired by Gide; simply, one must recognize that his 'soties' have done much to make the technique of the novel more supple . . . and first of all the technique of the novel he himself would write" (Claude-Edmonde Magny, *Histoire*, p. 239).
10. *Latinité*, January 1931, p. 47.
11. Rivière-Fournier, II, 338.
12. *Hommage à Jacques Rivière*, p. 550.
13. *Nouvelles Etudes* (Paris, 1947), pp. 253–260.
14. *Ibid.*, p. 264.
15. *Ibid.*, pp. 266–293.
16. Charles du Bos, *Journal, 1926–1927*, Tome III (Paris, 1949), p. 304.

17. Claude-Edmonde Magny, p. 243.
18. *Ibid.*, p. 282.
19. The two essays are reprinted in *Nouvelles Etudes.*
20. Rivière-Fournier, II, 373.
21. *Ibid.*, II, 415.
22. *Latinité*, January 1931, p. 112.
23. Rivière-Fournier, II, 59.
24. *Hommage à André Gide*, p. 131.
25. In conversation with the author, November 1950.
26. Jammes et Gide, *Correspondance*, p. 128.
27. Rivière-Fournier, II, 265–266.
28. Letter of November 5, 1922, *Lettres de Charles du Bos et réponses de André Gide* (Paris, 1950), p. 49.
29. Charles du Bos, *Le Dialogue avec André Gide*, p. 145n; letter of Rivière to Gide, January 3, 1911, in *Hommage à Jacques Rivière*, p. 766.
30. *Hommage à André Gide*, pp. 131–132.
31. Letter of March 12, 1909, in *Hommage à Jacques Rivière*, p. 762.
32. Taken in conjunction with Du Bos's *Journal* and with the *Lettres de Charles du Bos et réponses de André Gide, Le Dialogue avec André Gide* may serve as a model of distorted criticism — the more so because Du Bos was capable of subtle analysis and trenchant phrasing. The habit of dictation usually led to a Jamesian verbosity; even when he is most grotesquely wrong Du Bos seems self-assured and patronizing. The reader is hedged in by so many scrupulous qualifications, by such an intimate friendship with the author under examination, that he is likely to be intimidated. The *Journal* reveals transparently two serious vices: (1) to classify and order even the most intractable material; (2) to quote the author against himself even when the two or more passages have, taken in context, no real connection. For an example of Du Bos's orderly tactics of ill-will, which omits all that is praiseworthy in the texts to be cited, see *Journal*, III, 321–322.
33. *Nouvelles Etudes*, p. 230.
34. Claudel et Gide, *Correspondance*, pp. 29 (note 3), 219.
35. *Ibid.*, p. 249. From an interview with Dominique Arban, in *Combat*, March 28, 1947.
36. We learn, for instance, that *Le Retour de l'enfant prodigue* is in part an answer to Claudel's missionary efforts (p. 16); that the double plot and Freudian motivation of *La Porte étroite* had no part in the original plan (p. 104); that, as late as 1914, Gide had kept his homosexuality unknown from the ambulatory Claudel and even from such a close associate as Rivière (p. 234), and that he hoped to keep it secret because he was married (p. 218).
37. Claudel et Gide, *Correspondance*, p. 245.
38. *Ibid.*, p. 217.
39. *Ibid.*, p. 220 (my italics).

40. *Ibid.*, p. 245.
41. *Ibid.*, p. 145.
42. *Hommage à Jacques Rivière*, p. 465.
43. Rivière-Fournier, I, 411, 92, 157, 330; II, 46, 59, 112.
44. *Ibid.*, II, 110.
45. *Journal*, December 3, 1922.
46. Rivière-Fournier, I, 121, 197.
47. Letter of January 3, 1911, in *Hommage à Jacques Rivière*, p. 767.
48. Letter of January 4, 1913, *ibid.*, p. 779.
49. *Ibid.*, p. 771.
50. Rivière-Fournier, I, 308; II, 48.
51. *Nouvelles Etudes*, pp. 174–175.
52. *Ibid.*, p. 307.
53. Rivière-Fournier, I, 392.
54. *Hommage à Jacques Rivière*, p. 766.
55. Jacques Rivière et Paul Claudel, *Correspondance, 1907–1914* (Paris, 1926), p. 1.
56. *Ibid.*, pp. 7, 78, 184, 192. See also pp. 11, 12.
57. Rivière-Fournier, I, 79–80, 131, 132, 38.
58. *Ibid.*, pp. 375, 376.
59. *Ibid.*, II, 229.
60. *Ibid.*, p. 247.
61. *Hommage à Jacques Rivière*, pp. 491, 504, 507.
62. J. Chaix, *De Renan à Jacques Rivière: dilettantisme et amoralisme* (Paris, 1930), p. 121.
63. See Gide, *Journal*, June 12, 1926, and *Hommage à Jacques Rivière*, pp 497–502, 773, 775.
64. *Hommage à Jacques Rivière*, pp. 498–499 (tr. AJG).
65. *Le Dialogue avec André Gide*, p. 168.
66. These figures are given in Yvonne Davet's *Autour des Nourritures terrestres* (Paris, 1948). The ensuing comments on *Les Nourritures terrestres* are all cited in her book: see pp. 166; 141–142, 147, 128; 103; 130; 126, 122, 124, 129.
67. *Ibid.*, p. 128.
68. From *La Belle Saison* (tr. AJG). See *Autour des Nourritures terrestres*, pp. 226–227.
69. *Le Sabbat*, p. 257, cited in *Autour des Nourritures terrestres*, p. 222.
70. *Autour des Nourritures terrestres*, p. 233.
71. *Ibid.*, pp. 230–231.
72. Cited in Maurice Sachs, *André Gide* (Paris, 1936), p. 43.
73. "Introduction au Théâtre de Goethe," in *Attendu que . . .* , p. 128 (tr. AJG).

APPENDIX (1969): THE POSTHUMOUS REVELATIONS

1. Roger Martin du Gard, *Notes on André Gide* (London, 1953), p. 35.
2. Claude Mauriac, *Conversations avec André Gide* (Paris, 1951), p. 87.

3. André Gide, *Madeleine*, trans. *Justin O'Brien* (New York: Knopf, 1952), p. 16 © Copyright 1952 by Alfred A. Knopf, Inc.
4. *Ibid.*, pp. 20–21.
5. *Ibid.*, pp. 30–31.
6. *Ibid.*, p. 49.
7. Jean Schlumberger, *Madeleine et André Gide* (Paris, 1956), p. 14.
8. Gide, *Madeleine*, p. 64n.
9. Schlumberger, p. 170.
10. *Ibid.*, p. 136.
11. *Ibid.*, p. 159.
12. *Ibid.*, p. 61.
13. *Ibid.*, p. 117.
14. *Ibid.*, p. 14.
15. *Ibid.*, pp. 187–188.
16. *Ibid.*, p. 188.
17. *Ibid.*, p. 210.
18. *Ibid.*, p. 169.
19. Roger Martin du Gard, *Notes on André Gide*, p. 23.
20. Jean Delay, *The Youth of André Gide*, abridged and translated by June Guicharnaud (Chicago, Ill.: University of Chicago Press, 1963), p. 291.
21. *Ibid.*, p. 298.
22. *Ibid.*, p. 297.
23. *Ibid.*, p. 64n.
24. *Ibid.*, p. 346.
25. *Ibid.*, p. 405.
26. *Ibid.*, p. 441.
27. *Ibid.*, p. 452.
28. See above, page 263.
29. Davies, p. 74.
30. Delay, *Youth of André Gide*, pp. 306–311.
31. *Ibid.*, p. 350.
32. *Ibid.*, pp. 447–448. And see Roger Martin du Gard, *Notes on André Gide*, p. 44.
33. See Preface, p. xvi.
34. Delay, *Youth of André Gide*, p. 395.
35. *Ibid.*, p. 396.
36. *Ibid.*, p. 407.
37. *Ibid.*, p. 405.

INDEX

INDEX

"Black Notebook, The," 55
Blafaphas (*Les Caves du Vatican*), 138
Blake, William, 31, 153
Blida, 8–9
Blum, Léon, 14, 25, 227
Bonheur, Raymond, 227
Boris (*Les Faux-Monnayeurs*), 155, 157, 160, 162, 163, 167, 173
Bouhélier, Saint-Georges de, 14, 193
Bourget, Paul, 21, 81, 99, 106, 146, 187
Bowen, Elizabeth, 176
Breton, André, 187, 199, 233
Brod, Max, 196
Brunetière, Ferdinand, 21, 193
Bute (*L'Immoraliste*), 105
Byron, Lord, 211

Cahiers d'André Walter, Les, 7–8, 11, 13, 14, 48–49, 52, 54–58, 63, 94, 98, 174, 194. See also André
Cahiers de la quinzaine (Péguy), 20
Caldwell, Erskine, 96
Caligula (Camus), 200
Caloub (*Les Faux-Monnayeurs*), 155
Camus, Albert, 4, 14, 71, 132, 135, 187, 193, 198, 200, 201, 205
Carlyle, Thomas, 185
Carola (*Les Caves du Vatican*), 131, 134
Casimir (*Isabelle*), 126
Cassou, Jean, 188
Castle, The (Kafka), 152, 178
Caves du Vatican, Les, 11, 62, 71, 76, 82–84, 93, 94, 95, 128–138, 139, 148, 174, 175, 178, 195–196, 197, 227, 230, 232
Céline, Louis-Ferdinand, 187
CFSO, 25–26
Champel, 8
Chance (Conrad), 119
Chants de Maldoror, Les (Lautréamont), 62, 195
Chardonne, Jacques, 30
Charles (*L'Immoraliste*), 105, 107, 114, 116, 117
Chartreuse de Parme, La (Stendhal), 95, 128
Chemins de la liberté (Sartre), 163

Chronique privée de l'an 1940 (Chardonne), 30
Claire, Aunt, 6
Clarion (*Le Voyage d'Urien*), 66
Claudel, Paul, 16, 21, 81, 89, 119, 186–187, 188, 191, 207, 208–209, 212–220 passim
Cocles (*Le Prométhée mal enchaîné*), 77
Cocteau, Jean, 21, 187, 188
Compagnie Forestière Sangha-Oubanghi, 25–26
Condillac, Etienne de, 135
Condition humaine, La (Malraux), 198
Congo, 24–26, 34, 48
Conrad, Joseph, 3, 4, 13, 14, 17, 24, 53, 78, 94, 95, 96, 110, 112–113, 119, 142, 145, 161, 175, 180–185 passim, 205
Copeau, Jacques, 16
Coppée, François, 19
Correspondance (Stendhal), 95
Corydon, 13, 85, 124, 203, 232
Crémieux, Benjamin, 154, 224
Crime and Punishment (Dostoevsky), 100
Criterion, The, 199
Curtius, Ernst Robert, 145
Cuverville, 10, 12, 34, 78, 79, 80

Dada, 139, 195, 199, 233
Daedalus (*Thésée*), 91
Daumier, Honoré, 156
Davet, Yvonne, 188–189, 194n, 229
Death in Venice (Mann), 113–116, 118
De Goecklin, Miss, 6
De Renan à Jacques Rivière (Chaix), 224–225
Dialogue avec André Gide, Le (Du Bos), 210–211
Dickens, Charles, 96, 156, 178
Dimitrov, Georgi, 4, 206
"Dindiki," 24
Dostoevsky, Fëdor, 4, 17, 22, 34, 39, 95–96, 109n, 111–112, 117, 132–136 passim, 145, 151, 152, 176, 177, 182, 193, 203, 220
Double, The (Dostoevsky), 111, 118
Douglas, Lord Alfred, 9